Ways of Knowing in Science

RICHARD DUSCHL, SERIES EDITOR

DESIGNING PROJECT-BASED SCIENCE

Connecting Learners Through Guided Inquiry

JOSEPH L. POLMAN

Foreword by Roy Pea

Teachers College, Columbia University
New York and London

Published by Teachers College Press, 1234 Amsterdam Avenue, New York, NY 10027

Library of Congress Cataloging-in-Publication Data

Polman, Joseph L., 1965–
    Designing project-based science : connecting learners through guided inquiry / Joseph L. Polman.
        p.   cm. — (Ways of knowing in science series)
    Includes bibliographical references and index.
    ISBN 0-8077-3913-8 (cloth). — ISBN 0-8077-3912-X (pbk.)
    1. Science—Study and teaching (Secondary)—Methodology.
    2. Science—Study and teaching—Activity programs.   I. Title.
    II. Series.
    Q181.P4694   1999
    507′.1′2—dc21   99-36981

ISBN 0-8077-3912-X (paper)
ISBN 0-8077-3913-8 (cloth)

Printed on acid-free paper
Manufactured in the United States of America

07   06   05   04   03   02   01   00   8   7   6   5   4   3   2   1

*For Mom and Dad, who showed me the wonder
and promise of learning.*

Contents

Foreword

Achieving a deeper understanding of the situated nature of educational reforms is an essential antidote to thick commission reports calling for more engaged learners ready for the cognitive demands of an information age, or prescriptions in the National Science Education Standards to foster students' learning science through project-based inquiry.

In *Designing Project-Based Science*, we see how deeply close analysis and well-crafted narratives of one teacher's experience can serve to reflect the preoccupations of a broad range of scholarly disciplines, and to offer up new insights on the challenges and opportunities of project-based learning useful to teachers, policymakers, and researchers alike. Scholars of narrative are fond of noting that fables are remarkably specific yet powerfully general. In a similar vein, the power of the particulars in this teacher's personal journey and the tales of his students engaged in inquiries about dinosaurs, hurricanes, planetary moons, UFOs, and earthquakes transcend the biographical. They serve as touchstones for thinking about and organizing one's own experiences in the classroom, as a learner and as a teacher. By turns, Polman's case study illustrates fundamental issues in the learning sciences, educational anthropology, educational policy, teacher professional development, conceptual change in science, collaborative learning and the design of learning technologies, and the classroom activity structures in which interactive learning environments must be functional.

Polman's strategy is to look from the inside out rather than the outside in as he provides an interpretive case study of one teacher's development in how to promote "learning by doing" in a high school classroom. The action takes place in the midst of a complex research project focused on learning through collaborative visualization (CoVis), which built upon constructivist pedagogy and a diverse suite of computer and telecommunication technologies. A number of crucial theoretical concepts are developed in the context of Polman's case study. We see how a teacher "appropriates" rather than "adopts" a project-based learning pedagogy and comes to perceive the affordances of software and telecommunication as supportive resources for teaching and learning. With the concept of "transformative communication," Polman illuminates the bootstrapping process by which learners and teachers engage in a reciprocal process of appropriating communicative actions toward higher levels of performance. Beyond these theoretical notions, there are practical lessons of considerable utility in how this remarkable teacher, Rory Wagner, evolves vocabulary and methods for guiding—with increasing effectiveness—learners' participation in inquiry-oriented learning. From launching inquiries to negotiating topics of appropriate scope, finding and using resources, marking progress with milestones, and coping with the constraints of time and grading, Rory Wagner's advances in how to structure classroom activity for project-based learning carry lessons for other teachers and ground the researcher in the pragmatics of classroom and school life.

In the difficult climb to a functioning project-based learning classroom, this case study speaks volumes about the resourcefulness of an amazing teacher and the documentary wisdom of an insightful observer. *Designing Project-Based Science* provides an important contribution to the growing sociocultural literature on the intersections of learning sciences, learning technologies, and educational reform.

Roy Pea
Center for Technology in Learning
SRI International
Menlo Park, CA

Acknowledgments

I am forever indebted to Rory Wagner and his students for sharing their lives and opinions openly with me. I hope what I have written here shows how greatly I admire Rory's perseverance and hard work, and how much I enjoyed spending time day-to-day with him and his students.

I am grateful to the National Science Foundation (under grant numbers RED-9454729 and MDR88-55582) and the Illinois State Board of Education (under the Eisenhower program) for funding this work. The writing was completed with the support of a grant from the James S. McDonnell Foundation (under the Cognitive Studies for Educational Practice program).

Thanks as well to the rest of my talented colleagues from the Learning Through Collaborative Visualization (CoVis) project, who contributed in innumerable ways to my research and ideas, as well as my life. They include my faculty advisors, Roy Pea and Louis Gomez; fellow students Laura D'Amico, Kevin O'Neill, Barry Fishman, Doug Gordin, Steve McGee, Greg Shrader, Sam Kwon, Raul Zaritsky, and Dan Vermeer; teachers Patty Carlson, Larry Geni, Mary Beth Hoffman, Ken Lewandowski, and George Dervis; and the rest of the team, including Eileen Lento, Danny Edelson, Joey Gray, Phoebe Peng, Susie Rand, Linda Ortega, and Lars Rasmussen. Special thanks to Laura D'Amico for survey data cited in Chapters 5 and 9, and Greg Shrader for another teacher's quote used in Chapter 11. Some of the issues raised here are also examined in research conducted by my colleagues; three other studies include examination of particular issues in Rory Wagner's class. Laura D'Amico (1999) studied assessment infrastructures, Kevin O'Neill (1998) studied "telementors," and Steven McGee (1996) studied the taught and learned curriculum.

In addition, I thank the other people who made graduate school what it was for me, including my fellow graduate students Brian Smith, Nichole Pinkard, Sandor Szego, Eric Baumgartner, Bill Sandoval, and Ben Loh, and faculty members Brian Reiser, Carol Lee, Richard Beckwith, Roger Schank, Larry Birnbaum, Joe Walthers, and Mike Ravitch.

A special thanks goes to my dissertation committee, who offered a balance of inspiration, prodding, and challenge. Thanks to Allan Collins for his gift of theoretical and descriptive clarity, as well as his difficult questions. Thanks to Louis Gomez for tolerating a different path, and for his daily warmth. Thanks to Bill Ayers for the inspiration of his writing and his unwavering confidence that I could in fact "take him there" with my own. Thanks to Roy Pea for encouraging me along this path in the first place, and for substantive feedback every step of the way.

Completing the final stages of this work was spurred in part by my new colleagues in St. Louis, especially Jim Wertsch. I look forward to our continuing work together.

Thank you to my family for making me who I am today: Mom and Dad, Sarah, Josh, Bill, Laura, Dee Dee, Taf, and Sofia. Also Grandma, Joe and Jo, Becky and Louie, Stan and Marge. I miss those who are gone and hope that my life will have as much meaning to others as all of yours have to me. To my brother, sisters, and nephew: we have been through a lot, but doing it together with you has made it better. It is amazing to think how we all have grown. Thank you to the Plax clan—Julie, Steve, Andy, Ted, Danny, Alison, Kate, James, and Charlie—for welcoming me, and for the gift of their interest in my work over the past few years.

And finally, thank you Katie for being my partner, my inspiration, and my beloved, as well as being my internal editor. Being with you these years has been the most wonderful thing to happen to me. Discovering and contemplating the world, each other, and our future is continually exciting. I look forward to planting a garden with you and seeing it grow for years to come.

PART I

THE GUIDE'S CHALLENGE

CHAPTER 1

A Particular Effort at Science Education Reform

In recent years, project-based and inquiry-based science education have been revived as means to promote active engagement with scientific phenomena. Most of these efforts are rooted in Dewey's ideas (e.g., 1902), and have been explored since then in the progressive movement (as chronicled by Cremin, 1961), reforms of the 1960s (e.g., Bruner, 1963), and in recent efforts of the 1990s (Krajcik, Czerniak, & Berger, 1998; Ruopp, Gal, Drayton, & Pfister, 1993).

The Learning Through Collaborative Visualization (CoVis) project followed in this tradition, seeking to aid in the reform of high school science toward a project-based approach (Pea, 1993a). The CoVis project was funded by the National Science Foundation from 1991 through 1997, and grew from involving six teachers at two high schools to a national testbed of thousands of students and over 100 teachers at 45 middle and high schools. I joined the nascent group of CoVis university-based researchers and reformers as a research assistant in January 1993. We began with a set of theoretically and historically motivated educational ideas and networked computer tools assembled by the university-based staff, and fleshed out with high school teachers and computer industry representatives.

CoVis could be described as an educational intervention designed to explore "what could be" in science classrooms if things changed quite a bit from the status quo. Students are not often expected to learn by conducting project inquiries into scientific phenomena. Yet theoretical arguments (see Chapter 3) and some empirical studies (e.g., Aikin, 1942; Kyle, 1984) support the worth of project-based approaches. In addition, teachers do not often have classrooms equipped with the latest in technology—typically, schools lag years behind industry (Pea & Gomez, 1992). Yet new technologies are increasingly important in the practice of science, and they can be instrumental in creating authentic learning environments for project-based science. For instance, access to computers and the Internet can enable students to find and analyze real, large-scale data sets to answer research questions they formulate themselves (Gordin, Polman, & Pea, 1994). Communication over the Internet can enable students to work with practicing scientists and other experts as mentors (O'Neill, 1998); provide a larger knowledge-building community (Scardamalia & Bereiter, 1991); and serve as a means of breaking teacher isolation through exchange of ideas over networks (e.g., Bruce & Rubin, 1993; Schwab, Hart-Landsberg, Reder, & Abel, 1992).

THE APPROPRIATION OF PROJECT-BASED SCIENCE REFORMS

With such ideas and tools, we hoped to create an extended learning community whose participants conducted authentic, collaborative scientific inquiry. But as countless experiences in the past have shown, neither the creation of technologies nor the ideas of researchers or policymakers determine how classrooms are run. Ultimately, teachers accomplish classroom activity with their students in the schools (e.g., Ayers, 1993; Cuban, 1986; Sheingold & Hadley, 1990). Critics sometimes accuse teachers of stubbornly resisting all outside ideas, but a good deal of research shows that good teachers *must transform* outside ideas for their own classrooms. To be effective, they must customize reform ideas somewhat to their particular school contexts, and to the individual personalities and needs of their students.

I refer to the use of ideas and tools in particular contexts and for particular tasks as *appropriation* (Leont'ev, 1981; Newman, Griffin, & Cole, 1989; Pea, 1992) rather than *adoption* to highlight the transformations that teachers and their students must make to such abstract notions. Saying that teachers (and their students with them) simply *adopt* project-based science methods and networked computers to accomplish them would imply that they use them exactly as conceived in the abstract, and that all teachers can or should use them in the same way. Saying that teachers and their students *appropriate* project-based science methods and networked computers stresses that they must transform them for their specific situation, which includes numerous cultural, historical, and social factors.

This book is a study of one teacher and his students' appropriation of the CoVis project-based science reform. The teacher and his class are by no means typical of CoVis participants: they are unique in the amount of time dedicated to project-based science (100% of class time after the first quarter of the year), and the degree of commitment to *open-ended* research projects that students fundamentally help to design. I present this exceptional classroom in order to explore "what could be" (Schofield, 1990) were more teachers to attempt this sort of appropriation. As Schofield uses the distinction, studying what could be involves "locating situations that we know or expect to be ideal or exceptional on some a priori basis and then studying them to see what is actually going on there" (1990, p. 217). As stated above, CoVis was explicitly an exploration of what science education "could be" if teachers appropriated project-based approaches in technology-rich, networked classrooms. In this case study, I explore "what could be" if an experienced, reflective, and adventurous teacher attempted to design an entirely project-based science class. Studying his classroom allowed me to build a more complete model (Erickson, 1986) of how projects could be organized and supported in networked science classrooms.

THE RESEARCH PARTICIPANTS AND SETTING

Rory Wagner (his real name, at his request) had been teaching Earth Science at Lakeside High School (a pseudonym) for over 20 years when he began participating in CoVis in September 1992. He is an active white male in his 40s who was born and raised nearby. After attending a small midwestern college and receiving his degree in science education, he took the job at Lakeside. He has taught at the school since, except for the period he took off to complete his master's degree in geology.

Lakeside is a public high school situated in an affluent, mostly white community in the suburbs of a large midwestern city. The "campus," and the word aptly describes the grounds, is large and well-apportioned, although the buildings were built half a century ago. Students who arrive at school carrying Starbucks coffee cups do not look out of place. According to the 1990 census, the average per capita income in one town in the district was $62,000 (Krieg & Wheelan, 1995). The average spending per student for the just under 3,000 students at the school was $12,000 in 1995 (Krieg & Wheelan, 1995). The demographic makeup of students at Lakeside as of 1994–95 was 85% white, 2% African-American, 11% Asian or Pacific Islander, and 2% Hispanic, and less than 1% American Indian, Eskimo, or Aleut (Sunspace, 1997). The demographics of Rory Wagner's Period 1/2 class reported on in this study are thus not atypical: of the 28 students enrolled, 25 were white, 2 Asian-American, and 1 African-American.

Although there is an average student/teacher ratio at the school of 12/1, the size of Rory's classes over the past three years has ranged from 15 to the 28 in the group detailed in this study. The difference between Rory's course and the overall average is in part because of a variety of specialized courses that have much smaller enrollments, such as those in the drama department. Drama is one of the areas of excellence for which the school is known.

At Lakeside High, the Earth Science course, along with some other courses such as Anatomy and Environmental Science, are considered "alternative" science courses and are taken by fewer students than are chemistry and physics. The core sequence of science classes is biology (which most 9th graders take and all students must take at some point), chemistry, and physics. As is often the case with elective science courses, Rory's classes routinely consist of 9th through 12th graders. The class detailed in this study consisted mostly of older students, however: 1 9th grader, 4 10th graders, 13 11th graders, and 10 12th graders were enrolled. Throughout all Rory's classes, he has slightly more older students than younger students, but individual classes are skewed one way or another by the fact that students in a given year tend to have similar schedules. The class I observed the previous year had a large number of freshmen and sophomores, in contrast to this class.

Roughly 80% of residents in the enrollment area are college graduates (Krieg & Wheelan, 1995), and there is an obvious expectation that all students should attend college. Most *will* attend college. In late spring 1996, the student newspaper published a list of all seniors' "destinations." The top ten in 1996 consisted mostly of large Big Ten schools. A number of students have gone on to Ivy League universities or Stanford and Berkeley, as well as a variety of community colleges and small liberal arts colleges. Of the approximately 700 student destinations listed, 4 were explicitly *not* attending college or university (to work or take a year off), and 40 were "undecided." On that spring day, students ranging from first to fourth year in high school pored over the list and commented to one another about their peers' futures.

Like a number of public schools in the area, Lakeside and its community have a long tradition of involvement in education reform efforts, including the progressive movement (Progressive Education Association, 1943; Zilversmit, 1993). In addition, the Eight Years Study, which documented the success of students educated in progressive elementary and secondary schools when they went on to college (Aikin, 1942), included students from this region. This history, combined with the high teacher salaries, may help contribute to an atmosphere among the faculty and administration of acceptance for a multiplicity of teaching practices. As Rory said, there are

> some schools, where everybody who is teaching biology is essentially on the same page, doing the same lecture, doing the same lab. It's all lock step, and they all give the same test at the end of the unit . . .

That's their way of quality control, to make sure that every kid has the same experience.

[At Lakeside, though] at least in our department, . . . we're kind of like, "Yeah, you do whatever you want. You're a highly educated and well-paid professional, and you know what's important in your discipline" . . . We deeply cherish this right . . . [1]

Throughout the period of this study, the principal and science department head supported participating CoVis teachers such as Rory in the various initiatives each was taking to implement reform. Like other teachers in the department, Rory Wagner was afforded the opportunity to teach using his own combination of new and traditional approaches.

RATIONALE FOR THIS INTERPRETIVE CASE STUDY

What can educational researchers, practitioners, and designers learn from this study? Looking at learning environments as *functional systems* can reveal how they work and how they change through the reorganization of activity (Cole & Griffin, 1980; Pea, 1985; Sproull & Kiesler, 1991). Taking a systemic view implies considering how the components of a system work together, not how any one of the components acts alone. The components of a learning environment are not like mechanical cogs in a very important way—many of them are persons making sense of their situation and acting on the sense they construct of that situation as it develops. As Erickson (1986) puts it, the "meaning-interpretations" humans make are causal. The context and possible meaning-interpretations differ in important ways from school to school, teacher to teacher, and even from a given teacher's first period to sixth period class. But better understanding one such learning environment in all its complexity can provide important insights for educators. Alan Peshkin (1988) has pointed out that understanding complexity is a key benefit of qualitative inquiry. Understanding Rory's and his students' intentions and actions situated in this particular environment will raise important issues we must face in other learning environments with similar goals of introducing project-based science, but different particulars.

In order to understand the complexity of Rory's classroom, I have conducted what I refer to as an "interpretive case study." According to Erickson (1986), "interpretive" research refers to any form of participant observational research that is centrally concerned with the role of meaning in social life, enacted in local situations. For details on my interpretive research methods and data collection techniques, see Appendix A.

As Erickson (1986) has recommended, the focus of my interpretive research is *particularizability* rather than generalizability. Erickson describes particularizability as being achieved by examining "concrete universals" in particular, detailed cases, and comparing them with one another. By considering the different layers of context that are shared with other settings, the interpretive researcher can begin to indicate what aspects of the concrete case under study may apply to other cases, but the applicability of the case studied and described is left to the reader (Firestone, 1993). For instance, Ayers (1989) shows how widespread social problems are manifested in particular preschool teachers' work, and Kotlowitz (1991) shows how urban violence, the drug trade, and housing policy affect the particular lives of two youngsters in Chicago. In this study, I show how such issues as traditional schooling practice affect this implementation of project-based science teaching.

Although I ultimately leave readers to make decisions about what they can learn from this study and apply in their own setting, I nevertheless feel obliged to address one possible conclusion some readers might draw from the description of Lakeside's district. Some might feel that the affluence and overwhelmingly college-bound student body make the lessons from Lakeside *completely* inapplicable to other settings in urban or rural communities, where students have a lower socioeconomic status. I view this conclusion as erroneous, and side with teachers in the Coalition of Essential Schools who have pointed out that it is possible to learn important lessons when we

> put aside the notion that one can learn only from teachers who teach in the same kind of school, the same aged kids, the same discipline, and who work with kids from the same economic background. Techniques, strategies, structures, personal reflections, and big ideas can and do transcend all of these personal identifiers. (Wasley, 1994, pp. 9–10)

My inclination is to encourage readers to think about how the *cultural beliefs* about schooling and learning described here apply to other settings, and how the *structures* for classroom work and organization and the *strategies* of interaction and guidance described here can aid reform in other school settings. For example, there may be important differences in how grades act as a motivator for students in some other settings compared to the students at Lakeside (where a competitive, college-bound atmosphere reigns, albeit to a somewhat lesser degree in Earth Science class than AP Physics); but there will likely be important similarities in how *interest* and *student voice* work as motivators.

It is worth noting that figuring out how to particularize strategies to situations is exactly what teachers like Rory do on a daily and yearly basis.

Thus, my portrayal of Rory's iterative design situated in the classroom should give readers a model for how he has adjusted and refined his particular strategies over time. Readers of this and other such studies are not told *exactly* how the findings in these cases apply to other settings that share common issues, such as the challenge of changing from traditional school practices. But by gaining a fuller understanding of how the larger issues particularize to these cases, readers are in a better position to apply these findings to other situations.

A final word about the utility of this interpretive case study. The form of the text itself, with detailed narrative cases and vignettes, is designed to aid *the reader* in particularizing the findings from the study to their own setting (Firestone, 1993). A range of cognitive theorists argue that narrative forms and cases are primary vehicles for learning and extending understanding (e.g., Bruner, 1990; Schank, 1990). I invite readers to take advantage of this feature, and use the narratives reported here as thinking devices for effecting changes in educational practice elsewhere.

THE PLAN FOR THE BOOK

In the following chapters, I will describe what doing science research projects means in this specific classroom, and how Rory Wagner and his students interactively accomplish project work. I will particularly focus on aspects of the teacher's work that involve designing systems for supporting students' inquiry learning and actively guiding them on a daily basis. Specifically, in Chapter 2 I will present a "day in the life" of Rory Wagner's Earth Science class to show the promise and challenges of such an endeavor. In Chapter 3, I will review some historical background on child-centered educational practices and the appropriation of technology to support teaching, as well as describe relevant emerging views of learning. In Chapter 4, I will describe Rory's personal background leading to his interest in projects. In Chapter 5, I will describe the background and attitudes of Rory's students and some of the basic challenges of involving them in a nonstandard form of schooling, along with some of Rory's early frustrated efforts. Part II shows in detail Rory's work guiding students. In Chapter 6, I will describe the groundwork Rory lays for conducting research projects starting with the first day of class and continuing until the end of the first quarter. In Chapter 7, I will show how smoothly running student projects take advantage of the activity structure for projects that Rory has designed, enacted, and refined over the years. In Chapter 8, I will describe how lack of time and perception of time can both cause and enable students to fall through the cracks in Rory's class. In Chapter 9, I will detail how the

traditional culture of schooling changes students' perceptions of Rory's reform teaching practices, and affects (in mostly negative ways) Rory's efforts
to guide student participation in scientific inquiry. In Chapter 10, I will
describe strategies Rory uses to try and maintain a balance between taking
too much control from students and letting them be responsible for learning. In Chapter 11, I will summarize the lessons learned for others interested in project-based science. The purpose of my description and analysis
throughout will be to create guideposts and models for other designers of
project-based science.

NOTE

1. The source of this and all other unattributed quotes of Rory Wagner and
students are interviews with the author conducted outside of class, with the exception of directly reported classroom action.

CHAPTER 2

Expeditions to Mt. Everest: Daily Life in a Project-Based Science Class

Period 7 Earth Science class is about to begin at Lakeside High School on a spring day in 1995. Seventeen 9th through 12th graders sit in clusters scattered about the large laboratory room equipped with sinks on either side. Some students are sitting at the movable work tables in the middle of the room, and a few are sitting at the six tables in the front and back of the room with computers hooked up to the Internet on them, monitors facing in. The students' attire leans heavily toward the casual looks of skateboarding shorts, torn jeans, baggy flannel layered over T-shirts, and worn baseball caps with college logos; a few sport khakis and button-down shirts, while a couple of the young women are in dressy silk pants and blouses. The room is much wider than it is deep, with the "front" defined by the blackboard and maps on the north wall facing the hallway. In front of the blackboard is a tall, permanently attached demonstration table with a sink—clearly, the teacher's base. On a stool behind the table sits the teacher, Rory Wagner. Rory is wearing brown corduroys, a blue chambray shirt, and a wolf tie—casual for a teacher, with a touch of the outdoors he loves. He is tall, with ruddy skin and dark black hair. His looks and fitness make it difficult for students to discern his age. Rory is talking with Alex and his research group about possible project topics. The students began working on their final quarter-long project of the year a week earlier. For their projects, they design and conduct research within the broad domain of Earth Science.

As the three students converse with Rory at the front of the room, the volume level in the room is high, with multiple conversations going on. At the Macintosh computer just to Rory's right, two students read electronic mail one just received from Israel. A young man browses the World Wide Web at the computer to Rory's left. A group lounges in their usual back corner of the room to Rory's left, in the vicinity of another computer. Nearby, three other students sit at a table trying to figure out what kind of project they can do on comets. Two young women sit at another computer in the back of the room, while one reads a message from the graduate student who mentored their last project, and the other pulls some books on soil out of her backpack. Four more students are gathered near the center of the room in an animated conversation. A lone young woman works on something from another class. On the board behind Rory, the day's announcements detail "Things past due" and "Next due."

BEGINNINGS

The bell rings and no one calls to order, or reduces the volume of conversation. Some of the student groups ask Rory if they can go to the library, and then take their backpacks with them out of the room. Rory continues his conversations with students, and also notes in his book who is here today, asking for "re-entrance" forms from those who were absent yesterday.

Rory has tried to "make this class a little bit different" from other classes since the first day, when they walked to a nearby beach on a lake to collect sand samples. There are many obvious ways in which this class is different from other classes—not many students use electronic mail or computers on the Internet at Lakeside or any other high school, and not many high school classes are as informal as Rory's. But technology use and informality are not the main issue for Rory—the "motivating factor," for him, is "the idea of *doing research*. . . . I wanted people to actually try to figure something out—observe some scientific phenomena, take measurements or collect information on it, and try to come to some conclusion about how it worked, or what was happening." Rory's been working with these kids since last fall on how to do research, when he took the role of project manager on the sand analysis project. Since then, students have worked in groups of their own choosing, on topics of their own choosing. Letting them pursue topics of their own choice is a second "motivating influence" for Rory, since "if students are involved with doing things that they pick and design, they're more apt to be . . . energized by that, and take more interest in and ownership in it."

Today Rory's students are in the beginning stages of their fourth and final project of the 1994–95 school year. Last Friday they were supposed to let him know their project teams and broad topics, as the notice on the blackboard reminds them. All but one group have done that; they're still trying to decide, and they soon get into a conversation with Rory about it.

NEGOTIATING A TOPIC OF INTEREST

Kevin and Alex (pseudonyms, as are all student names) are part of the "grunge" crowd, who style their dress after the music scene that started in Seattle, with untucked, oversized flannel shirts and old jeans. Alex almost always wears a gray knit cap, and sometimes finishes off the outfit with reflective wraparound glasses. For their last project, they tried to prove the existence of UFOs, using examples such as the oft-cited government "coverup" in Roswell, New Mexico. They weren't able to marshal much data to use as evidence, though, and Rory is trying to help them find a more promising topic. Kevin suggests hemp and its uses, but not surprisingly, that gets deflected as having more to do with botany than earth science. Kevin then suggests toilets, and "why the water flushes down counterclockwise in the northern hemisphere and clockwise in the southern hemisphere." Rory tells him that has to do with the Coriolis effect, which also affects wind and storms; it's a possible project. It doesn't catch their fancy, but they keep searching. Alex mentions volcanoes, and Rory suggests that scientists have been having trouble describing hot and cold magma flow. Kevin moves on to whether suicides in Alaska are related to what he calls the "Aurora Borus." Rory doesn't think that's the reason, but he knows there is a real effect of greater suicide rate. "You could compare suicide rates in several places, and also include longitude, number of sunny and cloudy days, amount of rain, and so on." Kevin thinks that may be too much work. They try refining it into a workable project for a while, but then Kevin suggests geysers. Rory says they could try to figure out if there is a pattern to the geyser eruptions. Kevin finally seems interested in pursuing one of the ideas. He goes to a computer and asks where you could find data on geysers. Rory suggests Alex search on the Internet for Yellowstone in Wyoming.

This sort of interaction between Rory and his students is not uncommon in this phase of projects. It doesn't always turn out this well—sometimes none of the promising ideas take hold, sometimes the students get frustrated, and sometimes Rory gets frustrated. As Rory told me after class, he's been trying to be more open to students' ideas, even when they seem at first like dead ends, because he believes they might be able to turn them into projects that work. Sometimes students' interests lead them in directions in the broad field of earth science where he has little expertise. He has a graduate degree in geology, but earth science also includes atmospheric science, oceanography, and astronomy. Access to scientists over the Internet relieves him to some extent of "being the expert on everything." This year he began posting messages to Usenet newsgroups on the Internet such as "sci.geology" and "sci.astronomy" asking for volunteers to mentor students conducting projects in their areas of expertise. He connected several groups in each of his classes with graduate students and Ph.D.s in various fields, and they communicated by electronic mail. Kevin and Alex didn't end up contacting the potential mentor he told them about today, though, satisfied with the leads they had found themselves.

FINDING AND USING SOURCES

As Kevin and Alex search the Internet, Rory goes next door and looks up the name of a contact he has on the pattern of eruptions, from a project some students did on geysers the previous year. He gives it to them, and then turns his attention to other groups while Alex and Kevin work on the computer. They've been using the World Wide Web for work and fun since the fall, when Rory had them learn how to use it by searching for earth science information. Kevin has a favorite Web site, "Yahoo," which has links to many different places, as well as search capabilities. Within ten minutes, they've found the "Yellowstone Home Page."

The search for data relevant to a group's chosen topic does not always go as smoothly as Kevin and Alex's search does, however. As Rory says, "Finding stuff [on the Internet or in the library] isn't always as easy as it seems." Many students need to work on their research technique—they often just "look for the one book that has [their] topic title on it, . . . or . . . to do Internet searches, they type in their word and they don't find anything."

Sophia and Alison, sitting to Rory's right at a computer, are having trouble with their own search for books on the Dead Sea. Alison, who tends to wear dark clothes that complement her black fingernail polish, told me yesterday that Sophia wanted to do a project on the Dead Sea "just because it's in Israel." Sophia is really interested in her Jewish heritage, and has a correspondence going with an Israeli soldier over e-mail. After the success of their last project on the mineral contents of obsidian, they have high hopes. But they are having trouble finding anything. Alison says "if only" they could find one book with good data, they'd be set. Rory pipes in, wondering about the possibility that the "one book" could be inaccurate. Wouldn't it be better to have multiple sources? Alison responds, "Why would they publish a book full of lies?" Rory reminds them of all the books others found on UFOs. Do they think all those are true? Sophia then suggests exploring "What made the Dead Sea salty?" Rory thinks it's worth exploring, but Alison thinks it will be a black-and-white answer in a book. Alison and Sophia's frustration with the search shows during this period, but within a couple of weeks, they have learned about a number of salt seas in the world, and they are investigating the differences between them.

WORKING WITHIN A GUIDING STRUCTURE

Amanda and Jeff come into the room with a printout from the library on comets. Jeff says, "Now we have to come up with a question." He is referring to one of the components they need for the next "project milestone" they will be turning in. When Rory first started doing project-based science in his class two years earlier, he didn't have deadlines every couple of weeks as he does now, built around a project paper format. Instead, the requirements for the project report, due at the end of the nine-week period, were largely left open. As he tells it:

> I thought that I was setting them on top of Mount Everest and saying, "Look, the whole world is here for you to look at. Isn't that great? Look what you can study." And they felt like I was sticking them on top of Mount Everest, and they felt like "Oh my God, I'm gonna fall, I could die up here, this is horrible, I'm gonna freeze to death, I'm gonna fall off the mountain."
>
> [We had] two totally different perspectives. I thought I was setting them free and they felt like they were being abandoned. And when they felt abandoned they got angry.

Arguments and long discussions ensued, which Rory credits with forcing him to articulate and refine many of his own ill-formed ideas about projects. He also had discussions about how to guide and structure projects with other teachers and researchers in the Learning Through Collaborative Visualization (CoVis) project, especially the other CoVis teachers at Lakeside. Together, they developed a paper format for projects that each of them modified for their specific purposes. The paper format "became almost the blueprint for doing projects." Each section from the introduction to the method and on through the conclusion represents a milestone that the students turn in to Rory for feedback along the way, until they put together a final paper followed by a presentation to the rest of the class. Although he has set up a structure for students to follow, which he says is like the scientific method in some ways, he doesn't believe "Moses [came] down from the mountain with the scientific method written in stone." He tells his students, "Science happens in a lot of different ways," so it makes sense to let them get their projects done in a lot of different ways. The milestones he has them turn in along the way provide a "framework for them to work in," but he's "trying to give enough flexibility within this thing, and yet have them accountable at short steps." Thus, he seems glad one group are working backwards from the presentation. As a group member put it, they "planned it all out and will fill it in along the way." The teacher's main goal is that students keep moving, and don't put the whole project off until the night before they're due. Details on how the paper format structures activity are found in Chapter 7.

ANTICIPATING PROBLEMS WITH GRADING

In addition to the tensions about the amount of structure and guidance Rory provided students, he encountered related tension about grades, "because all of a sudden they didn't know how to play the game, and yet they were being graded on how they were playing." Evaluation still causes frequent conflicts, despite Rory's efforts to "head them off early." He now maintains a spreadsheet on the computer network with current marks and outstanding assignments according to his records, where all the students can look up their status by their school ID number. The system has helped, especially with concerned students who check their grades frequently, but there are still problems. For instance, one student had failed the course in the fall, and had been working much harder since Christmas. She recently found out she was getting a C, and confronted Rory, shouting at the top of her lungs "I got a C! . . . I got the lowest grade in the class. I can't believe it . . . How could I get the same grade as people who just sat around and didn't work?" She stormed out of the room, and had been absent since. Grading is one of the issues of school culture that affect Rory's work with projects, and is discussed in Chapter 9.

DEALING WITH TIME

The demands on Rory's attention continue for the rest of the period. Sophia talks further with Rory about the Dead Sea project. A student who's looking for information on rainforests carries a bunch of Earth Science books to her desk. Sophia and Alison go to the library to look for books on the Dead Sea. Jeff looks up comets in Yahoo on the World Wide Web. A student who has watched a video on his topic recommends the strategy to Alex and Kevin, and later Rory helps them find and view a videotape on geysers in Yellowstone Park. The bell ending the 40-minute period rings, and some of the students head out to the hallway to take a break. Others continue working. On Mondays and Wednesdays, they have a double period, supposedly for labs. But every day is part lab and part office and part lunchroom in Rory's class—it's just that on Monday and Wednesday, they have more time.

The plasticity of time constantly confronts Rory. For him, there's never enough time to support the 8 to 12 different projects going on simultaneously in each of his three classes. He spends many periods going from one request (or frantic cry) for help to another. As he told me at the beginning of the year,

> I've never had so many kids *needing* me so much. And it's not like when someone has a question in a [traditional] lab and they ask, "Um, I don't get this—what's this about?" Here they're like, "Mr. Wagner, I need to talk to you *now*." It matters to them much more, so there's more pressure on me.

Since so many students are constantly seeking Rory out, he tends to have fewer interactions with the few who do not actively seek him out.

For some of the students, his deadlines leave too much time; for others, they don't allow enough. He tries to get around this by making them somewhat flexible, giving bonus points for assignments turned in early and accepting them late with moderate penalties. But giving different deadlines for different people is not viewed by students as "fair," unless they are taking the class for higher-level credit, as two students in this class are doing. A detailed look at issues relating to time limits and perceptions can be found in Chapter 8.

GETTING FROM BROAD TOPICS TO RESEARCH QUESTIONS

During the break, Christina asks Rory for a book on rainforests. He goes next door to the cubbyhole he shares with the other Earth Science teacher. While Rory is out of the room, two former project partners get in a minor skirmish that ends when Rory reenters the room. Rory hands the book, *The Rainforest* from Time-Life books, to Christina. He has brought these books in from home to help students get basic information on the wide variety of topics in Earth Science that interest them. He asks them to read up on topics once they have decided what they want to study, and encourages them to formulate research questions based on what they study. Christina dutifully follows this model by reading through a number of books on rainforests. Two years ago Rory hoped students would be able to formulate good, researchable questions directly out of their interests. But he has had to adjust that expectation along with many others. He found that the initial questions students came up with, before learning about their topic, were often dead ends. Rory's conversation with Jeff and Amanda during period eight provides a case in point.

Jeff finds a FAQ—a list of Frequently Asked Questions—about comets on the Internet, and begins looking for some images of comets at the NASA Web sites. He hopes to paste them into a PowerPoint slide show for their presentation in five weeks. But after a while, he becomes frustrated with being unable to get in to the NASA servers because of heavy network traffic, and begins playing games on the computer. Amanda, in the meantime, has been trying to come up with a project question. Eventually, she says to Jeff, "How about 'Why does a comet revolve around the sun?'" Jeff replies, "I'm sure that's already answered." Amanda laments, "I know, but that's all I can come up with." Jeff turns back to his game, but Amanda is determined, and calls Mr. Wagner over for help. Rory finishes up helping Kevin with something on the computer, and comes over a minute later. Amanda begins to suggest a question, but Rory first asks, "What do you know about comets so far?" Amanda says not much. Jeff begins to read off something from one of their FAQ printouts: what comets are made of, how big they are, and some other information. Rory says, "So size is important . . ." Amanda pipes in, "Here's a question. 'What relation do comets have to the sun?'" Rory relates that idea to what Jeff has read, about how the chunk of rock has a tail, called a coma, which is caused by the sun. Amanda complains, "We need a question," but Rory says "That's like asking for your conclusion before you start. You need to learn something about comets first somehow before you can come up with a good question . . . you could do a comparison of comets' tails." Amanda suggests "Why they have tails." Rory points out that Jeff already knows that. The struggle continues, but the idea for investigating the relationship of a comet's core and tail size takes hold with Jeff, and he continues trying to help Amanda see why that kind of question might be more fruitful and less settled than "What is Halley's Comet?"

ONE DAY IN SUMMARY

During the second period of the class, Rory continues his brisk pace. After he runs up to check on his students in the library, he continues having short conversations with students. At the end of the 85 minutes, he has had some 20 separate interactions with student groups all around the room. Student questions and the conversations they spur with him range from the technical to informational to strategic to scientific. Sometimes students want to share their excitement, at a find in the library or a message received over the Net.

Other times, they just want to complain: "This proposal is hard. We looked at different questions, and they all have simple three-sentence answers." In some cases, Rory ends up sitting down with students and walking them through a procedure on the computer, like sending e-mail or searching the Net. In others, he offers advice, like narrowing a research question or searching under vertebrate paleontology. In still others, he volleys questions back at students: "What kind of data would answer that question?" "What interests you about eclipses, anyway?"

Eventually, the bell ending 8th period rings. The students pack up their bags, having completed another day of project-based science in Rory Wagner's class. But they'll pick up from here tomorrow.

THE COMPLEXITY OF PARTICULAR REFORM EFFORTS

As stated in Chapter 1, the vision of a reform like CoVis depends on the work of many teachers in particular contexts, and how they appropriate the ideas and tools in their classrooms every day. The April day in Rory Wagner's classroom described above makes apparent the complexity of creating and maintaining an environment to support project-based science.

First, teachers like Rory must decide what "projects" should mean in their classes, and then they must enact their vision with their students using the resources at their disposal. The way this works depends on many particulars of the situation. For instance, Rory holds particular beliefs about what is important in science and how it is practiced. These beliefs affect what kind of projects he would like to encourage and where to challenge students the most. Since he believes science is more than "knowing facts," he wants them to learn something about how to "do science," which involves answering questions like "How do you come up with a problem . . . and then solve it. What's your evidence, [and] how do you prove that you solved it?" There are no "cookbook" procedures or lists to memorize in his class. His particular view of how children learn affects how much he directs students as well—as he put it, "It's not enough for me to *show* them or *tell* them what is going on, what they should do, or what they should know. The students have to somehow *make it their own.*"

The particular values Rory holds toward student responsibility and student–teacher relationships affect his willingness to prod students who are goofing off, as well as the level of informality acceptable in his classroom. The particular culture and atmosphere of the school and community Rory works in has encouraged innovative techniques and technologies; it has also dictated an open campus policy that both benefits and frustrates Rory. The affluence of the community may at times highlight the importance of grades as levers for getting into "good colleges." The particular students Rory works with in every class change the strategies he takes—he spends more time trying to focus one student's energy, and more time trying to challenge another's ideas and open her to new ones, for instance. Finally, the particular tools and resources Rory's students have access to, from the library to data on the World Wide Web to scientists on the Internet, enable him to offload certain supporting functions. Paradoxically, though, *he* must often facilitate students' use of these same resources before their effective use can relieve the pressure on him.

All of these particulars, and many more, ultimately combine to create the meaning and significance of project work enacted in Rory's classroom, just as they would in any other particular classroom. In order to gain a better understanding of the challenges and complexities of such an endeavor, I have conducted in-depth research on Rory's continuing journey designing and implementing a project-based science class.

THE NATURE OF LEARNING ENVIRONMENT DESIGN

In talking with Rory and observing his class in the three and a half years after he began doing projects in 1993, I was struck by how he has, as he puts it, "evolved." This evolution has included everything from "how to get resources" to "how to convince kids this is a good idea." His initial desire for doing projects was influenced by reading the LabNet book (Ruopp et al., 1993) chronicling high school physics teachers' use of project-based methods. His desire was also influenced by discussions with other CoVis teachers and researchers, and the powerful learning he'd experienced in his own master's thesis project. But as Pea (1993b) and Suchman (1987) have pointed out is the case for educational and work activity, desires that lead to action are often diffuse and ill-specified. They don't prescribe a clear set of steps to follow. Rory said he felt "like I was making things up as I went along, so I thought the only way to do it now is to jump in and actually do it, and see what happens, and troubleshoot, and fix things up as you go along." The characterization Rory makes of his work as evolving, in reaction to what he tries out and adjusts along the way, with important contributions by other educators and students, resonates with ideas in the design literature. Specifically, I believe viewing the structures and practices that constitute projects in Rory's classroom as the object of *iterative, participatory, situated design* may prove useful.

Let me return to Rory's class to illustrate these design terms. The design of these projects is *iterative* in that Rory goes through cycles of upfront planning of the activity, followed by implementation of these plans with midstream adjustments to the situation as it develops, retrospective reflection on the projects, and redesign for the next round. Between 1992–93 and 1995–96, Rory completed eleven such cycles. The upfront planning consists partially in structuring project activity through the refinement of the paper format that serves as a blueprint for students' project work. Rory has changed the document detailing the paper format over time. The midstream adjustments Rory makes are countless, ranging from the negotiation of project topics such as those described with Kevin, Alex, Amanda, and Jeff, to looking for ways to deal with grading conflicts. Such adjustments midstream are like "design in use" of the upfront plans (a term borrowed from Allen [1993]; this has affinity to Suchman's [1987] "situated actions" and Schön's [1982] "reflection *in* action"). Reflection on the projects in earlier cycles led Rory to see a need for a structure that students could follow, and to encourage students to find out more about their chosen topic before designating a final "question" to answer through their project (similar to Schön's "reflection *on* action"). The design of individual student projects is also iterative, in that students hand in milestones and receive feedback from Rory before incorporating them into their final paper.

The design of projects is *participatory* because it is socially constructed. This social construction of design takes place at several different levels. Rory and students like Jeff and Amanda interact to define and implement each and every project. Sometimes these interactions involve what Pea (1994) has termed "transformative communication." In such interactions, Rory helps the students transform the moves they make in the research process with limited understanding into more sophisticated moves that neither he nor the students would have originally predicted (see Chapter 10 for further details and examples). When the students present their projects to one another and they are discussed and critiqued publicly, they are participating in the group's sense of what valid projects are and how to conduct good projects. Thus, the "Aliens" project conducted by Alex and Kevin earlier in the year became emblematic of how important it is to use data effectively to construct an argument *and* to question the veracity of information sources. Finally, students' ideas for projects often act as seeds or sources for later projects: Rory's introductory sand analysis project this year grew out of a project that two students devised but had trouble implementing the previous year. Rory's input to Kevin and Alex on their geyser project was based on another project from the previous year.

Designers often talk about the set of given resources and/or constraints in the environment, each with certain *affordances* (a term introduced by Gibson, 1986, and elaborated by Norman, 1988). In Rory's particular *situated* work, students' interests are a resource, affording a means of students making problems their own, about topics such as salt lakes. Rory's skills at collaboratively constructing ideas with students facilitate building on students' interests in ways that his experience suggests will be productive and instructive. The paper format Rory and his fellow teachers constructed affords a way of structuring classroom activity around milestones corresponding to paper sections. Network tools such as the World Wide Web afford searching for information and data that can inform students' inquiry. Usenet News and electronic mail afford contacting and communicating with scientist mentors. Constraints for Rory include the structure of the school day, limited amounts of time with many student groups working on different problems, and the culture and practices of schooling that students encounter outside of Rory's class. Making a strong distinction between "resources" and "constraints" can be misleading, however, since "constraints can be turned into resources, and resources can turn out to be severe constraints" (Brown & Duguid, 1990, p. 38). Specifically, one aspect of the same environment or task can be seen as a resource by one person and a constraint by another, or a resource for one purpose and a constraint for another. The open campus policy at the school, for instance, acts in some ways as a resource that affords freedom of movement for students to accomplish aspects of their projects, but acts in other ways as a constraint on Rory's ability to track student activity.

Designers need to try to optimize for certain purposes, but will often be faced with tradeoffs (Pea, 1993b). This points to a further reason why I believe viewing the work of teachers as *designing* learning environments can be beneficial. It makes apparent the constructive, intentional nature of the work. As Shweder put it, "intentional persons" interact with and transform cultural meanings and social practices (1990), including the meaning and practice of conducting projects in a high school science class. Teachers such as Rory have the power to effect change at the classroom level, and are more likely to succeed if their teaching practice is reflective (Schön, 1982) and iterative, in a manner similar to the concept of spirals of reflection and action in the tradition of action research (Lewin, 1946) and also to the kinds of "design experiments" Collins (1992) recommends.

CONCLUSION: LEARNING FROM EXPEDITIONS

What can we learn from Rory? We can learn what paths he has taken. How he has helped his students to work together. How to judge the winds and unexpected storm clouds. How to survive the bitter cold of the night. How to find and work with a myriad of guides. What kind of grapples and knots he uses in different situations. Where the key footholds are in precarious situations. And above all, what these heights can look like and feel like to the guide and participants in these expeditions, and how they find ways to improvise their way toward the top.

CHAPTER 3

Historical Background:
Haven't We Tried This Before?

Rory Wagner's struggle to enact project-based science teaching in his class-room may not seem terribly unique. The historian of education might well ask, "Hasn't this all been tried before?" And with good reason. The idea of project-based science education is firmly rooted in the tradition of child-centered education spanning two centuries prior to the 1990s. In addition, agricultural educators after the turn of the 20th century introduced the idea of doing "projects" (Alberty, 1927), Dewey and later progressives refined the concept (Cremin, 1961), and reformers of the 1960s revived it (Ravitch, 1982). The very fact that project-based approaches have been tried before, showed success, and yet remain rare today, begs investigation. What happened to all these previous efforts? What can we learn from them? Do we have any reason to believe the outcome can be different now or in the future?

In the following pages, I will begin to address these questions. First, I will explore related efforts that have been tried in the past, and what we have learned from them. I will then consider why, at this particular historical moment, educators, other researchers, and concerned citizens have come to reconsider and reconceptualize the potential importance of project-based approaches to science learning. Along with this, I will examine some of the ways in which the nature of today's attempts at project-based science are shaped by historical particulars. This leads to consideration of the real settings in which the necessary changes will take place—class-rooms—and the kinds of research and practice that offer promise to under-standing and fostering such changes.

HASN'T THIS BEEN TRIED BEFORE?

A fundamental insight that has driven child-centered educational ap-proaches is that the mind is active and imposes meaning and structure on

23

experience. In two works influential on education from the 1760s—*Julie* and *Émile*—Jean-Jacques Rousseau stressed the importance of starting with the child's own experiences and dispositions and building on them, rather than imposing ideas that are relevant only from the perspective of the adult or society (Archer, 1964). Building on children's natural dispositions implies that all students cannot be treated the same. Instead, teachers must work to diagnose and cultivate those dispositions. Learning must also build from the child's personal experience: instead of learning geography from maps of distant locations, Émile is better served by studying his own area and constructing his own map (cited in Farnham-Diggory, 1990). Dewey's philosophy that "learning is active . . . it involves reaching out of the mind" (Dewey, 1902, p. 42) has much affinity with Rousseau. The importance of children's interests was stressed by both Rousseau and Dewey. Dewey noted that genuine interest linked to both the means and ends of the task at hand fosters true learning, whereas "sugar-coating" of tasks with extrinsic rewards fosters simply the appearance of attention (Dewey, 1895). Teachers need to diagnose interests as indicative of children's development and readiness to learn (Dewey, 1897). The child's every whim should not direct the educator's every action, however. As Rousseau put it, "No doubt [Émile] ought only to do what he wants, but he ought to do nothing but what you want him to do" (cited in Bantock, 1984).

Numerous schools and movements have been influenced by these basic child-centered principles. Froebel and Pestallozzi founded schools in Europe, which Americans such as Francis Parker observed in their travels. Parker later led reforms in Quincy, Massachusetts, and at the Cook County Normal School in Chicago based on the theories of Rousseau, Froebel, and Pestallozzi (Farnham-Diggory, 1990). In both cases, he replaced the traditional curriculum with projects more relevant to students' lives. John and Evelyn Dewey founded their laboratory school at the University of Chicago after visiting Cook County Normal School (Cremin, 1961). At the Dewey lab school, students participated in a series of cooperative projects of increasing complexity. The youngest children worked on practical projects such as building a house or planting a garden, while older children studied formal subjects such as botany. The projects had both instrumental and intrinsic purposes: they afforded a means to foster intellectual and social growth vital to participation in a democracy, and also met students' immediate interests (Cremin, 1961).

Dewey's lab school, philosophy, and leadership at the University of Chicago were immensely influential on the progressive movement (Hofstadter, 1963), which carried on through the 1930s. The notion of hands-on projects picked up growing numbers of adherents as well. Alberty (1927) traces the first use of the term "project" to 1908, when agricultural educators in Massachusetts used it to denote the *growing* of crops as opposed to studying *how* to grow crops. The activity of successfully growing plants had intrinsic interest to the students, and could even result in financial gain. As in Dewey's projects, the knowledge gained in agricultural projects had more than practical purposes—it was integrated with formal and abstract principles of the discipline. In the case of the agricultural projects, disciplinary principles were provided through textbooks and lectures (Alberty, 1927). The application and meaning of the term "project" to other subject areas was debated among progressive educators, but some themes were common. Many projects involved the use of concrete materials to solve some problem in a natural setting (Horn, 1920). Projects also had to engage student interest—the interest should be high (Kilpatrick, 1925), and the students' goals should match the teacher's (Alberty, 1927).

SO IT HAS BEEN TRIED BEFORE—WHAT HAPPENED?

So child-centered instruction, including project-based teaching, was tried on a large scale in the progressive movement. But by the late 1940s, it had died out. Why did schools and teachers fail to sustain these ideas? An obvious explanation would be that these methods didn't work. The Progressive Education Association's influential Eight-Year Study (Aikin, 1942) documented the contrary. In this study of 1,475 pairs of students, each consisting of one student from 30 participating progressive schools and one from another secondary school, the effectiveness of progressive education was supported. Students of progressive schools, who were otherwise like their peers from other schools in gender, age, race, scholastic aptitude, home and community background, and interests, were more successful as judged by 11 separate measures (Cremin, 1961). These measures ranged from academic honors and grades to curiosity, resourcefulness, and precision in thinking. Kyle (as cited in Cole & Griffin, 1987) reports similar positive findings for the hands-on, inquiry-oriented science reforms of the 1960s and 1970s:

> Evidence shows that students in such courses had enhanced attitudes toward science and scientists; enhanced higher-level intellectual skills such as critical thinking, analytical thinking, problem solving, creativity, and process skills; as well as a better understanding of scientific concepts. (Kyle, as cited in Cole & Griffin, 1987, p. 21)

The failure of the child-centered and project-oriented reforms, from the progressive era as well as the 1960s, to sustain their hold on educational practice requires some explanation, and many have been offered over the years. I will briefly review some before offering a synthesis.

Downfall One: Misguided Implementation of Reform

Hofstadter (1963) argues that the importance of interest in Dewey's theory of education led to serious mistakes on the part of later progressives. Dewey's own work (e.g., Dewey, 1902) stressed that the developing interests of children should continuously interact with the direction they get from adults. But the stress placed on the importance of students' interests led some progressives to become slavish to student whim:

> Having once put the child so firmly at the center, having defined education as growth without end, Dewey had so weighted the discussion of educational goals that a quarter of a century of clarificatory statements did not avail to hold in check the anti-intellectual perversions of his theory. (Hofstadter, 1963, p. 389)

As Hofstadter mentioned, Dewey criticized later progressives for proceeding "as if any form of direction and guidance by adults were an invasion of individual freedom" (Dewey, 1938/1950, p. 9). This critique of progressivism amounts to placing the blame for its eventual failure on misguided and thus ineffectual implementation of the reform. Sarason (1971) identified the same important issue of teachers' lack of understanding of a reform effort in the case of the New Math.

Studies of the California *Mathematics Curriculum Framework* in two classrooms provide detailed examples of how the goals of reformers are transformed by teachers' understandings about subject matter. Deborah Ball (1990) studied a teacher for whom she used the pseudonym Carol Turner. Ms. Turner appeared to run a classroom where children were actively engaged, consistent with the goals of the reform. On closer examination, it became clear that Carol understood mathematics not as a living and growing domain of inquiry, but as a set of static tools to be learned. This fundamental view led her to overlook the possibility of children formulating problems themselves or evaluating alternative mathematical claims. Instead, there was always a "right answer" "out there" (p. 256). Carol knew those right answers, and tightly structured activity so as to instill them in the children. Classroom discourse was characterized by teacher instruction and questions followed by terse student answers. Because Carol was able to foster student participation in classroom discourse and make creative use of multiple teaching modalities to reach students with different strengths, she saw no need to change. David Cohen (1990) studied another math teacher in California who "revolutionized" her teaching by using a new curriculum and text, incorporating concrete materials and physical activities. Although she was open to and used all these new mathematical topics and devices, she too "used them as though they were a part of traditional school mathematics . . . as though mathematics contained only right and wrong answers" (p. 312).

Downfall Two: Interference of School and Task Structures with Reform

Other factors have been shown to hinder reform as well. Just when the progressive movement was gaining momentum, "education for all" was gradually becoming a reality (Nasaw, 1979). The large numbers of students needed to be handled in some way, and factory models—such as platooning—for moving children through the day with limited resources and optimal order proved useful. Larry Cuban (1984) argues that platooning and other school and classroom structures hindered the spread of child-centered instruction as much as ineffectual implementation. Schools and teachers use the various "batch processing" methods that today constitute the standard "grammar of schooling" (Tyack & Tobin, 1994) to cope with the demand of teaching and keeping in order groups of 30 children at once. These methods include school structures, such as Carnegie units of academic credits, age-graded grouping, and isolated classrooms; classroom-level structures, such as desks in rows and whole-group question-and-answer dialogues and lectures; and "task structures" (Doyle, 1979), such as worksheets and textbook assignments. Task structures such as projects, however, can be at odds with the teachers' priority of maintaining order, as well as with the students' priority of getting an optimal grade, because they increase ambiguity on how to perform to achieve a good grade and therefore increase perceived risk for the students. It is interesting to note that Dewey himself warned that "the mechanics of school organization and administration" (Dewey, 1901, p. 337) often doomed reforms, but his warning did not prevent such factors from affecting his own efforts.

Downfall Three: The Social Control Role of Schooling

Theorists such as Nasaw (1979) argue that schools play a social controlling role in society. According to this view, students are "sorted" in order to channel them toward "appropriate" careers, ostensibly based on intellectual capacity. The aspiration of American education to be a "meritocracy" (Lemann, 1995) in which students succeed on the basis of merit alone has long been unfulfilled in the face of differential treatment based on social class, culture, gender, or race. A historical example is the "life adjustment" education of the 1930s and 1940s. Nasaw showed how life adjustment was targeted primarily toward poorer populations, and closed opportunities for financial advancement through traditionally elite professions at the same time that it enhanced opportunities in working-class careers. In addition to encouraging students from different groups to take different classes, treatment within the same class has been shown to lead to group-based sorting. In classroom interactions between teacher and students, numerous researchers more recently have shown how language differences from the mainstream disadvantage African-Americans and other minority groups (e.g., Au & Mason, 1981; Heath, 1983) and how hidden assumptions about gender-based competence lead teachers to undermine young women, especially in math and science classes (Eccles, 1989; Sadker & Sadker, 1994; Tobin & Garnett, 1987). Since project-based reforms do not fit well into traditional testing paradigms and demand different norms for classroom interactions, the pressure to sort students in familiar ways may both consciously and unconsciously exert pressure to return to traditional methods of instruction.

Downfall Four: The Culture of Teaching and Beliefs About Teaching/Learning

Larry Cuban's (1984) analysis suggests that the three explanations described above—schooling as social control, school and task structures, and the implementation of reform—partially account for the remarkable constancy in teaching practice throughout this century, parallel with pockets of change. The culture of teaching and beliefs about teaching and learning also provide partial accounts (Cohen, 1988b; Cuban, 1984). Cuban and Cohen argue that the culture of teaching tends to be conservative due to recruitment of people who affirm rather than challenge the role of schools. In addition, informal socialization to previously existing practices is accomplished through 12 years of personal experience, and interactions with other teachers once on the job. The complex demands placed on new teachers also tend to reinforce reliance on remembered strategies and folklore passed among practicing teachers. New teachers must establish routines so that students are not disorderly and/or confused, convey prescribed subject matter to large groups of children, and evaluate all of those children. Reforms often explicitly threaten the culture of teaching by demanding changes in practice, and implicitly threaten aspects of the ethos of teaching by encroaching on the vacation time viewed as an essential feature of a profession that lacks significant financial rewards. In addition, folklore and beliefs about traditional practices that constitute a "real school" (Tyack & Tobin, 1994) are strong among parents and the population at large. Finally, child-centered instruction rests on the premise that learning is an active process of construction. But this belief is still a relatively radical notion among teachers (Cohen, 1990; Cuban, 1984), who more commonly believe that knowledge must be directly transmitted to young people and remembered as conveyed. In addition, everyday views and practices outside schools—among parents, business leaders, and students themselves—tend to buttress the belief that knowledge is transmitted rather than constructed (Cohen, 1988b).

Downfall Five: The Social Context of Teaching and Learning in Classrooms

The experience of school for teachers and students is not wholly determined by cultural beliefs about teaching and learning, however. Penelope Eckert (1990) has shown that schools are cultural institutions that serve many social purposes other than teaching and learning in classrooms. Primary among these purposes is student participation in social networks represented by social categories such as "jocks" and "burnouts." The dynamics created by these social networks affect what courses students take, and how they view participation in the courses they do take. According to Eckert's account, high schools offer jocks an avenue for performing meaningful social roles outside the parents' home. High schools also offer jocks an opportunity to participate in activities inside and outside the classroom that will help them build their careers. For jocks, participation in classroom activities is more driven by conservative career-building than by interest in what is going on. They thus tend to chafe at innovative and challenging classes, which reforms to project-based science represent, because they complicate climbing up the hierarchy and challenge the value of received knowledge that can be displayed for status. In the burnout network, on the other hand, cooperative learning where students share information and initiate much of the activity is more highly valued. Thus burnouts may be more receptive to project-based science courses where teachers act as facilitators to students' active construction of knowledge, rather than passive reception of knowledge.

Building on Eckert's research, Lave (1990) points out that according to the worldview generally held by researchers on learning, "students appear to occupy a peripheral role as objects or clients on whom services are to be performed . . . students are not viewed as powerfully influential on teacher, subject, pedagogy, or the learning that transpires in the classroom" (p. 253). Lave argues that this worldview is fundamentally flawed. Learning and classroom activity are socially situated, as Eckert's research demonstrates. Thus, I claim that the meaning of classroom activity, including that based on reform, can only be understood relative to the broader social situation in which it is embedded.

Research on science teachers, for example, has shown that students' reactions can be an important constraint on their teachers' actions. As Jay Lemke put it,

> While teachers "officially" have greater power and authority in the classroom,
> . . . students retain an absolute veto over activities the teacher tries to impose.
> Even the threat of that veto, student noncompliance or uncooperative behav-
> ior, is enough to keep most teachers . . . within the standard classroom rou-
> tines and activity structures that students have learned to expect and have be-
> come comfortable with. One result of this is that teachers who try to innovate
> in the classroom can expect to meet with considerable student resistance, at
> least at first. (Lemke, 1990, p. 71)

Brickhouse and Bodner (1992) demonstrated that a beginning middle
school science teacher's work with students was strongly influenced by the
students' concern with grades. Although the teacher believed scientists were
motivated by the pursuit of knowledge, his students continually connected
classroom activity to the pursuit of high grades. In turn, the teacher began
searching for ways in which students experiencing trouble with their grades
could succeed, and began limiting his own conception of rewards for good
work to grades. This finding is in line with the more general insight that
classroom activity and success are an interactional achievement of the student, teacher, and context, not determined by any one actor alone or the
environment (e.g., Doyle, 1979; Mehan, 1989).

Downfall Six: Economic and Political Pressures

Economic and political pressures have affected many reform efforts as well.
Nasaw (1979) documented how the business community in the National
Association of Manufacturers became involved in educational policy during the early 1900s, by funding the National Society for the Promotion of
Industrial Education, to ensure a steady supply of appropriately trained
American workers. Today, business-driven organizations such as the National Skill Standards Board (Houghton, 1996) and others are again increasingly driving educational reforms and standard-setting (Resnick,
1995). Similarly, promoters of progressive education and reforms of the
1960s garnered economic as well as political clout by aligning themselves
with powerful foundations (Tyack & Tobin, 1994). Ravitch (1982) and
Cuban (1990) have described the changing political climate's affect on education. Ravitch's account focuses on the conflict between "progressives"
and "traditionalists" since the 1940s. At that time, progressivism was dominated by "life adjustment education," and critics began to complain of
anti-intellectualism. With the Sputnik incident, the traditionalists' calls
were heeded, and "excellence" initiatives in subjects such as math and science were begun. Following the cataclysmic events of the civil rights movement and the Vietnam War, the work of progressives (e.g., Kohl, 1967;

Neill, 1960) became prominent again and ushered in the "open education" movement. Although Cuban (1990) criticizes the pendulum metaphor Ravitch and others use, he concurs that "value differences . . . become transformed by media and political coalitions into pressure on schools to change" (p. 8).

Dow's (1991) account of the origins of "Man: A Course of Study" (MACOS) in the Sputnik era and its eventual obliteration by conservatives on the local and national level, is a compelling example of politics' effects on reform. The "Anti-American" implications that conservatives saw in the MACOS social science curriculum based on cross-cultural studies led to its demise, despite the fact that it was intended primarily to align instruction with university scholarship. Because of such strong political and economic pressures, local practitioners often make *symbolic* and *external* changes in schools rather than making the *substantive* changes reforms often demand (Fullan & Miles, 1992). Examples of empty symbolic changes are the purchase of new books that are taught in the same way as older books, and task forces at schools that popularize the use of new labels such as "cooperative learning" for the same old practices. The knowledge that previous waves of trendy new ideas and buzzwords have been ineffectual naturally makes teachers and other educators skeptical of new ones, and to some extent encourages surface adoption of the latest trend (Sarason, 1971) rather than more fundamental appropriation.

A SYNTHESIS—SITUATIONALLY CONSTRAINED CHOICE

Cuban (1984) introduced the concept of "situationally constrained choice" to explain the relative stability in teaching over the past century, amid pockets of change. Cuban's description synthesizes many of the insights provided by the partial explanations described above, and accommodates the additional factors discussed here that he didn't explicitly consider. He describes situationally constrained choice as follows: "The school and classroom structures . . . established the boundaries within which individual teacher beliefs and an occupational ethos worked their influences in shaping practical pedagogy" (p. 250).

School and classroom structures serve as constraints on the environment. These structures are influenced by political and economic realities, such as the acceptability of certain curricular topics, the importance of order, and the number of students per teacher. The structures are also influenced by social realities, such as the meaning ascribed to them by students. The structures that dominate, such as chairs in rows, recitations, worksheets, and textbook assignments, successfully solve the daily problems presented by the task of teaching groups of children in limited time while maintaining discipline. But there is potential for change, particularly through changes in teacher beliefs. Effective reform efforts and the gradual encroachment of the view of learning as active construction on popular consciousness (Cohen, 1988b) can and have influenced beliefs, which in turn influence practices. But putting beliefs about the nature of learning into practice is seriously hindered by the constraints of schooling and teachers' relative lack of autonomy.

Ultimately, instruction occurs in individual classrooms, and some teachers make efforts based on their beliefs about how learning occurs. Due to the unavoidable constraints of school structures, however, such efforts meet with some degree of frustration. Dealing with this frustration relates to two primary reasons cited by researchers for teachers' lack of change in classroom practice: the cost in time and energy to prepare and deal with the effort, and the lack of extra help or resources in putting complex ideas into practice (Cole & Griffin, 1987; Cuban, 1984; Office of Technology Assessment [OTA], 1995). Sarason's (1971) account of the failure of the new math in a school system provides evidence for the importance of both time and resources. In order to implement the reform, elementary school teachers, many of whom had little math background, were asked to learn a great deal of math and new teaching methods within a short workshop and the few weeks following it before the upcoming school year. Once the school year began, there were scant resources for supervision and ongoing work with the teachers. They were left on their own to flounder or flourish.

CAN COMPUTERS AND NETWORKING
PROVIDE SUPPORTIVE RESOURCES?

Recently, reformers have stressed that computers and networking can perhaps provide vital support for teachers attempting to put project-based science into practice (e.g., Blumenfeld et al., 1991; Pea, 1993a). But the history of reform related above, as well as Cuban's (1986) study of how new technologies have failed to alter teaching practices, should serve to temper optimism.

Cuban (1986) documented how several waves of technology in this century failed to significantly alter the practices of teaching. The promoters of radio, film, and instructional television predicted revolutionary changes in the efficiency and effectiveness of instruction through technology. But as with other changes, teachers ultimately made choices based on their situation: "Teachers *have* altered practice when a technological innovation helped them to do a better job of what they already decided had to be done and matched their view of daily classroom realities" (p. 66). Thus, instructional television encountered problems because it lacked flexibility. Trying to schedule classroom activity around a haphazard schedule of broadcasts, as well as signing out and setting up the equipment, proved to be obstacles working against the very efficiency they were supposed to enhance. On the other hand, some elementary school teachers used films and television in the afternoon to some degree, as entertainment and motivation for their students rather than integral parts of instruction.

The kinds of changes radio, film, and television were intended to provide were more a matter of degree than kind, however. They hoped to offer more efficient and entertaining *transmission* of information to students. Since these technologies failed for the most part to provide greater efficiency in doing the same thing most teachers were trying to do, it was not surprising to see them neglected. In contrast, computers and networking, the latest technologies to be heralded as revolutionizing instruction, have consistently been linked to reforms toward child-centered instruction.

Seymour Papert, for instance, argued in *Mindstorms* (1980) that the LOGO programming language could put children in an active position of constructing knowledge of how to use powerful ideas from science and mathematics. Papert's early work focused primarily on what the computer could do for children, and seldom described how it fit within classroom life. But as Mehan's study of microcomputer use by teachers in language arts classes confirmed, "when used in educational settings, the microcomputer is always a part of a larger social system" (Mehan, 1989). Thus, it's not surprising that the spread of LOGO in the early 1980s resulted in uses that were in line with the kinds of teacher-centered priorities Cuban has documented. By 1990, Papert's group had been roundly criticized for the lack of consonance between the claims made in *Mindstorms* and the practices implemented in classrooms across the country. Once again, reformers were reminded that computers, like other technologies, are not themselves agents for change; rather, teachers and students are (Harel & Papert, 1993; Mehan, 1989).

The question of whether and how computers and networking can serve as resources for educators who are agents in the change process remains. Recall Brown and Duguid's (1990) insight that whether a given "objective fact" is viewed as a constraint or a resource depends on interpretation as well as creativity. Since the same "objective fact" can be interpreted as either a constraint or a resource, it might be fruitful to consider how teachers have "situationally resourced choice" along with "situationally constrained choice" in environments incorporating computers. I turn now to a discussion of how today's efforts to change instruction toward project-based science differ from previous reform efforts, due to cultural and historical particulars.

A PARTICULAR HISTORICAL MOMENT

Understanding the context of efforts at change requires looking at this particular historical moment. In the 1990s there is a renewed interest in child-centered approaches to learning science, such as inquiry and projects (e.g., National Research Council, 1996). There is also widespread belief that technology can effectively support changes to such approaches (Dede, 1990; Means et al., 1993; Office of Technology Assessment, 1995). The reasons for interest in child-centered approaches, inquiry-based approaches, technology use, and their interconnections are embedded in theoretical, political, and economic developments that deserve some explication.

Emerging Views of Learning

Theoretical advances in our understanding of learning have transformed the reasons for recommending open-ended projects in a rich social setting. Constructivism, shaped by the research of Piaget, provides an explanation for the importance of active engagement. In this view, all experiences are filtered through existing mental models, and either alter those constructions or are assimilated to them (von Glasersfeld, 1989). Vygotsky's theory of learning provides an explanation for the importance of learning embedded in a social setting. According to Vygotsky (1978), language and social interaction mediate learning. In other words, operations that take place on the interpersonal level (i.e., activity-in-the-world involving multiple people) are transformed into *intra*personal operations in learning (i.e., representations in the mind). This leads to the concept of the "Zone of Proximal Development," in which learners accomplish with the help and cooperation of others (e.g., teachers) what they could not do alone, and push their individual capabilities to new levels by internalizing the process.

Building on Vygotsky's work, later theorists have argued that all cognition and learning are situated in particular environments (Brown, Collins, & Duguid, 1989), and that thinking is distributed across physical as well as social aspects of the environment (Pea, 1993b). Since knowledge is indexed and recalled according to aspects and interpretations of the environment in which it is embedded, *authentic* settings for learning become extremely important (Brown et al., 1989). In order for the knowledge gained in a learning setting to be useful in the actual domain under study, the setting must be consonant with the cultural practices and tools of the domain. This perspective provides further justification for project-based learning,

> so that students can face the task of formulating their own problems, guided on the one hand by the general goals they set, and on the other hand by the "interesting" phenomena and difficulties they discover through their interaction with the environment . . . in projects, students learn first to find a problem and then, ideally, to use the constraints of the embedding context to help solve it. (Collins, Brown, & Newman, 1989, p. 488)

Based on the situated nature of learning, Collins et al. (1989) argue that a strategy of "cognitive apprenticeship" is promising for schools. Taking a cue from the practices of craft apprenticeship, cognitive apprenticeship offers some metaphors for teachers' work. Teachers can model expert activity and make their tacit knowledge explicit. They can also coach students while they carry out tasks, "offering hints, scaffolding, feedback, modeling, reminders, and new tasks" (p. 481). Scaffolding provides support for accomplishing goals in students' "zone of proximal development," and is often later faded so that students can exercise their new skills to perform the activity without teacher support. In addition, finding ways to encourage student articulation of their ideas can push learning.

Emerging Importance of Computing and Networking Technology

One means of promoting student articulation is through shared computer environments (Edelson & O'Neill, 1994; O'Neill & Gomez, 1994; Scardamalia, Bereiter, McLean, Swallow, & Woodruff, 1989). Computer technology also lends authenticity to the practices of science today (McGee, 1996), which make increasingly sophisticated use of high-performance computing, such as visualization and modeling (Fishman & D'Amico, 1994; Gordin et al., 1994), and communication such as electronic mail (Fishman, 1996; Sproull & Kiesler, 1991).

Computer technology is important today for political and economic reasons as well. Collins (1991) argues that since computers are so vital to work in today's world, they are bound to have an effect on education. Skills in working with computers are vital to participation in the emerging information economy, so schools will face increasing pressure to incorporate their use into instruction. Based on previous research, Collins argues that once computers are introduced into the classroom setting, regardless of the purposes, their continued and committed use are likely to result in several changes. For example, computer use should foster student engagement and necessitate small-group instruction instead of whole-group instruction and coaching instead of lecture and recitation. In effect, this argument maintains that computer use will introduce constraints that over-power the standard constraints of schooling described by Cuban. In order to provide students with more computer time, for instance, teachers who have a limited number of computers in their classrooms face constrained choices about how to reorganize instruction. Two common solutions that Mehan (1989) identified were incorporating computers into small-group work for one group at a time, and sending pairs of students to work at the computer during time set aside for individual seatwork. Both these options involved a grouping strategy, peer interaction, much different from whole-class instruction. The teacher no longer directly supervised the students' work. Instead, students used one another as resources and talked through their work on the computer, thereby surfacing confusions. They also ex-plained their understandings to one another, which caused them to articu-late and reevaluate those understandings. Meanwhile, the teacher no longer initiated all interaction—the students called for the teachers' help and coaching when they encountered trouble.

Cuban (1993) agrees with Collins's (1990) prediction that increased technology use will foster change in some settings, but does not concur that such changes will occur in all settings. Specifically, Cuban argues that Collins's vision will be implemented in elementary schools, but that change at the high school level will not be generally forthcoming due to the greater constraints placed on high schools. These constraints are of three types: the economic pressures for training in complex subject matter, the structural constraints associated with limited teacher contact time with students, and political pressures from accrediting associations, college entrance require-ments and exams, and job market requirements. In this view, pressures for computer competence would be forced into didactic, isolated parts of the curriculum to continue meeting the demands of other constraints. At the elementary school level, Cuban believes there is enough flexibility and less pressure, which is likely to allow for greater use of computers across the curriculum.

Nonetheless, there is some indication that changing cultural beliefs combined with economic transformation may bode well for sustaining re-form. Teacher beliefs in more active learning and models of teaching offer a window of opportunity for change, even within highly constrained school environments (Cuban, 1984). Cohen (1988b) argues that the active view of learning is still relatively new, and is only slowly encroaching on the more common everyday conception of learning as transmission. Over time, more teachers, students, parents, and business people may be subscribing to these views. In fact, businesses have already begun to call for more active problem-solvers, rather than passive direction-followers. The Secretary's Commission on Achieving Necessary Skills (SCANS, 1991) argues that the information-oriented and service-oriented sectors of the economy require such dispositions. Even the manufacturing sector, inspired by international competition and changing technologies, has begun to appreciate the active contribution all their employees can make (Houghton, 1996).

Finally, interaction is possible between new constraints introduced by technology use in classrooms and teachers' beliefs about learning and instruction. Although it is often true that practices follow beliefs, McLaughlin (1990) has suggested that beliefs can be changed by participation in certain practices, even if they are mandated practices—the experience of the Rand Change Agent study, a large-scale evaluation of reform efforts, bears this out. Evaluators of the Apple Classrooms of Tomorrow showed how regular access to computer technology was indeed instrumental in changing teachers' beliefs as well as their practices (Dwyer, Ringstaff, & Sandholtz, 1991). Teachers in the study began by using computer technology for traditional practices, but when they mastered the technology themselves and saw some of the work their students were able to accomplish, they began to take more risks. This risk-taking, combined with the uncertainties introduced by the new constraints that computer use put on teachers' work, often led to a reappraisal of beliefs. But Dwyer et al., along with others (e.g., Brickhouse & Bodner, 1992; Cole & Griffin, 1987), maintain that teachers do not always have the opportunity to reflect on the relationship between their beliefs and their classroom practices, nor the latitude to make all the changes they would like.

Thus, we would do well to remember Seymour Sarason's advice about single solutions:

> It is not that these single . . . solutions are in themselves wrong or inadvisable but rather that they are viewed as ends, which if reached will in some mystical way change the quality of life in the classroom and school. (Sarason, 1971, p. 225)

Computer technology, like the project method of teaching, does not mystically change the quality of life in schools, but rather interacts with the many cultural and material constraints and resources I have described.

THE IMPORTANCE OF EXAMINING CHANGE IN DETAIL IN ONE SETTING

I have described several reasons to recommend project-based science learning in computerized, networked classrooms, and the growing interest in such efforts. But ultimately, these aspirations must be met by individual teachers in classrooms within actual schools. Based on her experience in a large-scale evaluation of reforms, Milbrey McLaughlin argues that change is a "problem of the smallest unit" (1990, p. 12). In other words, local realities determine the outcomes of change more than global policies or visions. Bruce, Peyton, and Batson (1993) highlight this truism by stressing the difference between an innovation's "idealization" and its many local "realizations." As the review above has demonstrated, the local realities that determine realizations include teacher and student beliefs and practices, the resources and expertise available, political and economic realities, and traditions and social circumstances in the school. Bruce et al. also sketched some of the paths of change in which values and technical capabilities interact to bring about new possibilities. It is important to remember that such paths are not deterministic—they involve a series of implicit and explicit choices made by individuals such as teachers. These choices are affected by factors at many levels, as this chapter has illustrated.

In Schön's influential work (1982), he called for research in professions such as teaching that could contribute to what he calls "frame analysis" by providing an inside view of practice. He said:

> This sort of frame analysis would help practitioners to experience the world they would create for themselves if they adopted a particular way of framing the practice role. It would convey the experience of problem-setting and solving, the self-definitions and the definitions of success and failure, that would be inherent in a particular choice of role frame . . . it would help the practitioner to "try on" a way of framing the practice role, getting a feeling for it and for the consequences and implications of its adoption. (p. 315)

Such research is clearly needed on the complex project of putting project-based science teaching into practice. By studying in depth a single teacher's work at a single site, I will show how he frames and reframes his role and the problems he faces across multiple situations with a wide variety of students. I will examine the implications these choices have for his further work with students. As this review has illustrated, this will require examining how multiple levels of sociocultural context and situated actions affect his and his students' work. Making "adventurous teaching" (Cohen, 1988b) such as project-based science work requires complex negotiation of constraints and resources.

Just as practitioners face such complexity, research should. As Sarason (1971) pointed out years ago, researchers and practitioners should "avoid the understandable but self-defeating tendency to flee from complexity at the expense of relevance" (p. 32). In this endeavor, I follow the recommendation of Cuban:

It is important to policymakers, practitioners, administrators, and researchers to understand why reforms return but seldom substantially alter the regularities of schooling. The risks involved with a lack of understanding include pursuing problems with mismatched solutions, spending energies needlessly, and accumulating despair. The existing tools of understanding are no more than inadequate metaphors that pinch-hit for hard thinking. We can do better by gathering data on particular reforms and tracing their life history in particular classrooms. (Cuban, 1990, p. 12)

In this way, I will describe a journey, not a blueprint (Fullan & Miles, 1992). Blueprints for school reform and other social change generally fail, since they assume an ability to rationally plan for all the possibilities of complex and varied situated environments. Suchman's (1987) work on the difficulty of creating expert help systems for copy machines convincingly shows that such prescriptions are doomed to inadequacy in the face of real situations in myriad settings. I will characterize the types of decisions a teacher has made and continues to face in his journey, the range of possible choices, the tradeoffs and implications involved in his choices, and the conflicts and interactions between the many available courses of action. The description and analysis of this one journey will thus serve as a guide for future travelers along the paths of reform.

CHAPTER 4

A Teacher's Journey: Finding Shoes That Fit

Understanding what Rory does in his classroom requires some consideration of his "life narrative" (Ayers, 1989). In this chapter, I will examine some pertinent aspects of Rory's life narrative that led him to venture into project-based science teaching and continue struggling to improve his approach, despite early difficulties putting projects into practice.

SWIMMING UPSTREAM

Like many careers, Rory's career as a high school Earth Science teacher did not come about as a result of a clear, linear plan. It was a "big, long, complex, twisty windy road." He once said, "I don't have a life plan . . . I've never had a plan . . . how the hell did I get into teaching? I didn't plan to be here. I didn't plan to be here for 22 years. I had no idea where I was going." Rory had spent his first year in college as what he calls an "Intro major"—someone who takes introductory courses of all types. But then in his second year, geology captured his imagination and attention: "I was wandering through the forest looking for something interesting, and I found geology." Before, "rocks were things that you threw at your little brother," but now they revealed fascinating stories about the world. His interest grew, and he experienced early success. But during his junior year in college a course in geophysics, where "a new Ph.D. . . . was throwing formulas and stuff around the room like boomerangs, and [Rory] was getting hit in the head too much," convinced Rory that graduate school in geology was not for him. He didn't have a strong college math background, and he believed at the time that would not bode well for graduate studies. So he considered his options, and decided he could still work in geology if he became a teacher. Becoming an Earth Science teacher would also mean being involved with astronomy, another class that had "literally broadened

[his] horizons." When he was taking astronomy in college, he'd "looked out at the sky and wondered at how far away the stars were and even further the other galaxies were." He took education courses, and found that he liked them, too.

In his work as a teacher, Rory "wanted to share all the cool stuff that [he] learned." As already mentioned, one of the most powerful sources for teachers' ideas on teaching practice is previous experience in school (Cohen, 1988b; Cuban, 1984). To figure out what to do, Rory turned to the model of some of the good teachers he had had, like the paleontology professor who gave great lectures, including one in which he impersonated an ancient coral. Most of what they had done, and what he began doing, was "telling people about [phenomena] . . . 'here's how things work.' You know. Here's what happens in an earthquake, and here's what happens in a volcano, and here's plate tectonics. Here's how ocean currents move." He typically divided up the year into four topics, corresponding to the four subfields of Earth Science: geology, oceanography, meteorology, and astronomy. He still takes pride in some of the skills he developed—drawing illustrations on the board, such as diagrams of plate tectonics and ocean currents, and explaining how these phenomena work, and answering students' questions.

But there were downsides—engaging students' interests, finding ways to get students' "hands dirty" in Earth Science, and maintaining his own interest all proved difficult. Throughout, Rory "felt like a fish swimming upstream." Even worse, he "felt like a salmon swimming up Niagara Falls." Rory tried many different ways to get the students engaged and interested over the years, all within the basic framework of "lecture-lab-demo" science teaching. After beginning to teach with projects, Rory summed up his previous practice like this:

> You go through the year, and you do your lectures. You cover your stuff. You have your labs. You grade your labs. You wade through all the paperwork. You add up all the points. You give the grades. You give the tests. You know, very standard. Very boring . . .
>
> At the same time, you're trying not to be boring. You're trying to come up with activities . . . that are exciting, that make kids think, and understand how things work, and hopefully some of it works.

To make things work better, Rory tried varying the order in which he covered topics, depending on "the way things worked the year before." He added in videos and laserdiscs that he found thought-provoking. But the students' interests seldom seemed to match his own:

And then that leads to all kinds of things like falling asleep, [and] doing other homework . . . and then *my* feelings are hurt 'cause they're
doing their history while I'm trying to do my world's best lecture on
plate tectonics, and they don't want it, 'cause they don't need it,
'cause they have a history test next period, and couldn't give a shit
about plate tectonics.

Rory also tried new labs almost every year, but he was "frustrated by the
nature of the laboratory activities in Earth Science." Their vicinity is not a
terribly exciting area for Earth Science study—except for glaciers, lakes,
and weather, there was nothing much to "get your hands into." And the
laboratory exercises that tried to address other interesting issues, like earthquakes and volcanoes, were "the basic cookbook kind." The problem was,
"You get down to the end, and you're supposed to get something out of
it, and most of the time nobody does."

Finally, Rory himself "got bored . . . [with] talking about the same
thing over and over again," especially with four classes on the same subject
in the same day.

At the time he became involved in CoVis, in September 1992, Rory
was not sure he would be teaching for much longer. After 19 years, the
process had become too frustrating. He had been "trying to get them to
think a little bit . . . whether it [was] critically, about a particular problem,
or what's out there, that they haven't ever heard before." He had tried
for a long time to get the students excited about a subject he enjoyed so
much—geology—and a process that he found so fascinating—science. But
he felt over and over again that the "kids aren't interested—I am. . . . They
don't care about it."

FISH OUT OF WATER

In September 1992, Rory's department head suggested he go to the CoVis
meetings that other teachers at his school had begun attending the previous
summer, to see if he was interested. Given the background described above,
it is not surprising that Rory was intrigued by the idea of getting students
involved in doing science research. This approach was one that he had not
tried, and he felt that "if students are involved with doing things that they
pick and design, they [will be] more apt to be more energized by that, and
take more interest in and ownership in it." Instead of him saying "do this,
do this, do this," the students would get to make decisions. But he had a
dilemma: "How do I explain what I want them to do without telling them

exactly how to do it?" He and the other teachers in CoVis discussed this and other issues of introducing projects into their classrooms. Most of them decided to wait until the fall of 1993 to begin projects, so they had longer to discuss and plan. But after reading *LabNet* (Ruopp et al., 1993) and thinking hard about what he was trying to accomplish, Rory decided to step out of the familiar upstream struggle he'd been waging. In the second quarter of 1992–93, he decided to throw out his textbook reading assignments, lectures, and "cookbook" labs. He was uncertain how exactly he would go about helping his students do projects, because the LabNet teachers had all been working on physics projects, and he was unsure how to accomplish what they were doing in his Earth Science class. At the time, he said, "I felt totally like a fish out of water. Because I had no idea what I was doing. So I was really—you talk about winging it. You know? This was really winging it."

One reason he was "winging it" was that his personal experiences in secondary school and undergraduate studies did not provide him with models for this kind of teaching. So instead he turned to the model of the graduate research project. As mentioned previously, Rory avoided graduate studies right after college, but years later he decided to pursue a master's in geology. He studied the mineral compositions and fracture patterns in rocks in Wisconsin, under the guidance of a graduate advisor. Now he hoped he could get his students to play an active role in defining research problems, designing approaches to the problems, and performing the analyses, much as he had done for his master's. He would provide mostly feedback and advice, as his advisor had done.

He assigned students a quarter-long, open-ended project with no formal requirements other than that it have something to do with mapping, and that they give an oral presentation at the end. He himself had what he later characterized as a "vague" sense of what he wanted his students to accomplish, but felt they would enjoy the freedom of studying almost anything about the Earth they wanted. As related earlier, however, he was reminded that "things . . . don't always work the way you expect them to work"—his students felt as if he'd abandoned them on top of Mount Everest without a guide. Rory attributed some of the students' frustration to the fact that he had started the year out traditionally, then changed the "rules of the game" to a nontraditional model. When he told the students they would be doing real research, like graduate students, this only further daunted them. As he recalls it, their reaction was, " 'We're only fourteen and fifteen. How do you expect us to do projects that . . . scientists are working on?' " He wanted the students "to do all the work," and he was confident they could do it with his guidance. But he had to become comfortable with that role, rather than the role of disseminator of packaged knowledge. To avoid being overly directive, Rory often left students completely to their own devices.

Rory's initial swing away from teacher-directed pedagogy to a student-directed version is well described in a study by Rogoff (1994). As Rogoff describes, lecture-based classrooms depend on transmission of knowledge from an active teacher to a passive learner. When trying to get away from this model, teachers often move to the contrasting model of unguided discovery, which depends on acquisition of knowledge by an active learner with the teacher remaining passive. Rogoff suggests instead the model of community of learners. It "is based on the premise that learning occurs as people participate in shared endeavors with others, with all playing active but asymmetrical roles" (p. 209).

But the class was not functioning well as a community of learners. The frustration level in the class during that first project was high. Not only were the students expected to play this new game, but they were also "being graded on how they were playing." And they were "very vocal about not wanting to do this." I vividly recall seeing a red-faced student in those early days shout at Rory, "Just tell me what to do and I'll do it!" In addition, the students' parents "were of the type who would call the school and complain that their students aren't getting the traditional [instruction]."

LESSONS FROM THE "PRACTICAL TINKERER"

Rory still says emphatically that "lecture-lab-demo was easier than [project-based teaching]," but he persisted because he was committed to the idea of students doing science. Rather than abandoning project-based science, Rory modified what he was doing to make it work better. He credits his grandfather with teaching him that

> things don't always work right the first time, but then you keep on trying, you modify. . . . If you're patient enough, chances are you can get it done. And things that seem insurmountable aren't if you take them in small little pieces. And there's always a way to do *something*. And if you want to do it, then find a way to do it.

Rory spent a great deal of time as a child and adult with his grandfather, whom he calls a "practical tinkerer." When his grandfather needed to have an air conditioner on the second floor but didn't have a 220-volt line up there, he "drill[ed] a hole in the wall and [ran] a conduit down the outside of the building down to the basement," despite the fact that he wasn't an electrician. He just "learned how to do this stuff, either by watching other people or by doing—just by figuring it out himself." And when his grandfather ran into adversity, he was undaunted, even when he got to be over 60:

> I owned a house in the city for a couple of years, and we were doing some electrical work, and one image that always comes back to me is: it was a hot summer day, and we were in this crawl space, maybe we were between floors or something like that—there was a false ceiling on the first floor—and we were doing some wiring. And [my grandfather] was screwing something in, and he's sweating like crazy. And he's got these glasses. I don't even know how he could see, 'cause he had sweat all over the glasses. It must have been like looking underwater . . . and . . . I don't think I ever saw him get mad. You know? And there were really frustrating things . . . if [one thing] didn't work, then he'd try something else . . .

To this day, Rory works on projects around the house the same way, remembering his grandfather's example. When he needed heat in the laundry room in his house but there was no heating vent, he figured out a way to add one. He thought to himself,

> OK, there's a crawl space, and heating ducts. I know what heating ducts are, [but] I've never done any heating [work] before . . . I need this piece. I connect this piece to here, and this piece to here, and cut a hole in the floor, [and] put a vent in.

When Rory needed a lock for the sliding glass doors in his house, he tried all kinds of "store-bought gizmos" that didn't work, but eventually made a custom lock out of eight dollars' worth of [PVC] pipe and corners from the hardware store. He says that project is "still in evolution, as is everything that I do." His attitude both inside and outside the classroom is to figure out what the problem is, and "invent something that [will] fix it."

THE HIKING SHOES FIT

Rory's continued interest in project-based science teaching despite adversity has partly to do with personal style:

> It's a real shift, and the good thing is that it feels much better to me to do things this way. It's like an intuitive . . . kind of a thing. The way I described it to somebody . . . was kind of like having shoes that

fit, but they just . . . they don't *quite* fit right, and your feet hurt after you wear 'em for a while. They start out OK, but then they get kind of—they hurt. They're still OK, but they hurt. So then you get a new pair of shoes that just fit, perfectly. Your feet love it, and you can walk forever, and [your feet] *never* get sore. That's the way [project teaching] feels as opposed to [lecture-lab-demo]. It was *okay*, but it was always quirky, there were too many rough edges that I couldn't seem to get off.

So this fits better, I like this fit.

The reasons project-based science teaching "shoes fit" Rory relates to the reasons he found a summer Alpine Ecology course in Colorado to be "one of the best times" he ever had. It was a course offered to students at Lakeside, and Rory was asked to simply be a chaperone—he had no official teaching duties. After the students did some introductory lessons in the classroom, Rory went with them to the mountains of Colorado for a week of field study. The program involved "hiking, looking at flowers, the food web, the food chains, the ecology, the geology, and whatever kind of came up . . . [along with] free time to go horseback riding . . . go climbing in the rocks, [or] whatever." He told me what was so special about it:

We were walking around, and I didn't want to . . . force myself on kids as "Joe Geologist." Because then I'm like a teacher, and I didn't want to do that. So I was just kind of . . . out there, and we'd go on hikes, and I'd stop and look at things that I found interesting. [I'd] find a whole wall like this [gesturing expansively in front of him] that was all polished smooth and shiny from the glaciers. And [I'd] stop, and just look at it, and go, "Wow! I mean, this is really neat."

And just by . . . looking at something, kids go, "Hey, what are you looking at?"

[I'd answer], "Glaciers . . . See that U shape? Wow, that's really cool."

[The] kids go, "Oh, wow."

So then we went hiking one day to this old silver mine, and we were looking at rocks, and kids were saying, "What's this? What's this? What's this?" 'Cause they wanted to know what the stuff was . . . and I remember one time there was this kid, and we were taking a hike—it was a long hike—and we were going up over this pass. And kids were asking what these rocks were. "Eh? Feldspar. It's quartz. It's whatever."

Pretty soon . . . this one kid picked up this rock, and he went, "Oh, just some more crappy feldspar," and he threw it. "Feldspaaaar, heeeey!" So kids were learning things. It was funny. And there was one kid on that trip who was gonna be a biology major in college, and he switched to geology because he had so much fun out there. Not that I had that much to do with it, but something changed, in him, because of what he saw.

For Rory, the trip "was a great experience" because he wasn't telling them, "You *have* to know this," with them responding "I don't *wanna* know this," or "This is stupid." It's as if choosing to teach project-based Earth Science has allowed Rory to put the hiking shoes that he wore on that summer field study back on, and wear them into the classroom. In his class, students can follow up on their interests within Earth Science, and grow new interests. As Rogoff (1994) suggested, Rory does play an active and unique role, as a guide and spur to thought, rather than a disseminator of canned information. Learning to wear the shoes of the guide has required Rory to refine his unique role of modeling and structuring activities in the classroom so that students can learn to conduct scientific inquiry. I next examine the students' backgrounds that necessitate the refinement of this role.

CHAPTER 5

Students' Journeys: Bootstrapping New Practices

Three weeks into her first Earth Science project in Rory Wagner's class, a bewildered student came up to him and said, "I need to talk to you about my project. I'm at square zero."

Rory launched into part of the litany of suggestions he has developed over the previous three years of running a project-based class. He said, "OK. Basically, you need to pick a topic—anything that you're interested in. Say, volcanoes. You then learn about that, and then focus down. Say, on volcano lava, or the pattern of volcano eruptions."

The student continued, "I'm having trouble understanding the point of this project."

Rory reiterated his most familiar line, "I want you to *do science*."

The student retorted, "You can just read it in a book."

Well, you can certainly read *about* science in a book, but that is a far cry from *doing* science, as Rory well knew. But many of the students in Rory's class had never been challenged to take an active role in framing and solving scientific research questions. He settled in to a more extended conversation, hoping to make some progress.

WHERE THE STUDENTS ARE COMING FROM

In order to understand the meaning of doing projects in Rory Wagner's Earth Science class, it is necessary to go beyond what *he* is trying to accomplish, and look at how his students are positioned to interpret the course. In this chapter I will describe the relevant background of the 28 students in Lakeside High's Period 1/2 Earth Science class from 1995–96 that is described in the action detailed in Section II. As in the rest of this suburban school, most of the students are white—the exceptions are Cheryl, who is

African-American; Barb, whose parents are Asian; and Mark, whose parents are from the Middle East.

Interest in Science and This Class

To see how the students in Rory's class compare to other students, it is informative to compare the results of their responses to a few survey questions we asked 1,662 students at more than 30 urban and suburban schools participating in CoVis during the fall of 1995 (see Table 5.1).

In general, students in CoVis do not express much enthusiasm for science or science classes in the survey. Nevertheless, Rory's class come out below the means on all survey items that relate to students' enjoyment of science, expectations about future use of science, and participation in scientific activities. In addition, larger percentages of Rory's students give the lowest possible ratings on these survey items: for instance, 31% are emphatically *not* science people, compared to 16% among all other CoVis classes, and 69% say they will "definitely not" major in science in college, compared to 36% among other students.

My interviews with focus students in Rory's class provide a closer look at the reasons students sign up. Although they are not required to take the class, most students tend to sign up for Earth Science less out of interest in science in general or Earth Science in particular than a variety of other reasons—from getting credits out of the way to doing project work to working with computers. Steve, the freshman in the class, is one of the few, along with Adam, who come in with a strong interest in science. Since he is a freshman, Steve didn't know much about the course or the way it was taught before arriving. He signed up because he wanted to do something different, and most freshmen take biology. Besides, he didn't expect to enjoy biology as much as Earth Science—he hoped they might "go out in the field and use geologist's hammers" and so on in this course. Since Lakeside requires two science credits to graduate and one of them must be in "physical sciences" (Earth Science, Chemistry, and Physics), some of the juniors and seniors in the class, like Patti and Beth, are taking the course to get their final science requirement and avoid the other choices they and most of the other students in the class perceive as more difficult. Patti does not like science, whereas Beth says she likes science, but doesn't consider herself good at it. Patti also took the class to be with some friends who were signing up. Cheryl, too, was attracted to the Earth Science course in part because she expected less math than the AP science courses she saw as an alternative. Cheryl is also an example of a student who is definitely not a math or science person—she is a senior much more interested in English and theater, and is "not really interested in [Earth Science] as a subject"—

TABLE 5.1. Mean student responses to survey items on science interest.

Item & Scale (all are 1-5 Likert ratings)	Mean, Wagner classes (N=26)	Mean, other CoVis classes (N=1592)
1 = I am NOT a "science" or "math" person 3 = Neutral 5 = I AM a "science" or "math" person	2.5	3.2
I enjoy classes in science. 1 = disagree strongly 3 = neutral 5 = agree strongly	3.2	3.5
Can you see yourself becoming a scientist? 1 = definitely not 3 = maybe 5 = definitely yes	1.6	2.0
Can you see yourself majoring in science in college? 1 = definitely not 3 = maybe 5 = definitely yes	1.8	2.4
Can you see yourself using science in your career? 1 = definitely not 3 = maybe 5 = definitely yes	2.7	3.0

Note. Twenty-six of 28 students responded to this survey.

but who is taking the course with an eye toward college more than any other factor. Competitive colleges are said to prefer more science credits than the two that Lakeside requires. In addition to getting her fourth science credit so her college applications will be stronger, Cheryl thought the course "sounded just like what [her] friends described college as." By this she means Rory "doesn't dote on you all the time," pressuring you to get assignments in, which she sees as more like professors in college than typical high school teachers. Dave also liked the prospect of doing the project work for the class, but his reason was different—he "like[s] group projects." When I ask Dave why he likes group projects, he says,

> It's good to have a bunch of different opinions, you know . . . a lot of times . . . you think your natural opinion is good, and then . . . you'll get another idea from someone else that's just as good . . . [And] it's just nice to have a bunch of people in the same boat, working on the same thing.

Cheryl, Beth, and Dave had all been attracted to the computer component of the class. Beth says her father and brother are very much "into" computers, but she was never comfortable with computers and would like to learn more. Dave considers computer skills "something he could really use . . . that's gonna be more valuable to [him] in the future than anything [he's] done in any other science course."

Even though Rory's students are less enthusiastic than many other students about science, their academic confidence and performance is almost the same as the larger group of CoVis students surveyed at other schools. The average self-reported GPA of Rory's students is 2.9 out of 4, whereas it is 3.1 in all other CoVis classes. Also, both Rory's students and other CoVis students average just slightly above neutral in their agreement with the statement "I do very well in my science classes."

Experiences in Other Science Classes

Rory works under the assumption that students haven't "ever done a project" like the ones in his class, where they have to build their own interests into a research study they design and go beyond what they read to make their own scientific claims. Rory has the impression that most students have done "descriptive" reports where you "find out all you can about a subject and [then] report on it." He wants them to be able to go beyond just saying "here's what I know" to adding "here's what I don't know" and addressing "how do I figure out what I don't know, and how do I make that into something I know?" He also has a general sense that some research projects and group work are going on at the school. To see how Rory's perspective matches that of the students, I explored what previous science classes students have taken, what those science classes were like, and whether students had done projects in *any* other classes.

According to students' responses to a survey on teachers' goals (D'Amico, 1999), the overwhelming majority of the students (95%) have taken high school biology previously. The only exception is Steve, the freshman. More than half the students (53%) have taken chemistry in addition to biology. A small number (21%) have also taken physics. In interviews outside of class, the five students I asked described their previous science classes as more lecture- and textbook-oriented. A "normal" or "usual" science class at Lakeside is considered by these students to be one in which students work on one topic a week. During that week, students do lab experiments that Patti describes as "all laid out for you" on two lab days, turn in a lab report, hear lectures on the topic where they are expected to take notes, read about the topic in the textbook, possibly complete worksheets, and then have a test or quiz on Friday. Friday is designated the "science test day" at Lakeside. About her biology class taught in this style, Patti says, "It was all very constructed, and like, step by step by step. It, like, hand-feeded [sic] you." In her opinion, she "didn't learn anything from that class, basically," because they were just copying things down. All the students do not view their other science classes as negatively as Patti, but the differences Rory expects between his class and the other science classes students have taken were echoed by all the students I interviewed.

As far as project-like work in nonscience classes, students differ somewhat in their experiences and perspective. Cheryl saw work in their English classes, especially the "Junior Theme" each student at Lakeside has to complete, as very similar to the projects in Rory's class, except for the fact that they are completed individually rather than in groups. Like Rory's project, the Junior Theme involves long-term research and results in a similar "expository paper," in her opinion. Cheryl's statement about the similar nature of Rory's final report with Junior Theme was made prior to the completion of her first Earth Science project, however, not long after she made the statement, "I don't see why we can't write a report on [UFOs] if people have written whole books on it." As I will discuss later, at this stage Cheryl had not yet grasped the importance of original data analysis to Rory's goals. All the other students I interviewed pointed out that projects for other classes, like English and an interdisciplinary English and history course, are less open-ended than the projects in Rory's class. For the projects in those other classes, students have to turn in note cards and/or outlines in specific formats, and in many cases are given topics and specific subquestions. An example is the project Patti did in an integrated history/ English class a few of the other students had also taken. The students were given the topic of cultural diversity in the U.S. during the 1800s, and each group particular questions such as, "What culture clashes were there between groups like the Indians and English?" As Beth put it, "the teacher tells you [everything] to do to complete it." Beth echoed Rory's intuition that students had not been asked to play a role in figuring out *how* to answer a research question. In addition, Steve, Beth, and Dave pointed out that the primary work in their projects in other classes was finding and organizing facts that others had established about a topic—what Rory terms "standard library research." Again, Beth echoed Rory's intuition about how his projects were different from those in other classes when she said she had "never had a project where there hasn't been like really an answer, or someone who's already found the answer."

THE NEED FOR BOOTSTRAPPING

Given this student background, it is not surprising that Rory's first efforts at teaching science through projects were not easy, and students' first efforts at understanding what he means by doing projects have proven difficult each year. In Rory's view, the main feature of "lecture-lab-demo" teaching that made it easier than project-based teaching was *control*. With his switch to project-based science in 1992–93, Rory initially relinquished almost all control over student learning in the classroom, but now he controls some aspects of what is learned by having all his students work through a common framework. In the encounter at the beginning of the chapter, he referred the student to the first step in this framework, selecting a topic. The specific topics and questions students learn about are still largely controlled by the students, though. This is a significant change from lecture-lab-demo, in which teachers "don't have to respond" to the students' interests. Rory believes that connecting to student interests "gets to a much better model of education."

A model of education in which learning is achieved through participation in the activities of a community of practice has been extolled by researchers and theorists time and again. Papert (1980), the proponet of LOGO, aspired to the kind of intergenerational learning that takes place in a "samba school" for a Brazilian festival: experienced adults work with novice children on teams over an extended period of time, supporting learning and passing on expertise naturally through the construction of displays and the production of street theater. Similarly, Lave and Wenger (1991) describe how apprentice tailors gradually learn their craft by aiding master tailors in ever-expanding portions of work they are hired to do. Brown et al. (1989) have described the general processes of modeling, coaching, and fading as important means by which more experienced members of a community help novices learn to contribute to activities. For educators like Rory interested in fostering meaningful learning in school classrooms, however, models such as the samba school and classical apprenticeships can seem frustratingly distant from any reality they face or can create with students.

For Rory's and his students' daily work in high schools, the most salient community is found in the individual classrooms that change on a period-by-period basis. One obvious difference between traditional apprenticeship models and classroom communities is that the group the teacher leads is entirely reconstituted at the beginning of each year. At any one time in an apprenticeship, most of the members of the community have some experience and a few are novices. In a high school class at the beginning of the school year, only one person in the classroom has experience in the specific practices of that specific class—the teacher (Wasley, 1994). As Rory puts it, "When you start out a new year you have a whole new group of kids, and they have no idea what happened the last year."

Although the classroom group may be new at the beginning of the year, students are familiar with common school practices from previous years' experience. Thus, teachers who conduct their classes in the most typical fashion can take advantage of the shared experiences students already have, even though they don't know the students personally. Such teachers using the most typical pedagogy will have an easier time at establishing shared understanding of what is expected in the class than those whose pedagogy departs from the norm. Teachers like Rory who go outside the norm not only lack the shared understanding of how school works that more traditional teachers use; they must at times actively *resist* students' assumption that the class is or should fit the accustomed model.

The lack of experts and the opposition to the standard culture of schooling create a unique problem for a teacher like Rory leading reform-oriented classrooms: he must create an environment in which students can take actions to begin to "pull themselves up by their own bootstraps." Before turning to the Rory's more recent efforts at conveying what he means by doing projects, I will briefly describe his efforts to use a modeling strategy.

MODELING SCIENCE RESEARCH PROJECTS

After his frustrating first year with projects, Rory knew he faced a challenge in conveying what he meant by doing a project. The second year (1993–95) he began with a PowerPoint slide show answering, among other things, the question "How do you do a project?" in a step-by-step outline. After laying out this framework, and along with conducting activities introducing the classroom technologies, Rory orchestrated a model project in which he acted as the "project manager." In the literature on cognitive apprenticeship, *modeling* is discussed as an important aspect of how experienced practitioners can help novices learn new skills and ideas (Brown et al., 1989; Collins et al., 1989). Rory hoped that leading them through a whole-class project of his own design would provide them an opportunity to "observe and build a conceptual model of the processes that are required to accomplish the task" (Collins et al., 1989, p. 481). During the first quarter, Rory directed the students in measuring and then mapping the size and extent of a local sand beach, collecting historical maps and data, and using these data to analyze how the beach had changed over time. He then directed them in measuring hills and elevations at a local park to create a contour map of the land elevation. Each of these model projects included students working on vital parts of the process, such as systematically collecting and organizing data and creating graphical representations of the data.

After the model projects were completed, Rory gave another presentation and passed out handouts describing the steps they would follow for doing their own Earth Science projects. He used the model beach project as an example to describe the steps. For the crucial step of narrowing a research proposal from a broad topic, he described how he brainstormed about the broad topic of beaches to come up with a focused research question and a research plan. He suggested a five-step process of brainstorming for the research proposal, and described what he had done for these steps in the case of the model project on the beach in an attempt to make his thought processes and decisions explicit, as recommended by Collins et al. (1989).

The beach- and hill-mapping projects certainly succeeded in sending the message that "this class [is] a little bit different" by holding class on a beach and in a park for the better part of two weeks. But Rory did not feel that the students were able to transfer the experience to their later projects, in which they were responsible for the research design. Instead, students "started doing your basic library research paper," which he saw as fundamentally different from original science—mostly due to the lack of analysis of empirical data. Looking back a year later on the mapping projects, Rory attributed at least part of the problem to the conceptual difficulty of mapping compared to some other topics. In addition, most of the empirical data students could use in their later projects did not require heavy analysis of maps, but instead involved tables of numeric values and graphs of them. Since these issues may have prevented students from grasping and applying the lessons about doing projects, Rory decided the following year to do a sand analysis project that focused on two of the other questions he had brainstormed earlier: "Is all the sand the same on one beach? If it's different, where and why?" The results of this effort would be graphs that were more like what students typically worked with in their own projects.

During the first quarter of 1994–95, the model project that Rory directed was one of three strands of activities Rory conducted on alternate days (the others were lectures providing an overview of Earth Science, and introduction to the networked computer tools). Once again, the intention of the beach sand analysis project was to model a process of data collection, analysis and coming to conclusions that the students could later utilize when they were conducting their own projects. Rory described the project as follows:

> Student groups analyzed sand samples collected from the nearby beach. They collected the sand [at three locations], sieved it to find the amounts of different-sized grains, and examined each different-size sample with a hand lens to determine the roundness and smoothness of the grains. Each group made . . . graphs of their data; grain size vs. percentage of total sample, grain size vs. roundness, grain size vs. smoothness. They then put the data into a spreadsheet and each group made the same three graphs for the class data. Looking at a map that showed where the samples were taken from on the beach, they then had to see if there were any patterns in the sizes, smoothness, or roundness of the sand either up and down the beach or away from the shoreline.

Students were able to complete the activities, and made brief presentations to the class. But Rory gradually became convinced that his goals for the activity had not been met. He felt at the end that students "were not paying attention to this—they were just doing it." When students completed their first round of projects, he had "little evidence . . . that the [sand analysis] exercise had any meaning for the students other than to get it finished." Although Rory had designed the sand analysis project to cover three parts of doing science research projects—data collection, analysis, and conclusions—the students were not yet in a position to think of the activities in the same way as Rory. Rory summarized the problem as follows:

> Most of [the students] were just missing completely how this fit in, 'cause there was no context. They hadn't ever done a project, so it didn't make any difference to them what part of the project it was.

Thus, when the students were asked during the second quarter to do data collection, analysis, and coming to conclusions in their own projects, Rory intended students to think about the sand data collection, organization and graphing of sand data in a spreadsheet, and reaching conclusions about the beach sand. Ultimately, the sand analysis project fell into the same kind of trap traditional labs do—students never took interest or ownership, and were able to follow step-by-step orders without considering how the steps fit into the bigger picture of how to design and carry out a science research project. For instance, Rory distributed instructions on exactly what graphs students should make, including how the graphs should be labeled and what data should be in them. Students did not need to consider why the graphs they made were apt. There was not enough parallel in the students' experience during this first project that Rory managed and the later projects that the students managed themselves for the students to build a conceptual model they could use; the model project "never really accomplished [Rory's] goals."

Due in part to lack of student engagement and transfer, Rory decided that he would drop the model project strand from the introductory activities in the 1995–96 school year. I would note, however, that Rory's experience with model projects does not necessarily imply that such projects could *never* prove useful to students. Rory's experience does, however, highlight some of the important pitfalls of this strategy. Most importantly, teachers must find ways to engage students in actively considering the rationale behind the model project while working through it, and students' *experience* in the model project must parallel their experience in later projects for transfer to be successful. In Rory's 1993–94 and 94–95 efforts, there was a structural parallel that *Rory* saw between the model project and the framework for student-designed projects, but *students* did not necessarily see the parallel because they played very different roles at the two times.

Model projects could be designed and conducted to address the pitfalls Rory encountered. For instance, the teacher could supply students with a driving question for which he or she had considerable expertise and/or resources. The teacher would then challenge *students* to "think about the question, and have them help decide how to answer the question," rather than supplying a canned procedure. The teacher would also challenge students to think about how their decisions along the way fit into a larger plan to answer a research question. Such a strategy could avoid the pitfalls of students never taking ownership of the problems and never building a conceptual model of research project design. In fact, Rory and a colleague had conducted an activity like this in previous years, with somewhat better success. They had challenged students to map a complicated plot of land using only string, meter sticks, and their own wits and bodies. In these projects, Rory and his colleague consciously held back from offering their own solutions, and instead supported student decision-making by asking questions based on their own knowledge of map-making and the issues involved. Rory flirted with implementing a strategy like this in the 1995–96 school year on the beach sand theme: the focused question could be, "What is the sand size distribution on the beach?" Focusing on just one variable, he believed, would allow him to concentrate on the process of research design and implementation. "Instead of giving them the step-by-step of how to do it," he would ask students to figure out "what do we need to answer this question" and "how are we gonna collect this data?" After they had the data, he would work with them on how to organize the data, graph it, figure out what the graphs meant, and explain why the sand size might be distributed the way it is. He would not provide the answers; he would ask important questions.

In the end, though, Rory opted to jump directly from the Earth Science lectures and activities introducing the network tools to the students' first project. In this way, the class would "get to the real stuff instead of talking about what they're going to do." And Rory could "work with [the students] a lot, and maybe share with the class and brainstorm together" about each of the parts as each group considered how to design and carry out the research projects they owned. In effect, he would model subskills and provide scaffolding embedded within the larger activity of conducting a student-designed project, so that students would not lose the context.

PART II

AN EXPERIENCED GUIDE IN ACTION

CHAPTER 6

Laying the Groundwork for Projects

Another school year begins on a hot late August day in 1995. Before school, Rory meets me outside the cinderblock cubbyhole office he shares with the other Earth Science teacher. Shuffling through his briefcase, he talks to me about the upcoming class with nervous excitement. "Things are crazy," Rory says. It's been a while since he had a 1st period class, and it doesn't seem like there's enough time before the period to get ready. Plus his e-mail account and the printer are not working, and he is responsible to fix them in his new role as technology coordinator for the classroom. Another teacher calls to inform him their Internet connection is not operational, even though it worked fine when Rory tested it the previous day. Rory tells her he will try to get it up and running before her class.

We go into the classroom next door a few minutes before class, and Rory sets up for an electronic presentation about the course. The bell rings at 8:40 to begin class.

Right after the bell, easily projecting his voice so the whole class can hear, Rory says, "OK, I've got some additions to make, so if you just bear with me . . . if anybody's got more schedule changes, bring them up." Three more students walk in late and find a place, getting no comment. Rory opens the three-ring binder in which he keeps class lists and attendance and grade sheets. Looking up from his writing, he says, "OK, welcome back." Then he smiles wryly and adds "I'm sure we're all glad to be here." Gesturing to the board, he continues, "This is Earth Science 114 and 119 . . . We meet every day Period 1, and Monday and Wednesday we have a double lab period. I'll be handing out a paper tomorrow explaining the expectations for the class." He then goes on to attendance, asking students to correct his pronunciation or tell him preferred nicknames, and telling them they can call him either "Rory" or "Mr. Wagner."

Rory then informs his students that the class textbook will not be used for assigned readings, but instead as a "reference book" with "facts . . . that you don't need to remember . . . but if you need to look 'em up, they're there." He is trying to head off problems he has had in the past.

Last year, some students kept asking him during the year, "Why don't we ever use our textbook?" and felt they had wasted the money on the book. So this year he is giving students the option of acquiring any recent Earth Science book should they need to look up some term or find a basic explanation for a phenomenon.

Once attendance and the other preliminary comments are completed, Rory turns to his presentation about the class. He gets a remote computer controller and turns on the large televisions hanging above the class, which are set to display the image from the computer monitor. He opens up the slide show on a computer in the front of the room, and an animation of an approaching globe plays, followed by the title "Earth Science and CoVis Project." The use of multiple technologies is not an accident: Rory wants to "model for the kids using the technology as a tool" within the everyday activity of the class. Rory then explains the term "CoVis":

> The "Co" stands for "collaborative" and the "Vis" for "visualization." You are automatically part of it by being a part of this class, or any other Earth Science class at [Lakeside], for that matter . . . CoVis is . . . about trying to change teaching from lecture-lab-demo—the way most classes are taught—to doing more long-term projects that interest you . . . CoVis means we'll be using a lot of tools . . . You'll have to sign a couple of forms, take a survey or two. That's it.

This sketchy summary glosses over a host of complex issues, but it begins to indicate some of the ways in which the abstract ideas of CoVis have been appropriated by Rory to fit his own particular circumstances and goals. As already mentioned, Rory's particular realization of CoVis differs in ways from other teachers' and the abstract vision. Rory's particular appropriation, which focuses more strongly on the "Co" in CoVis than the "Vis," is conveyed and realized in situ throughout this day and over the next few months.

Next, Rory moves into a set of animated slides on Earth Science, which split activities up into "Content" (maps, weather and climate, the universe, geology, and oceans) and "Process" (measure, observe/collect data, classify, describe, create theories, make and test models). He says, "There are two parts to what scientists do: the body of knowledge, and how they go about getting that knowledge. Most classes concentrate on just the body of knowledge. In this class I'm more interested in the process—how you go about getting knowledge. It's kind of like sports—a lot of people aren't satisfied just reading about sports and studying them. They want to *do* them. Scientists want to *do* science, not just learn facts . . . that's one of the shifts I see in this class."

Rory then goes on to explain that as part of CoVis, his Earth Science class involves three things: projects, technology, and collaborations. The definition of projects on the slide is "collaborative investigations of Earth Science 'phenomena' of your choice." He tells the students, "Projects are what *you* want to do, not what I want. I do recognize that you often don't want to do much at all . . . I'm trying to change that . . . My job is to light a fire, but like the saying says, 'You can lead a horse to water, but you can't make it drink.' If you don't want to work, that's your choice. But your grade [will suffer]."

He describes the different possible collaborators. "Collaboration can be with other high school students . . . you will be partners with other students on projects, even students in other places. For example, you could have a partner in Ohio. That's the way scientists work—they work at different times and in different places on different parts of the problem." But students will have the opportunity to collaborate and communicate not only with their peers, but also scientists, including teachers, colleges and universities, museums, and "the rest of the world through the Internet."

In order to collaborate over the Internet, they have a suite of technology in the classroom. He stresses that technology is "a tool to help you do projects" and "this is *not* a computer science course." For communicating with others, Rory says, "you'll be using tools like electronic mail." He doesn't mention the World Wide Web yet, but later in the week, he will demonstrate it. Other technological tools besides these are mentioned on his slides, including tools for visualizing weather and climate data and the Collaboratory Notebook, a tool for storing, organizing, and structuring scientific inquiry developed by the CoVis staff. But as is the case during the rest of the year, Rory does not highlight the latter technologies in this initial presentation, instead focusing on communication tools.

Next comes a series of slides outlining how the students will be doing one project per quarter later in the year. Then Rory opens up the floor for questions. One student asks if they have labs, and Rory says no, because he wants to "replace traditional labs with doing projects." Rory tells them deadpan about quizzes and tests: "There is at least one." A number of students, disbelieving, say, "For the whole year?" He reassures him that is what he meant, and then elaborates that their grades will be based primarily on projects, for which he will try to be their "trusty Sherpa guide."

Just before the end of class, Rory introduces me, and explains that I am from the local university and doing research on the class, and so will be around often. I say a few words about my research and role, and let the students know that they will be kept anonymous. The 40-minute class is finished for the day.

OVERVIEW OF THE FIRST QUARTER

Throughout the first quarter of the year, which ends the first week of November, Rory conducts a series of alternating discussions and activities intended to "lay the groundwork" for conducting projects during the following three quarters of the year. These include a few periods discussing classroom policies on attendance and assignments, grading, and appropriate use of the computer tools and network,[1] as well as a discussion of how fundamental values can be played out in the classroom. The majority of the first quarter is spent on Rory's "lecture tour" and videos about the content of Earth Science, and on activities introducing students to the computer network and Internet tools for browsing the World Wide Web and for reading and sending electronic mail messages and Usenet news posts. Table 6.1 shows the breakdown of periods spent on these various activities for the class periods during the first quarter (each week has seven periods counting the two double periods).

COMPUTER ACTIVITIES: LEARNING TO USE NEW TOOLS

Starting two years earlier, Rory led his students through a series of activities designed to give them a basic familiarity with the Internet applications

TABLE 6.1. Number of periods spent on activities during the introductory quarter.

Type of Class Activity	Number of Periods
Content	
Lectures & Exams	28.0
Videos	9.5
Technology	
Teacher Demos	2.5
Student Activities & Exams	19.0
Discussions of Policies & Procedures	9.0
TOTAL	68.0

on the computers in the classroom. Students come into his class with a wide range of computer background and skills, and the CoVis classroom is the only one at the school hooked up to the Internet. This year, during the second week of the quarter, Rory gives a demonstration of the Macintosh, again using the overhead screens to show the whole class. He explains how to get around, open applications, switch between applications, open and save files, and work with windows. Then, he shows the students Netscape Navigator, a program used to browse the World Wide Web.

Afterward, he gives the students open time with Netscape on the six computers. He encourages them to browse for anything they are interested in on the Web—not just science. During the previous year, Rory introduced the Web only through an assignment in which students had to find scientific data, and one student later "wished he could spend more time [using Netscape] on the stuff they were really interested in, and didn't have to spend it all on science." On reflection, Rory felt the exclusive focus on science early on prevented some of the students from getting excited about the technology when they otherwise might have. He hopes they will better develop initial comfort with this tool through browsing Web sites they are intensely interested in. They will also develop the "patience" so they will "look further" when browsing for scientific information. This way, they can "really play with this in a recreational, and still educational way." He had intended to give a version of the data-searching assignment later this year, but ends up dropping the idea due to lack of time. His plan was to ask each student, "If you had to find data to answer this question [from a list of possible project questions he has compiled], what would you do?" He figured "that would kill two birds with one stone" by giving students further experience searching the Web, and initial experience thinking about the relationship between data and research questions in science.

During the third week, Rory demonstrates the electronic mail program they use, Eudora. He shows students how to read a message, reply, edit text, and write new messages, as well as some conventions such as including text from a previous message in a reply and using "emoticons," which are series of characters symbolizing emotions [for example, ":)" is a happy face, where the colon is the eyes and the parenthesis the mouth when viewed sideways]. This demonstration is followed by an assignment "to tell [him] something, some little personal thing about what you did over the summer," using e-mail. As the students gather at the computers and try to open their e-mail, all run into a technical problem in the setup of their accounts on the network. In his first year of using the computers and the Internet 2 years earlier, Rory found such situations difficult to handle. The pressure of four or five groups of students urgently calling for help with computer problems was difficult enough, but it was exacerbated by Rory's own lack of comfort with and mastery of the tools, which were new to him, too. As Rory described the first year afterward, "I had to help kids search on the computers [and] use the programs . . . and at the beginning of the year . . . that created a lot of frustration . . . because I didn't know what I was doing, and I couldn't help them with their questions: 'Why is this program doing this?' or 'How can I do this?'"

Throughout the past two years, Rory has maintained a strong personal interest in the computer tools, and makes frequent use of e-mail, the Web, and Usenet news outside of class for school and personal activities. Consequently, his knowledge has grown immensely, and although he is not always able to immediately fix problems, he is more confident in his ability to work through or around problems. Due to his personal interest and growing command of the technologies, Rory has taken on the role of technology coordinator for the CoVis classroom at his school this year. In years past, university staff had filled this role, but with a growing effort in many schools, we could no longer provide full-time support. In this case, Rory fixes the problem with the students' e-mail accounts in less than five minutes, and they continue the activity with scarcely a hitch.

By the beginning of the next week, Rory has sent a personal response to each of the students by e-mail. When he did this the previous year, he did not expect or ask students to respond, but he ended up beginning ongoing dialogues with a few students in a forum that allowed him to "learn about [the students] as people" in a way not common during class. This result fit in well with Rory's general goal of "be[ing] a little more open in my own personal dealings with the students . . . kind of retracting some of . . . the defenses and walls that I've put up over the years to isolate myself from students." One reason he was doing this was that he felt "different teachers 'get' the kids in different ways . . . It really may come down to the personal relationship between the student and teacher, and the teacher's genuine desire to 'share' instead of 'dictating' what they know."

As a result of the experience last year, Rory asks all the students this year to respond back once to his messages, in which he asks elaborating questions on their anecdotes, saying this will also give them practice at responding to messages. Many of the exchanges do not go much beyond simple descriptions of summer activities such as mountain climbing or whitewater rafting, working in stores or mowing lawns, or going to summer camp, but a few are more extensive. For instance, Tom mentions having fun working at his father's factory in the summer, and he and Rory discuss how hard work can be fun, especially when you work with friends. Rory had spent a summer loading boxcars, much like Tom's summer loading produce on trucks. Barb talks solely about punk shows she was able to see in the summer in her initial message, so Rory asks her about who her favorite music groups are overall and in the area. Although he knows almost nothing about the music she enjoys, during the course of exchanging multiple messages they discover that she saw a show at a bowling alley Rory knew, because he went there with his father to repair the bowling machines years earlier. TJ talks about his lacrosse playing at a national tournament during the summer, and since Rory used to coach the sport, the two continue to discuss it throughout the year. Sonia relates how she taught four-year-olds during the summer, just as Rory's sister does, and then the two get into an extended exchange about the rewards of teaching, her sense of guilt associated with growing up "privileged," and making a difference through community service. When Rory learns that Beth spent the summer with an aunt in New Mexico who studies wolves, he shares his enthusiasm for wolves with her, and they bring in pictures to share and discuss.

After a week of concentrating mostly on lectures, Rory introduces Newswatcher, a program to read and send posts to Usenet newsgroups on the Internet. As he had done in the previous year, he asks the students to open up one of the Earth Science–oriented newsgroups—sci.astro, sci.geo.geology, sci.geo.meteorology, and sci.geo.oceanography—and note the originating location of five articles in three different threads. In the process of completing this assignment, the students learn the basic terminology—news "articles" can be posted, and follow-ups to an article are arranged in threads—and how to get around within the interface of Newswatcher. In addition, Rory says, "by looking at the 'locations' [posts] came from, it might give [students] some sense of the worldwide communication." Since Rory will be encouraging students to post articles requesting information or leads later on in the course of doing projects, he wants them to know, and take seriously, the scope of the communication. Finally, in order to continue to "foster use of [e-mail] as a communication tool," Rory has the students turn in the assignment by e-mail to him. Rory is somewhat dissatisfied with the "artificiality" and lack of connection to students' interest in this Newswatcher assignment. Previously, he "tried just letting students browse" in Newswatcher, but "that didn't work." Until Rory finds a better way of introducing this tool, he will keep the assignment. It provides a relatively efficient means for students to learn the program, become familiar with the scientific newsgroups they may be posting articles to later, and learn how to use two programs—Newswatcher and Eudora—at the same time.

During all these activities, Rory encourages the students to help each other and work together at the computers. Finally, in Weeks 9 and 10, the students have to complete individual competency exams on the computer. Rory lets the students know what they will need to do, and then puts a sign-up list on the board for them to indicate they are ready. Two students,

Julie and Cindy, ask to watch others take the exam to help them learn, and Rory encourages them to do so. In the course of the exam, students must log onto the network, send e-mail, do an Internet search and save a file to their personal network folder, and use Newswatcher. Rory helps many of the students with hints along the way. After watching several, Cindy remarks that she is starting to get it. Rory suggests that she take notes, which she can use during her own exam. She begins to take notes, but watches eight more students over several days before taking the plunge herself. Rory asks once if she wants to do it, but doesn't push her. Gradually, Cindy progresses from asking students taking the exam questions about what they are doing to offering suggestions, and then sharing Rory's frustration at knowing what people need to do but seeing them flounder. Cindy finally takes the exam, and not surprisingly she passes "with flying colors—she didn't even use her notes."

LECTURES AND VIDEOS: CONTENT, SCIENTIFIC PRACTICE, AND SEEDS FOR PROJECTS

By the third week, some students are joking about why Rory's class is called Earth Science. They have spent most of their time discussing policies and values, and have just begun the e-mail activities. On the way out of class, one student says, "Is this class all about computers? I thought we were gonna do something about the earth." During the first week of class, Rory had begun his series of videos and lectures by showing an episode from James Burke's *Connections* series. But the program was not about Earth Science, and instead focused on how various technical inventions were historically connected and interdependent. Rory told the class that the reason he was showing the *Connections* video was that it shows "how things develop through time. The reason I think this is important is that it's a metaphor for how science works. It builds up, and leaps in science are putting ideas and things together. But they don't just come out of nowhere." Later in the third week, Rory begins somewhat more traditional material with lectures on astronomy. Although these do not yet deal with the earth (the full title of the course would more aptly be "Earth and *Space* Science"), the lectures are closer to "what [students] expect from a class."

Means of Covering Standard Content

On a Tuesday in the fourth week of class, Rory is preparing to give his fifth lecture on astronomy, after having shown a video about solar systems the previous day. One of the reasons Rory tries to "explain at least the big picture about how everything works" through lectures and videos is that "kids have misconceptions" about such things as the massive scale of our solar system, in which Pluto is *40 times* farther from the sun than the Earth. Through the lectures, he hopes to "make them at least think about [the materials] a little bit." The breadth of material in the fields of Earth Science that he covers in lecture over a brief portion of the year necessitates a shallow presentation. This contrasts with the greater depth the students will learn about the specific topics they research during their three projects later. Clearly, Rory's lectures are partly done out of the traditional notion of "coverage"—he figures that his Earth Science class and the other teacher's are so different that students' experiences will be largely different, but "they ought to at least learn some of the same stuff." As he said at one point, "I just think someone who took Earth Science should have seen rocks and pictures of planets," and some of the students would miss certain topics altogether if they were doing projects all year. Like most experienced teachers, he does not do strict lesson plans for his lectures, instead working somewhat improvisationally, drawing from years' worth of notes and experience. As Rory puts it, he goes through the big picture, "starting at the origin of the universe, and going up through geologic processes and geologic time, and oceans, and weather . . . and how they all fit together, and how they generally work."

Right now he is at the solar system, so he walks into class and writes "Today: Solar system notes" on the board. He mutters his way through the attendance. Marie asks if they get to work on the computers today, and Rory says they can read his responses to their e-mail for ten minutes at the end of class. He goes to the board and says, "We're gonna go over some of the solar system stuff. Put some flesh on the bones you got from the movie yesterday." He draws a schematic of the planets as he explains some things about each. "Where life evolved, where we are, is just a matter of accident. We're at the optimal point . . . if the sun were hotter or cooler, conditions might have been better on Mars or Venus for life to evolve." When he gets to Uranus, he chuckles, saying, "The name of Uranus was changed to be PC when Voyager was approaching it. They didn't want to have to have people saying Ur-*ay*-nus on the radio, so they call it Ur-*uh*-nus."

> As Rory draws Pluto's orbit, Marie asks, "Have we seen Pluto?"
> Rory replies, "Yes, with telescopes."
> Marie follows up, saying, "What do we see?"
> "Light reflected off it."
> Still wondering, Marie says, "What light?"
> Rory clarifies, "From the sun," and Marie nods.

Rory goes on to explain what the "plane of the ecliptic" is, and how Earth's orbital plane and all the other planets except Pluto are in this same plane. He describes some other ways in which Pluto is exceptional. Danny asks how long it takes Pluto to go around the sun, another student ventures a guess, and Rory looks it up.

Interlude: Dialogue Sequences Punctuated by Student Questions, Not Teacher Questions

When Rory first described his lecture series as "boring" to me at the beginning of 1994–95, I would not have imagined them being as interactive as they in fact are. Based on research conducted elsewhere, even this more traditional aspect of Rory's teaching differs from standard instruction. In Hugh Mehan's (1978) work on standard interaction sequences in school lessons, he identified the dominant structure of discourse to be what he termed "Initiation-Reply-Evaluation" (I-R-E). In such a sequence, the teacher *initiates* an episode by asking a question about an established fact or idea he or she wants to convey; students *reply* with bids for correct responses; the teacher *evaluates* the responses, and may initiate another round. Jay Lemke (1990) conducted similar research on discourse patterns in science classrooms, and identified an analogous dominant structure with a sequence he labeled "Question-Answer-Evaluation" (Q-A-E). In the sequence, the teacher opens with a *question*, a student *answers*, and the teacher *evaluates*. In Rory's lectures, this sequence is rare: out of 15 class days I observed in which Rory showed videos and gave lectures, he initiated only *three* Q-A-E sequences. The fact that a substitute teacher showed the last video and immediately initiated a Q-A-E sequence after stopping the VCR only highlighted the difference between Rory's style and standard instruction. The Q-A-E pattern is well suited for situations in which the teacher is trying to simultaneously maintain a high degree of control in the classroom and also probe students' current understandings to foster grasping clearly specified concepts. Consequently, Rory may not be proactively detecting as many student misconceptions as he would if he used Q-A-E.

On the other hand, Rory's lectures are punctuated by a significant number of what Lemke terms "Student Questioning Dialogues"—a total of 99 over the same 15 periods. A Student Questioning Dialogue is when "students initiate questions on the subject-matter topic and the teacher answers them" (Lemke, 1990, p. 217). Examples are the episodes above beginning with questions from Marie and Danny. When they are given the opportunity to ask questions like this, students have more responsibility for monitoring their own understanding, and potential control over their learning. According to Lemke, many teachers use a variety of strategies to discourage student questions, and privilege the Q-A-E format, precisely because it keeps more control in the hands of the teacher. Rory planted the seeds for this altered situation on the second day of class, when he told students they were going to have an exam on the lectures worth 25% of their first-semester grade, but that it would be "open notes." It became the students' responsibility to make sure that their notes were complete and they understood them, so that they could use the notes during the exam. Rory came up with the idea for the exam with open notes the previous year (1994–95), as an inducement for them to listen and take notes. He told me, "The important thing [about the exam] was that they listened to me . . . and if they needed further clarifications, they would ask questions." He is especially pleased with classes, like this one, and students who habitually ask good questions very relevant to the material, although he has noticed that some students and classes tend more toward "borderline" questions that may simply be ruses whose purpose is to waste time. As Lemke's analysis implies, that is one cost of relinquishing some control over their learning to the students.

Despite this difference between the dominant structure of dialogue in Rory's lectures and standard science lessons, there are some important senses in which Rory's lecture activity and standard science instruction are the same: specifically, "who's doing the talking" most of the time, and the underlying metaphor for learning. In Rory's lectures, he talks the overwhelming majority of the time, just as the teachers in Mehan's and Lemke's research did. In addition, the purpose of the lectures is primarily to transmit information about science content. In the three years he has been conducting this video and lecture tour of Earth Science, he says he has been "trying to come up with the quickest, easiest way to *transmit* the basic information" (my emphasis), using various combinations of technology such as videotapes, laserdiscs, PowerPoint presentations, and chalkboard lectures. As previously mentioned, the view of learning as transmission from teacher to learner is the dominant traditional view, in contrast to constructivist and Vygotskian models of learning. Rory has no illusions that all he says is transferred directly to the minds of students, but he is trying to at least get the information "out there" so that students can pick up some of it. The metaphor of learning as *construction* of knowledge, on the other hand, is better served by what Lemke (1990) terms "true dialogue," where teacher and students ask questions that don't necessarily have already established answers, and/or "cross-discussion" among students without the teacher. As will become apparent in subsequent chapters, project work in Rory's class is much more dominated by true dialogue and cross-discussion. But the groundwork for the projects is laid in part through teacher lectures and videos punctuated by student questioning dialogue.

Means of Conveying How Science Is Practiced

Back in the lecture, Rory elaborates on the motions of the planets, follows up on another student question, and then moves on to the size and scale of the solar system—the issue he wanted to be sure to cover today. He says that "the distance between the earth and the sun is called an astronomical unit, or A.U.," and "if it took one second to get to earth, it would take 40 seconds to get to Pluto . . . " After another brief diversion, he puts up a table showing the distance of all the planets in A.U. from the sun. Then Rory goes on to tell a story:

> Somebody [yesterday] asked "Can you see Pluto without a telescope?" . . . Before we had telescopes, you could see five other planets—Mercury, Venus, Mars, Jupiter, Saturn. An early astronomer noticed the progression of distances from the sun. See how they sort of double? And then he predicted there should be another planet around 3 A.U. from the sun. They looked for it and they found [the asteroid belt].

Rory went on to explain how they looked for another planet beyond Saturn, about twice as far away from the Sun, and found Uranus. Using this technique, scientists eventually found all the planets we know of in our solar system, and "are currently looking for Planet X," which the model would predict to be around 80 A.U. from the sun.

Rory told me in interviews, "I'm trying to—at every chance I get—to show examples of how scientists do science . . . and that scientists are people, and that they think, and they create." That's why the first video he showed was Burke's *Connections*. That's also why he mentions the "nuts and bolts," like looking for anomalies such as Pluto's revolution off the plane of the other planets, as well as large patterns such as the approximate doubling of the distance of each planet in our solar system from the sun. When I asked him whether his lectures had always been peppered with such examples of science in action, he said, "I might have told stories, but not with that express goal in mind." He told me the way he would have presented the same information about the distances of the planets from the sun:

> I would make this big table on the board, and explain how Bode's Law works, and show the planets, and their distances, and his predic-

tions, and that there should be something here and here . . . It [was] like, "You should know Bode's Law. Here's Bode's Law" . . . Bode's Law was the important thing . . .

[Now] Bode's Law is *not* the important thing. I mean, that's the shift. What's important now is that there's a *pattern*, and somebody *saw* the pattern, and *used* the pattern to find out something else. Which is what science *is* . . .

In this particular lecture he did not even mention the term "Bode's Law." Rory says this change in emphasis was "almost an unconscious shift" that may have come about because he thought focusing on how science is done would probably be "valuable and useful" later, during student projects. It clearly does not dominate all he is saying throughout his lectures, but it colors the way he presents material. On other occasions Rory will give examples of how a scientist "used supporting data to prove that his model was correct," and how "looping" patterns like those of air in our atmosphere and water in our oceans recur often in science. He will also mention his own experience as a geologist determining grades of metamorphism in rocks.

Seeds for Later Projects

Rory closes the lecture period for the day, saying, "OK, let's stop here. You can read your mail or whatever you want." From September until early November, he spends 28 periods on such lectures and 9.5 showing videos. The topics range from the origins of the universe; to stars, galaxies, the solar system, planets, and comets; to the origin of Earth; to igneous, metamorphic, and sedimentary rock; to plate tectonics and geologic history; to weathering and erosion; and finally oceanography and meteorology. In his first year of doing projects, Rory did not give any lecture tour like this, and he felt that was one of the ways he "cast students adrift." When he asked them to do Earth Science projects on anything in the field "that interested them," he was "presupposing" that they knew enough of "what Earth Science is all about" to see what they might be interested in. In 1994–95, when he decided to give the lecture and video tour, he did so because

if you want students to explore science they have to know something about it. . . . Actually, when I think back to my own high school years, if someone had done this to me, I would have been as clueless as my students, even though I was interested in science at some gen-

eral level. So they need to have some background. The "big picture"
[to] flesh out at a later date.

Rory's hope was that once students had been exposed to this introductory
material, it would "give them some framework on which to say, 'Oh, that
was kind of cool, maybe I could do a project on that.'" Indeed, some of
the students specifically mention getting the idea for their projects from the
lectures. Dave and TJ, for instance, were beginning to think about what
they should do for their first project at the end of the lectures. As Dave put
it, "You could . . . see which sections you thought were interesting while
you were taking the notes, and which you didn't." When Rory described
hurricanes, they latched onto that as a topic. Adam followed up on Rory's
comments in lecture by doing a project later in the year on Pluto's status
as a planet (or not) in our solar system. Steve and Rich also found the seeds
of their project on moons in Rory's lectures. Rich said the lectures "gave
[them] kind of an overview . . . of what we could do . . . to basically figure
out our subject." Patti concurred that the lectures and videos gave her "an
understanding of which areas [they] can go into, to look for a subject of
research."

Because students are using the lectures as springboards for projects,
Rory has become careful about how much he emphasizes certain topics.
An example is black holes, which are an interesting but extremely complex
phenomenon in astronomy. In years past quite a few students had become
interested in the topic through Rory's lecture and had no luck completing
successful empirical projects, so this year, Rory did not bring the topic up.
When a student asked "What's a black hole?" one day, Rory simply said,
"It's theoretical thing, based on Einstein's relativity. It explains some
things, but it's really hard to see," and then changed the subject. Nevertheless, Adam and Jane choose to negotiate a project on black holes during
this year, as I will discuss in Chapter 10.

Besides giving students an overview of Earth Science from which to
choose project topics, Rory wants to avoid students having to "start from
ground zero" in their project inquiry. In years past, when he had given no
lectures or just a brief few, he felt students "didn't even know any of the
names or the terminology about the stuff they were working on" when
they began projects. He hopes the more extended lectures will prepare them
better. Among the six focus students I interview outside of class, Patti and
Dave are the only ones who find the lectures very "helpful" in this way—
she feels they provide her with a basic level of knowledge about the topics,
which helps in starting more in-depth research for the projects. She says,
"You also have background information, so it's in the back of your head,
just like, 'Oh yeah, I remember that.'" Dave felt "a lot of the meteorology

[they] did [in lecture] was helpful." But other students, such as Steve and Rich, find little information in lectures beyond what they know from elsewhere about their topic, moons. The extent to which Rory's lectures help provide students with basic knowledge about Earth Science content inevitably varies based on (1) the extent of each student's incoming knowledge base; (2) the depth of Rory's coverage of each topic, which varies based on student questions and Rory's own interests (Rory's preference for astronomy and geology over meteorology and oceanography is reflected in spending 24 lectures on the former and 2 on the latter); and (3) the extent of the students' engagement during the portions of lecture and video that end up being relevant to their later projects.

LIMITATIONS AND PITFALLS OF THE GROUNDWORK ACTIVITIES

The third point above brings us to the limitations and pitfalls associated with the activities Rory uses to introduce the computer tools and the content of Earth Science. The "stability" of the groundwork inevitably varies. For instance, just as students enter the class with varying degrees of computer expertise and experience, they complete the activities with varying degrees of competence. Throughout the course of project work, Rory will still have to remind some students, such as Pamela, Sylvia, and Marie, how to send him or others e-mail; he will have to help numerous students conduct Web searches; and he will help students daily with small printing, saving, or document layout problems.

A perhaps more severe problem is associated with lectures and videos: student boredom and lack of engagement. As mentioned before, Rory is fully aware that students "aren't paying attention" at all times. In fact, there is a marked tendency for student questions to diminish as the lecture tour continues: in weeks 3 and 4, the mean number of student questions per lecture is 14 (minimum 9, maximum 17), whereas for lectures in weeks 7 through 11, the mean number of questions is 4 (minimum 2, maximum 7). Although the decline in questions may be partly attributable to students' greater interest in astronomy as a topic, Patti mentions in interviews that the lectures started to get "boring," and Dave said he was "glad to get the lecturing over with . . . it's nice to get that set aside." The problem of student engagement is to some degree inevitable given most students' relatively passive role during lecture. As Patti says, "I get annoyed [at lectures and tests], and then I'm like, 'Well, this is boring' . . . [it goes] in one ear and out the other."

To reduce student disengagement, Rory tries a number of strategies. First, he tries to break up lecture with other activities such as the introduction of computer tools. When the class has a double lab period, only one period is spent on lecture. Second, he tells them they will be given a written exam at the end of the lecture tour, during which they will be allowed to use their notes taken during class. As already mentioned, this places responsibility on the students for taking effective notes that they can use later. A further aspect of student note-taking that Rory could more explicitly emphasize is students using them as seeds for later projects, perhaps by asking them to take note of those topics that most interest them on a daily and weekly basis, or by asking them to note down potentially interesting project research questions that arise. Third, Rory tries to mix up the media he uses. Beyond standard "chalk and talk" at the blackboard, Rory tries to provide more "pizzazz" by showing some good videos and occasional multimedia presentation tools. He has found that the latter—whether it be commercial CD-ROMs or custom presentations he prepares—have the pitfall of making his own presentation slower and, paradoxically, boring students. Although he thinks multimedia is particularly well suited for showing certain things, like the process of plate movements in plate tectonics, he has concluded that their use needs to be limited, or the technology dictates the flow of presentation and discussion more than he and the students do. During his sessions on plate tectonics, for instance, Rory uses a CD-ROM and finds it difficult to not follow the program's slides sequentially, rather than jumping around and following up on student questions; consequently, the "lecture" extends over three days, with little student involvement.

As Larry Cuban (1986) has pointed out, one of the reasons blackboards are used more often than computers in most schools is that they are easier to fit flexibly into the flow of activities such as lectures (at least for most people, with the current state of the art). In addition, students have a great deal of experience taking notes off the blackboard, but don't necessarily have a sense of what to write down during multimedia presentations, where they cannot possibly take down every word, as they do with notes on the board. Nonetheless, the graphics still remain a problem: the images and animation are sometimes informative and compelling, but difficult for students to deal with in their notes, compared to the schematics Rory draws on the board. The difficulties Rory has encountered with multimedia presentations remind us that computer technology is not a panacea for content lectures any more than any other part of instruction, but instead introduces tradeoffs and unexpected complexities.

Beyond students' interest in the lectures, Rory's own interest plays an important role. On the negative side, he finds it frustrating to essentially repeat a lecture on a topic with multiple classes during the day. As he told me several times, it would be better "if I could have a big lecture section where I took all my classes, and lectured them all just once." On the positive side, his enthusiasm for the Earth and Space Science material can carry him away at times. This is one explanation for the fact that although Rory figured he "should" need "around 3 weeks altogether" for lectures, he ends up spending 28 class days on lectures. As Rory said when lectures started to drag on, "maybe the problem is that I can't get it all in . . . It's frustrating because I want to show them all the cool stuff there is. But I can never do it all. Even if I was [not doing projects], I'd run out of time. I used to run out of time every year."

CONCLUSION: GROUNDWORK ACTIVITIES AS A TRANSITION

The tools and content activities detailed in this chapter can be seen as means of transitioning students from more traditional modes of instruction to the projects commenced afterward. These activities do not constitute the same level of "guided participation in a community of learners" (Rogoff, 1994) that is represented by projects, but they are a gradual step in the direction away from traditional schoolwork.

Although Rory leads the students through lecture activities rooted in a transmission model of communication, the lectures have served the dual purpose of covering content *and* describing the practice of science students will attempt to participate in later. Thus, the content of these lectures is not only established, factual, scientific concepts, but also narratives and concepts of scientific practice. And although the lectures are dominated by teacher talk, they involve more student questioning and student control than is customary in traditional classrooms. Finally, Rory has told the students that he is less interested in their "memorizing facts" and "telling facts" than "thinking scientifically" with whatever tools and resources they can create or find; he has reinforced his comment by encouraging students to create notes to use on their computer competency and science content exams. Such practices are in line with Pea's (1993b) suggestion that "a principal aim of education ought to be that of teaching for the design of distributed intelligence" (p. 81) that is not just in students' heads but also in the tools and artifacts around them.

Teachers in other reform efforts toward project-based instruction, such as LabNet (Ruopp et al., 1993), have conducted similar lecture tours intended to prime students for later inquiry. Given the prevalence of traditional teaching practices and the difficulty of change for students, such transition activities take on a great deal of importance. Further research on the complexity and implications of designing and conducting such activities is needed.

But now it is time to move on to the primary work of doing projects. As Rory told his students, "Now you guys get to *do*, [and] I get to help." One way Rory helps students to successfully do projects is through the project activity structure, as we will see next.

NOTE

1. Network use policies will not be examined in depth here, but for a more complete discussion of their use in K–12 classrooms, see Fishman and Pea (1994). For the text of the network use policy Wagner adapted almost verbatim, see *http://www.covis.nwu.edu/AUP-archive/AUP-1.3.html*.

CHAPTER 7

How Structuring Activity Works

On Thursday, November 9, Rory officially begins the first round of research projects. He passes out two handouts, the first of which is "How to do an Earth Science project" (see Appendix B for the full text of the handouts). Instead of reading aloud what he has written about doing projects, Rory focuses the students' attention on some of the main issues. He reminds them, "What we're trying to do is really *do science* . . . Instead of pretending that we're doing science by doing little lab experiments that duplicate things that have already been done by a lot of people, we're gonna try and do some things that are maybe new. Maybe things people haven't looked at."

To give the students an idea of what he is talking about, he describes an example of a good project. The students who did the project first decided on volcanoes, and then specifically eruptions of the volcanoes, which was a good idea because "people write down when they occur." They then decided to focus on a small subset of volcanoes, specifically one type, and look for patterns in the time elapsed between eruptions. He stresses that "they looked at . . . a big problem, and then kept narrowing it down until it was something that they actually could do," while he stretches his hands out wide and then brings them together. He contrasts the narrowness and tractability of the volcano project to another project, where the students said, "We're gonna try and predict the effect of global warming . . . on the population in the next century." Such projects are "way too unmanageable," says Rory, even though they can sound appealing. The key is focusing them down. The students aren't on their own in figuring out whether their projects are focused enough "to be doable"; Rory is available at any time to help them. Rory then briefly describes another example project, on "Which group of dinosaurs lived longer, the carnivores or the herbivores?"

MILESTONES AS A GUIDE TO "COOKING
UP SCIENCE FROM SCRATCH"

The second of the two handouts is on "Project Milestones and Due Dates" (see Appendix B). The milestones he distributes for this second quarter of 1995–96 are as follows: (1) Group and Topic—3 days, (2) Background Information—2 weeks, (3) Research Proposal—1 week, (4) Data Collection—2 weeks, (5) Data Analysis—1 week, (6) Complete Research Paper—1 week, and (7) Presentation—1 week. Rory tells the students the reason for the milestones is his experience from the past. He says:

> I realized a couple of years ago . . . that I couldn't just say, "OK, let's go out and do research, and the week after Christmas your paper will be due. Go for it." Because what will happen is, everybody will sit here and play video games . . . and chat, and then over Christmas break a couple of you will get together and start working on it, and then that week before it's due everybody will say, "Wait! We don't have enough time. We can't get it done." Whatever. It's procrastination to its nth degree. And we know that happens because that's human nature.

Rory makes sure to tell his students that the sequence of steps he has laid out is not the *only* way to do science. He says:

> What I don't like about this is, it suggests there is a sequence of steps that you go through when you do science. The old scientific method. And in all reality the scientific method doesn't exist. There are things that you have to do to do science, but there is no step-by-step fashion, that you're led to believe, in doing experiment after experiment from grammar school up to now, that if you just follow the right steps, you'll get the right answer.

Despite their stepwise scaffolding, the series of milestones Rory has laid out are different from the recipe-like labs students may have conducted in other science classes. Traditional lab steps give such detailed directions for every step that students can almost blindly follow them and get the right results. Rory's milestones, on the other hand, provide a framework that breaks the multiweek project activity down into more manageable steps. Rory described the difference with an analogy:

> It's the difference between a cook who cooks from scratch and a cook who can only cook from following directions, or a cook who

can only heat up things in the microwave. There are different degrees of culinary expertise. Somebody will taste the sauce and go, "No, it needs a smidge of that." And that makes a difference . . .

As opposed to the person who just follows the directions . . . "Mix it up, put it in here. Boom. Here's how it came out. I don't care what it tastes like . . . that's what the directions said to do."

So there's . . . an artistic difference there. And there's an artistic difference between scientists also, which is very hard to capture . . . and tell you step by step how to do it. But we have to start someplace, and so, in order to start, I've given you the steps that I want you to follow, at least for this first project. And then we can go on, and do other projects.

Since the exact steps each student group will follow are not determined beforehand, there are no "right answers" in the sense that many traditional labs have right answers. Instead, there are multiple paths that students could follow to reach well-reasoned empirical conclusions about topics in Earth Science. Along the steps of these paths, they turn in intermediate written artifacts that require them to "use complex thought" (Blumenfeld et al., 1991) rather than the more trivial fill-in-the-blanks and prompted questions found in traditional labs. Additionally, traditional labs involve the whole class in the same lockstep activity, whereas Rory's students work on different problems of their own design and choosing.

In order to understand how the framework of milestones helps to structure student participation, I will describe two project teams who make effective use of Rory's activity structure.

THE HURRICANES PROJECT: COOKING UP
SCIENCE BY FOLLOWING THE PATH

The hurricanes project illustrates how two students who follow the path delineated by the project milestones can learn how to "cook up science from scratch" as Rory hoped they would. Part of the effective use of this activity structure is the way it provides multiple occasions for Rory to do the equivalent of tasting the sauce and discussing with the students what spices or adjustments might be advisable.

Who Are the Cooks: Choosing Project Partners

TJ and Dave are two experienced seniors sitting in the back right corner of the room. TJ is a stocky lacrosse player with long blond hair, and Dave is a hockey player with short hair. They are wearing one variation of their standard attire: TJ in jeans and a sweatshirt, and Dave in jeans and a casual shirt. As usual, their eyes are nearly obscured by ragged baseball caps with college logos. Right after the class discussion about how to do a project, they decide to work together on their project. They had discussed working with their friends Julie and Amy, as Rory had expected, but Rory wants students to work in groups of at least two and not more than three. Rory thinks three is ideal because they can break ties by voting, but there are not too many in the group so that students end up sitting around while someone else works. He told the students in his introduction that they can request an exception to the sizes he recommends, but they have to convince him they have a compelling reason. Since the four students have no reason for exceeding the recommended limit, they form two groups of two.

What's for Dinner: Choosing a Topic

After choosing partners, Dave and TJ have to choose their topic. On the first day of projects, Rory told the students, "You gotta figure something out that you want to study . . . it should be something you're interested in." Besides being something they're interested in, the topic must be part of Earth Science. Rory defines "anything in an Earth Science textbook" as acceptable; the shorthand he uses is, "If it's alive, it's probably *not* an Earth Science topic [and] if it's dead, or [has] never been alive, it probably *is* an Earth Science topic." For their project topic, TJ and Dave choose hurricanes, which attracted their interest during the weather lecture. When I ask what interests them about hurricanes, TJ says, "The destruction, to be honest. We also wanted to know how they fly into the storm. That's how they track them, you know."

Right away, they begin a pattern of turning in Rory's assignments in a timely fashion by sending their topic—"patterns and destruction of hurricains [*sic*]"—to Rory by e-mail a day early. They had noted Rory's comment that they get bonus points for turning in some milestones early. Although they later find out Rory only gives bonus points for turning in the last four written milestones early (the first of which is the Research Proposal), their enthusiasm serves them well.

Background Preparation: Learning about the Topic

Dave and TJ spend the first 2 weeks of the project diligently reading books about weather and hurricanes. On the first day of projects, Rory had told the students:

After you get a partner, and . . . general topic, then you have to do background research. That's where you start finding out all you can about . . . your particular topic. OK? So let's say you pick volcanoes. What you do is read everything you can about volcanoes. I generally would like you to start in your textbook. Read everything you can in the textbook. Then find other geology books . . . Find all the stuff on volcanoes. Read it, so you know how volcanoes work: where they are, why they erupt, why they don't erupt. Everything that you can. You have to become a mini-expert on volcanoes. That's your background research . . .

They borrow the books from Rory's collection in the classroom, and also begin to track down some hurricane resources on the Internet. They ask Rory to help them save an image showing hurricane paths they find on a Web site, and they include the image in the Background Information report they turn in a day early during the second week. Their report contains a descriptive overview of what hurricanes are, how they arise, and the destruction they cause, synthesized from the reading they have done. As an exemplary piece of what Rory terms "traditional library research," their background information earns the pair an A+.

Interlude: The Development of Milestones and the Paper Format

Up until this point, TJ and Dave's work, like that of the other students in the class, has been for the most part traditional, with the exception of adding Internet research to library research. As he mentioned on the first day, Rory has broken the long-term process of conducting science projects into a series of interim milestones that provide a "framework for [students] to work in," after seeing his students flounder in 1993 when faced with 10-plus weeks and a paper to turn in at the end. Dave and TJ are the beneficiaries of a set of milestones Rory has refined over the past few years, and it is worth reviewing the development of the milestones.

The original milestones Rory laid out in the spring of 1994 for getting the project done were: (1) choosing a research question; (2) doing background research on the question; (3) finding or collecting data that would answer the question; (4) analyzing the data; and (5) writing up the final paper. He encountered one major problem with these steps immediately: he found that students with little previous background were simply unable to come up with much beyond what Scardamalia and Bereiter (1991) term "basic information questions," such as the student's query in Chapter 2, "Why does a comet revolve around the sun?" In order to come up with more ultimately productive "wonderment questions" such as "How does a comet's core size affect its tail size?," students need a little more background on the topic area than they typically have. This is particularly crucial since Rory also found that one of the critical parts of doing a science research project is that you "have to come up with a question that you can work on." Therefore, Rory adjusted the milestones for 1994–95 such that Step 1 did not include deciding on a research question, but instead a general topic area that students then have time to read up on and, if necessary, learn more about. *Afterward*, they could come up with a focused research question.

But for the first project in 1994–95, students did not turn in Background Information *reports* like Dave and TJ's. Later that year, Rory added the report as a formal milestone to focus the initial period of learning about the chosen topic area, rather than relying on informally giving the students time to learn about their topic. The Background Information milestone simultaneously serves three purposes: (1) giving students an interim goal to focus the background research on their topic; (2) letting students apply the familiar model of library research or synthesis of established descriptions of a phenomenon (which they may have learned in other classes, especially English and History); and (3) making explicit the fact that they must go on to do something different in subsequent milestones and the final report and presentation.

Many of Rory's design changes amount to changing strategies from being informally *encouraged* to formally *required*. Rory used to encourage students to gather background information before trying to formulate a research question, and now he requires formal written Background Information. He also used to encourage students to assemble tables of data as part of their Data Collection, and graphs as part of their Data Analysis; now he requires students to include these features in these milestones unless the specifics of their project preclude such representations (in such cases, the representations are replaced by whatever else is appropriate, such as the maps TJ and Dave will have instead of tables).

Constructing Your Own Recipe: Brainstorming and Refining Research Questions

Too often in previous years, Rory saw students get bogged down gathering information about their topic—whether it was from books, journals, or the Internet—and they ended up with final reports that synthesized that information. Synthesis of known information is what Dave and TJ have done to this point in their project, and they've done it well. On the first day of the project, Rory told the students:

In a lot of papers . . . you'd be done after [the Background Information milestone], basically . . . But that's what's different about science. Because . . . you don't just take all the information you can find from all the different sources, and like, cut and paste and put them all together, and say, "*Voilà!* Here's everything that I know." That's [only] part of it.

There's more, though. Now that they've learned a great deal about their topic, Rory tells students they "need to focus it down . . . into something [they] actually can do some research on, something where either [they] can do an experiment, or look for data somebody else has collected, to try and answer a particular question [they] have." Whereas the background research is straighforward, narrowing down to a research proposal "*can* become kind of complicated" because "it's like taking a tree trunk and trying to whittle it down to a toothpick." Rory has tried to come up with ways to give the students more support at this critical phase. He decided this year to try brainstorming research questions and proposals with the class as a group. He decided to hold the session when all the groups were about to put their research proposals together, after the Background Information was returned. He figured that would provide for optimal participation and interest, since the discussion should help the students complete their next milestone (the Research Proposal). So Rory gathers the class together, saying:

> Remember, our next deadline is Friday. You need to have a workable, doable, researchable, very specific question based on your topic . . . I see three critical parts, basically, to doing projects, doing science. One is that you have to come up with a question you can work on. Then you have to find the data. And then you have to analyze that data to get an answer . . . Once you do those three parts, then everything else is kind of like . . . the dressing. It just kind of all fills in around there.

He then holds a whole-class brainstorming session on research questions, using a photograph of a wolf pack from his office. He asks the class "what are some questions that come to mind" based on the photo. After the class generates a number of questions, many of which are basic, he asks them to choose a question to pursue further. They follow several questions further, and he helps them to see that many of their broad suggestions would be difficult to address with accessible, numeric data, and that they need to be more specific. When one student mentions sizes of packs, he latches onto it, and suggests the even more specific "What is the average size, or the size distribution, of wolf packs in Minnesota?" Some students wonder, "How do we write a six-page paper on that? What is there to write?" But they discuss what data they would need to answer this question, and how they could construct a research report on it. He describes a possible report in detail, based on the outline he has distributed. The students seem somewhat reassured, but one asks, "What if you get all the information you can, but you have like a lousy question?"

Rory tells them, "I'm gonna try and not let you down the wrong path to start with." He also warns students that they will run into trouble if they "have a good question, but can't find the information [to answer] it." If they figure that out soon enough, they can try to adjust their question to a more manageable one. But "in the very worst-case scenario, you absolutely can't find anything . . . you can still report on what you did. That's still a scientific investigation, and that's still valid. Even if you don't find an answer."

In the end, Rory tells the students:

> I want you to continue to do this with your own projects. This is your job . . . to ask questions about your own project, and then continue asking questions about all your own questions . . . Try and keep it all on one sheet of paper, so it doesn't get lost. Questions about questions, or what information you would need to answer any one of those questions . . . keep in mind that you want to come up with . . . a very focused kind of a question at the end of this process.

By the next day, TJ and Dave have generated a list of questions, which they show to Rory. A short discussion ensues:

Rory: You've got some good things here. "What are the patterns?" is a good one. Like, what are the patterns over time?
Dave: Yeah, there are hurricanes every year, but this year it seems like there's more.
Rory: And why is that? You could look at how many there were every year, and it might expand to how many at what time of year. What about the sizes of them over time, or in any particular season? . . . For starters, I'd say the patterns one is the best, and also this one [about size] is kind of related, but if one of the others is related, it could become relevant, too.
Dave: OK.
Rory: I hope I helped.

At about this same time, Rory assigns Dave and TJ a mentor, a university-based scientist who specializes in atmospheric science and climate. As mentioned in Chapter 2, Rory had developed a system during the previous year for recruiting scientists who volunteered to act as mentors to his students through e-mail correspondence. He posted a message to Usenet newsgroups covering Earth Science content areas such as sci.astronomy and sci.geology, explaining the nature of his class, and requesting that interested scientists such as Ph.D. students, professors, and other practicing researchers e-mail him. The volunteers commit to responding to e-mail questions and requests for advice and feedback from a student group with whom Rory matches them. He matches scientists' expertise with student groups' chosen topic areas (for further details, see O'Neill, 1998; O'Neill, Wagner, & Gomez, 1996). Rory asks the student groups to introduce themselves to the scientists by e-mail, but does not make any other specific requirements at this stage; from time to time he does suggest that a group run an idea or question by their mentor, however.

Dave and TJ send a message and get a response from their mentor within a day, and Dave asks Rory, "Do we have the Web?" Rory explains that "the Web" is what they are looking at when they use Netscape, so they do have it. After Dave and TJ tell their mentor they have access to the Web, he sends them a number of library book references as well as Web site addresses about hurricanes. The students explore the Web pages he tells them about, and they follow links from these pages to other hurricane sites. Eventually they find a data set of yearly hurricane activity from 1880 through 1995 (Hurricane/Tropical Data, 1995). Dave and TJ are excited about all the maps and pictures they have found, showing among other things the paths hurricanes have taken in the northern hemisphere. They decide to propose a research question on the paths. Specifically, they propose answering, "Is there a preferred pattern of hurricane movement in the northern hemisphere?" They propose gathering several years' worth of data from the Web site to establish the patterns.

At the end of Week 3, TJ and Dave's proposal is approved by Rory, which is not surprising, since he collaborated in its construction. The students generated the initial idea of examining patterns of hurricanes after the brainstorming session and their Background Information report; Rory liked the idea and added the prospect of looking for patterns over some period of time; and the students refined their idea to focus on the patterns of hurricane *movement*, after finding images showing the paths of hurricanes with the help of their mentor.

Gathering and Organizing the Ingredients: Data Collection and Analysis

After agreeing on a research proposal, Rory tells students they need to "figure out where to get the information" they need. Like some other students, Dave and TJ figured out where their data would come from while deciding on their proposal, so they move directly into the next phase, gathering the data they need to answer their question.

Over the next two weeks, TJ and Dave work diligently to gather hurricane data off the Web. Rory tells me early in Week 4, "I have a gut feeling they don't know what they're looking for. They think it's a 5-minute process or they already have it." But Rory holds back, and lets them see for themselves what it takes to work with the images showing hurricane paths. It takes them a while to download images for a set of years, and they learn how to manipulate the images in graphics programs so that they can change the background color from black to white. They turn in a set of data just before the end of Week 5, and as they begin their data analysis, they realize they need to find a way to compare the paths from more than one image. TJ comes up with the idea of tracing hurricane paths by hand off the computer screen onto transparencies, which can be laid on top of one another. Now that they have gathered a body of data, Rory challenges them to go on to the next step of the project, figuring out "what the data say." The time-honored scientist's image of "talking with your data" comes in this case by way of Rory's master's advisor, a petrologist. For Rory's master's project, they "worked with igneous rocks, and the rocks became [the] data." Rory's advisor told him, "You have to talk to the rocks and the rocks will talk back to you." In turn, Rory tells his students, "You have to poke it, sift it, organize it, and it'll talk back to you."

By organizing the images and tracing hurricane paths, the students have gotten a definite impression of what the data say about how paths tend to be shaped. In an interview outside of class, Dave tells me most hurricanes "start southeast of Florida and east of the Caribbean, and then [they] swoop up toward the United States, and then they die in the Atlantic—they make a little semicircle." When I ask him to show me on paper how the hurricanes tend to move, he draws Figure 7.1.

However, figuring out how to turn this general impression into an analysis of data proves difficult for Dave and TJ, just as it does for most of the class. For their Data Analysis milestone, due at the end of Week 6, the students turn in four separate maps of hurricane paths for 1899 and 1993–1995, in electronic form and traced on transparencies. They just barely get the assignment together by the end of class on the due date, and hurriedly compose an ad hoc "Conclusion" in the e-mail message to which they attach the map images. Rory is unsatisfied with their use of the data to support conclusions. He asks why they chose those specific years, and they tell him they decided to compare "average years," which they found by "looking at maps." He told them,

FIGURE 7.1. Dave's drawing of hurricane paths.

You have to prove it to me, or the reader, that these are average years. You can't just say it. You can *say* you have four apples, but if three are red and one is green, you have to convince me they are all apples . . .

How do you define the average year? Maybe with frequency? Someone in another class is looking at the number of hurricanes per year. There's also the number of storms, tropical storms, and the number of each hurricane category . . . There were twenty-one hurricanes last year. Other years had five, eight, ten, and eleven . . . But maybe the average is not in terms of numbers, maybe it's in terms of paths . . .

Rory sees TJ and Dave's picking so-called "average" years based on no explicit criterion as an example of "generalizing a conclusion from inspection" of data. In this conversation, he discourages the students from making claims, such as the contention that the years they chose were average, unless they can back them up with reference to the data. When he generates the two possibilities that average years could be determined by the *number* of hurricanes or by the *paths*, separated by the qualifier "but maybe," Rory is also modeling the scientific practice of generating alternative hypotheses with means of disconfirming each. In this case the discussion does not lead to further analysis of what constitutes an average year, however, since that is not the main thrust of their project. Instead, the students concede the point that their sampling procedure of discontinuous years is questionable, so they need another strategy that they can act on with only a week to put together their complete research report. Rory makes a suggestion: "Why not twist the project to the last ten years, so you could use three you've done already?" On this advice, TJ and Dave use the sample from 1985 through 1995.

Serving the Meal in a "Spaghetti Bowl": Putting It All Together in the Research Report

The next step is putting together the research paper. Rory told the students the first day, "Once you've done data analysis, you should have a pretty good idea of what your question is, and what the answer is—then you can write your paper." Rory has designed the milestone assignments for the project so that they correspond to sections of the written research report. He tells them, "You're going to be assembling parts of your paper as you go along. So it's not like, 'OK, I'm gonna do all this work, *then* I have to start writing the paper.' This is actually designed for you to do parts of your paper as we go along, and by the time you get to [writing the paper], it's basically just finishing things up. It's analyzing, it's putting things into final form." Put another way, students' written milestones serve as first drafts they can revise and combine to create a draft of their final report. Figure 7.2 shows how milestone assignments correspond to sections of the paper (see Appendix B for the handout on the paper).

The design of project activities that Rory has developed for his class is powerful in part because of the synergy between the "activity structure" (Doyle, 1979; Lemke, 1990; Mehan, 1978) embodied in the milestone assignments and the "artifact structure" embodied in the format for the written report. Jay Lemke points out that activities in the classroom are structured in the sense that they can be broken down into "functional elements [that] have specific relationships to one another, including restrictions on the order in which they can meaningfully occur" (1990, p. 199). In his observational studies of standard classroom lessons, Hugh Mehan (1978) described how lesson activities are organized as sequences of events at various levels. The I-R-E sequences described in Chapter 5 are an activity structure at the most basic level, but multiple I-R-E sequences are often put together to form a classroom lesson—opening sequences to begin the class period, followed by topically related sets of sequences to cover instructional material, and closing sequences that end the class period. Extending this model, multiple class meetings can also have a structure or sequence: the typical five-day sequence at Lakeside, as described by students, is "Lecture-Lab-Lecture-Lab-Exam." Rory has designed and led the students through

FIGURE 7.2. Milestones as drafts of report.

Milestones	Final Project Report
Broad Topics and Partners	Title
Background Information	Abstract
	Introduction
Research Proposal/ Question	Method
Data Collection	Results
Data Analysis	Conclusions

an alternative activity structure with rich dependencies between the parts of the sequence. Some of the interdependence between parts of the activity, as well as the support Rory provides throughout the activity, is mediated by interim artifacts. The milestone artifacts are "shared, critiquable externalizations of student knowledge" (Blumenfeld et al., 1991; Guzdial, 1995) that Rory uses as occasions for feedback. The feedback can be naturally incorporated into the final milestones of paper and presentation. If each milestone were a freestanding, separate assignment, on the other hand, the teacher's feedback would be less concretely useful. The activity structure works in this abstract sense, but is nonetheless new and at times difficult for the students to carry out, as becomes apparent at this juncture in the hurricanes project.

After TJ and Dave download the remaining images for each year from the Web, they trace them onto transparencies. In an effort to get an overview of all the data, they create a composite image showing all hurricane paths from 1985–1995. The students and Rory come to refer to this representation of all the paths together as a "spaghetti bowl"—there is so much data covering other data in the image that it is difficult to make sense of the whole thing. At this point, TJ and Dave have to figure out how to put their burgeoning knowledge of hurricanes and their impressions of hurricane paths into a coherent written report, with conclusions supported by data analysis. The process proves difficult for TJ and Dave, just as it does for most of Rory's students.

On the day before the research report is due at the end of Week 7, the group has a long conversation with Rory about data analysis techniques. Rory asks them what the general pattern of hurricanes is, and TJ shows him the C-shape Dave had described to me previously (see Figure 7.1). Rory suggests they think about where the hurricanes occurred—they could define the rectangular area that defined the boundaries of the hurricane paths. Borrowing inspiration from the constituent mineral analysis he had done as part of his master's in geology, he also suggests the possibility of dividing the map up into cells of equal space on a grid. Then they could count up frequencies of the hurricane paths through each cell of the grid, to see where the highest "hazard potentials" were for the 10-year period. As they continue to look over the spaghetti bowl of data, Rory notices that not all the hurricanes follow the C-shaped path Dave and TJ had described. Some are straighter than the standard C, and others appear erratic. He then suggests they could devise a categorization scheme for path shapes. A valuable analysis, he tells them, would be to put a morphological name on each hurricane path over the years, count up the frequencies of each shape, and calculate the percentages.

The data analysis conversation was extremely productive and exciting to Rory. He tells me after class, "There are a lot of things you could squeeze out of what they did instead of just the paths." The only problem is, "the conversation [we] had . . . should have taken place last week. It generated more ideas, but there [is] no more time." Not surprisingly, Dave and TJ's incorporation of these ideas is only cursory in the report they turn in on time the next day. Like most of the other reports, Rory finds Dave and TJ's riddled with problems.

Adjusting the Seasonings for a New Course: Revising the Paper

Rory returns bleary-eyed the following Tuesday, after a long weekend, and announces to me,

> I was up 'til 2:00 A.M. last night working on this. It's really hard to figure out what they meant. They get into this verbiage where they're trying to sound like they know what they're doing, but it doesn't make sense. Maybe they knew what they meant, but it's not clear.
>
> Today is damage control day. They're gonna get these back and say, "Geez, I can't believe this. I worked hard on this and thought I did a good job, and look at my grade." For example, the hurricane group got a 51%, and it's a great project . . .

> The whole schedule is revised now. I can't make them do [presentations] on Friday. They need to revise this work . . . Presentations will then have to be in the second semester . . . Almost across the board there was no method or incorrect method. They have to fix it up. They'll have until finals to turn in a revised draft . . . then a week of creating presentations, and then the following week to [present] . . .

In his extensive commentaries written on the hurricane paper, Rory tries to be encouraging. On the front page, he begins with "Outstanding Effort! Don't quit now!" He tells them the "good things" are that they have "excellent data collection and manipulation," but the "bad things" are (1) "No Method," (2) "Data Analysis extremely weak—but fixable!," and (3) "can't support Conclusion from the Data Analysis." These major problems, compounded by a few minor formatting issues, have resulted in the low grade of 51% (the highest grade in the class was 64% on this draft). The neglected Method section was not merely an oversight; TJ and Dave are clearly unfamiliar with certain aspects of the scientific research report writing genre, as exemplified in the conversation that ensues during class. For instance, they don't know what the Abstract and Method sections are, and how they differ:

TJ: So is the method, you just recount everything, how you've done things?
Rory: How you did what you did. How you did what you did, and what you did.
TJ: I thought that was the abstract.
Rory: No, the abstract—
Julie: It's a summary of that—
Rory: What she said.

The group's statements in their Data Analysis are still not supported well by the data. Rory's comments on this section of their paper begin: "You have lots of good data to analyze. But, you just packaged all the data into a pile, saying 'here it is,' and you made statements in this analysis section *without* referring to the data once. You *can't* do that." He points out specific examples. TJ and Dave had written, "We found that most of the recorded storms began in the Atlantic Ocean, east of the Caribbean and made a C-like shape towards the United States and finished back east of the northern United States." Rory comments:

> In *this* statement, you need to *show/prove* this is true. Which diagrams show this? Of the total # of storms over this 11 year period,

exactly how many (and then, what%) of the storms had this "C-shape" path. You need to show, in step-by-step fashion, how you came up with your Conclusions/Results. *Back up* what you say with your graphs.

After these comments, Rory proceeds to expand in writing on the various analysis strategies they had begun to flesh out together during class the previous week. First of all, how they could classify each storm in the time period as having one of a set of path shapes, such as the C-shape they mentioned. He points out that a complete analysis of hurricane paths could include issues of location and not just shape: where the storms begin and end, perhaps where they turn if they turn, what the boundaries of the spaghetti bowl of storms are, and how often each cell in a grid dividing the total area was hit by a storm. Rory ends by writing, "Bottom Line: Lots of ideas, late in the game. Which ones are 'doable' in the available time? You decide."

For their revised report, the boys carry out many of Rory's suggestions. They categorize each storm as having one of three path shapes, and give the number of storms within each category among the 83 storms over the period. They also produce a pie chart showing the percentages of each shape (see Figure 7.3). The hurricane group's revised report is a significant improvement over their first draft, with a Method section and conclusions supported specifically by data analysis; the improvement is reflected in a

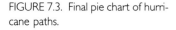

FIGURE 7.3. Final pie chart of hurricane paths.

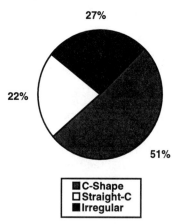

27%

22%

51%

■ C-Shape
□ Straight-C
■ Irregular

revised grade of 91%. (The earlier grade on the draft report does not affect the final grade.)

Final Presentation of the Meal

The final phase of the project is the presentation. As Rory told the class on the first day of projects, "Each group has to do an oral presentation to the class, telling the class what they did, and what they found." During the week before student presentations, Rory gives a sample project presentation using PowerPoint viewed on the overhead screens. Dave and TJ become excited about the program, and ask Rory if they can borrow it over the weekend to work on it. They complete an impressive series of slides explaining their research, and finish their first project pleased with all they have learned. Dave says they learned "a lot about hurricanes." When they did their presentation, it was "just second nature" because "you just really know what you are talking about." He thinks he learned more than he would have in a traditional class because "you're doing stuff that you really wanna do, and that you really wanna learn about." They also learned along the way about computer tools such as PowerPoint and the Internet. He says, "Coming in here I had no experience [on e-mail and the Net] . . . I feel like an expert now." He feels this has happened because they do so much and "you just learn stuff . . . when you're actually doing stuff so much better than really trying to memorize how to do stuff."

By guiding Dave and TJ through the activity structure he's designed for conducting projects in the classroom, Rory creates occasions for the students to "learn by doing." And along the way, Rory acts as a resource and facilitator as needed. As Dave put it:

> Whenever we . . . got into a jam . . . he always [had] a solution, or an example, or something new to do. Like, in our papers . . . he knew we could make 'em better, and so he, you know, let us all redo 'em. And each page, you know, was just filled with more ideas. [Some kids would think] that's annoying, but . . . from our first draft to our second . . . we made such an improvement. Just from all of his comments, and explaining everything. It really helped . . . I think it's definitely one of his strengths, it seems like he can solve any—answer anything that comes up.

Now that we have seen a pair of savvy seniors cook up science from scratch, guided by Rory and the activity structure, let's turn to another case. The activity structure facilitates these students' work, but not quite so smoothly.

THE "MOONS" PROJECT: ASKING "WHY?" OVER AND OVER AGAIN

Steve, a quiet freshman into skateboarding, and Rich, a straitlaced, quiet sophomore, are the youngsters of the Period 1/2 class. All the other members of this class are juniors and seniors.

Steve and Rich spend the first couple of weeks gradually focusing in on their topic. As Steve put it, "We first picked space, but that was kinda too broad, so we narrowed it down, to the solar system, and then the moons, and then we picked some moons so we could get some information." The last step is a crucial one: once they decide to focus on moons, Rory suggests they find some specific ones for which they can gather ample information and data. In previous years, Rory had seen groups focus in too far before making sure they could gather data on a topic, and end up without anything to analyze. For example, some students in 1994–95 went through three different proposals on astronomy topics for which they were never able to find relevant data, such as "Do red dwarfs account for dark matter in the universe?" They never tracked down data on red dwarfs *or* dark matter. On Rory's recommendation, Steve and Rich look both in library books and on the Internet, and then decide they can gather enough information to do something interesting with the Earth's moon, Saturn's moon Titan, and Uranus's moon Miranda. The books prove useful for general information, while the Internet is a good source for specific data such as temperatures, sizes, surface appearance, and gases. They collect some of the facts and figures into an outline for their background information report, with a section for each moon. Rory tells them they have a "good start."

The next stage is the research proposal. Although most of the projects in Rory's class are based on questions—like Dave and TJ's "Is there a preferred pattern of hurricane movement in the northern hemisphere?"— some successful projects are not really based on questions. So instead of calling the milestone "Research Question," Rory has begun calling it a "Research Proposal." One type of project students in the past have had success with that isn't really a question is compare-and-contrast. Along these lines, Rory recommends that Steve and Rich consider comparing and contrasting moons, and the students follow his advice. Their research proposal is "comparing and contrasting moons in our solar system." In Steve and Rich's case, however, the students have trouble getting beyond stating simple comparisons and contrasts to figuring out what they can learn from the differences—*how* the moons are different and *why*.

In the data collection phase, Steve asks Rory to help them construct a list of variables to contrast, and they generate one together. It includes size, mass, volume, distance from planet, orbit time period, and materials/

composition. The two boys begin laboriously organizing their data into tables, first in Microsoft Word, which proves too awkward. Rory introduces them to Microsoft Excel, so they learn to use a spreadsheet for the first time. Rich has almost no previous experience with computers, while Steve has a PC at home. Organizing and filling in gaps in the data takes them a few weeks. Eventually they've constructed a good table of variables, and then Rory helps them learn how to make graphs. The students end up with a graph for each variable showing the value for each moon; for instance, the sizes of Earth's moon, Miranda, and Titan are shown on one graph. Taking advantage of the flexibility of the graphics in Microsoft Excel, Steve and Rich make graphs in numerous styles, including horizontal and vertical bar graphs, line graphs, and 3-D graphs (examples are in Figures 7.4 and 7.5 below).

At this point, in the sixth week of the project, Rory begins to try pushing the boys into considering what they can learn from the data. While they are working on their data analysis in class, Rory talks with them about the variables. "Why are the moons the way they are?" he says. "Why are they different from each other? That's what we really want to know. Because we can . . . look at pictures of them and say, 'They're different,' OK. So what? Why are they different from each other?" After Steve and Rich turn in their data analysis milestone the following week, with many separate graphs of each variable assembled but their implications not described, Rory writes in his comments: "Nice graphs. But what do they prove?" Later, they show Rory a draft of the conclusion they are writing for their complete report, and they still haven't gotten far. As Rory comments to me, their conclusion "basically [says] some characteristics are the same and some are different." Rory's reaction is to reiterate, "Tell me *how* . . . look at why" the moons are the way they are. They are really trying hard at this point, digging through their data, making more and more graphs, but having trouble making sense of it all. In the course of discussing the final revision of their written report, Rory covers the same territory, saying, "Always think of *why*. Not just report what's there. What are the connections? . . . Ask the why question instead of just listing things." Recalling the first day of projects, Rory had stressed that science does not happen in a uniform, step-by-step fashion, as they may have learned previously, but "there are things that you have to do to do science." This is one example of such a meta-scientific issue: it is not enough to just list facts; instead, you have to do something like make connections, build models, or determine causal relationships.

This is new territory for Steve and Rich, though. They tell me later they are desperately looking for relationships in the data by this time, but they aren't sure how to find them. Steve says, "What was frustrating about

FIGURE 7.4. Orbital period of three moons.

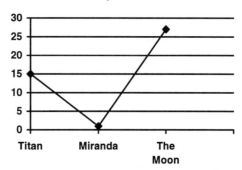

it . . . after we made all the graphs—we couldn't really analyze them, you know . . . it was really hard to analyze them, 'cause there was really no pattern" that they could see. But then Rory "kind of helped [them] out a little bit," as Steve put it, by helping them transform some of the work they turn in.

In the final draft of the paper, the students once again include only graphs of single variables, and then list each graph's interpretation separately. For instance, they include Figure 7.4, showing each moon's orbital time period in a line graph. In the text, they write, "The graph [of orbital period] shows that Earth's moon has the longest orbital period, 27.32 days, while Miranda has the shortest orbital period, 1.4 days." Another one of the eight graphs shows the density of the moons (see Figure 7.5).

Similar graphs in different styles are included for mass, surface temper-

FIGURE 7.5. Density of three moons.

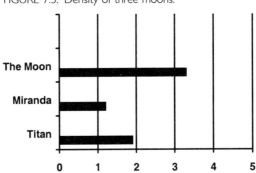

ature, and distance from planet. In the Data Analysis section of the paper, Steve and Rich do not mention relationships between variables, except in the statement, "Titan has a short orbital period in relation to its mass"— upon which they do not elaborate. But at the very end of the paper, buried in the conclusion, something more like a testable claim appears. They have written, "We have come [to] the conclusion that both Titan and Earth's moon [have] a much greater mass and density than Miranda, and that this could be why both Titan and Earth's moon have longer orbiting time periods." Rory latches onto this claim about how mass and density could be related to the orbital period of the moons, and shows Rich and Steve how they can directly test it using their data, with graphs combining variables. He sketches a number of graphs like Figure 7.6.

As in several other successful projects, Rory sees how something the students have done can be transformed to a more successful "move" in the "language game" of science (Wittgenstein, 1967); as I will illustrate further in Chapter 9, such transformative communication allows the students to participate in a new way in "talking science" (Lemke, 1990; Pea, 1992). In the course of working with the data and looking at the graphs over a period of time, Rich and Steve have developed a sense that this relationship exists; that is why they put the comment in their conclusion. Steve and Rich have "talked" with the data and it has "talked" back to them. As we saw in the

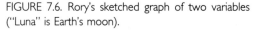

FIGURE 7.6. Rory's sketched graph of two variables ("Luna" is Earth's moon).

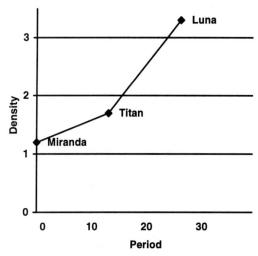

hurricanes case, however, a clear analysis technique may be difficult to find even after the data talk back to you. Here Steve and Rich do not know how to construct a graph to directly test their claim. In fact, the graphs they have in their data analysis are not conducive to checking the relationships the students themselves mention in their conclusion—as shown in Figures 7.4 and 7.5, one graph is horizontal while the other is vertical, and one is a bar graph while the other is a line graph. Rory sketches graphs of one variable against the other to directly check the claim: it appears that in the students' data, a relationship between density and orbital period is supported, but not between mass and time period. Using similar methods, Rory suggests that the students can create combination graphs for all the possible pairs of variables from their separate graphs. In this way, another apparent linear relationship is revealed, between the mass of a moon and its distance from the planet.

When Steve and Rich get the final version of the paper back, they are excited. As Steve put it,

> We finally saw, you know, what we were trying to find, with the patterns, by looking at those graphs. You know, we got all this information, now, and we finally saw what we wanted to see. With a little help from Mr. Wagner, giving some direction there. And that was . . . a good thing. Seeing relationships.

Although there is no provision for revising their paper again, the students get a chance to use this insight in their presentation. Instead of using Excel to make the graphs, they end up drawing graphs by hand on a poster. Interestingly, Excel's interface may have discouraged them from the kind of graphing they needed in the first place. In preparing electronic versions of the graphs, I encountered difficulty in constructing a graph of the form shown in Figure 7.6. Microsoft's Wizard, which automates graph-making from tables, did not lead directly to this kind of graph, suggesting instead putting density and orbital time period both on the same axis, in a grouped bar graph. This is a case of a general tool having embedded affordances (Norman, 1988; Pea, 1993b), or natural ways of using the tool, that do not easily match the task for which it is being applied—in this case, trying to show the relationship between two variables. In addition, the tool made it easy to create a variety of attractive styles, which had the side effect of making it even harder to find relationships. Rory's written comments on the group's paper speak to these pitfalls:

> Part of your graphing problem seems to be "different graphs." I know you were trying to graph everything you could to find things

that were connected. But, sometimes, the graph you choose is the most important "feature for success." You sometimes (always?) need to think about *what* you are graphing and how you want the graph to look. Then, does the graph show a "meaningful" relationship between two variables? If you start trying to compare line graphs with scatter plots with bar graphs (in more than one direction!) you are *increasing* the *confusion* about what the *relationships* are between the things you are graphing. Valiant effort to analyze the data! I think your "inexperience" in graphing and analyzing was the biggest negative factor here, but it's really not your fault.

Seeing these relationships is important to the students because it allows them to "come up with an explanation of why there [is] a pattern." They talk about this in their presentation to the class:

Rich: ... As I said, we were trying to find some patterns between certain things, and we did. We found [a relationship] between mass and distance. You can see here [he points to a graph like Figure 7.6, but showing mass on the y-axis and distance from planet on the x-axis, increasing on a nearly linear basis] ... We think that if a moon has a greater mass that might affect its distance from the planet that it, you know, comes from.

Also, we—between distance, uh, no, density and orbit time [he points to their drawn version of Figure 7.6]. Which also means if it has a greater density, that might affect its orbit time, meaning that it has a greater orbit time.

Steve: You know, a larger density would contribute to a longer orbit time, and a smaller density would contribute to a faster orbit time.

With these statements about one factor "contributing to" or being "affected by" another, Rich and Steve have finally moved into the realm of making empirically warranted causal arguments, albeit tentative and awkward ones. As in the scientific community, they are making their claims with the aid of particular types of inscriptions—in this case, somewhat crude graphs. The graphs make their claim more compelling and understandable (Latour, 1988). In addition, they are able to see possible extensions of the work they've done: unprompted, Rich mentions that a follow-up project could "compare even more data, put them together, [and] see if there's a pattern." Steve adds that he would "go into more depth on the ... graphs that we made, and see if [the relationship they saw] relates to the other moons in the solar system."

Steve and Rich were much less outgoing and experienced than TJ and

Dave, but the youngsters were consistently diligent throughout the project, and looked for advice from Rory at critical times. They had a great deal to learn about gathering, organizing, and analyzing data, but their project worked because they turned in milestone assignments and took Rory's feedback to the best of their ability and growing knowledge. They used the activity structure Rory had set up for projects well.

LESSONS LEARNED AND PROSPECTS FOR
FUTURE RESEARCH AND DEVELOPMENT

The moons project and the hurricanes project show various aspects of how Rory scaffolds students doing science. First of all, he scaffolds students with an activity structure that flows logically from one phase to the next, and is punctuated by interim deliverables that map into the artifact structure of the final written report. The Background Information phase of the project results in a written report on the students' selected topic, and serves as the basis for the Introduction section of the final research report. It also provides sufficient knowledge of the topic to formulate investigatable "wonderment questions" for the next phase. The Research Proposal serves as the beginning of the Method section of the final research report, and points to the data needed in the next phase. The Data Collection results in data tables and/or maps that will be included in the Results section of the final research report, and requires students to work with the data, during which time they may develop a sense of relationships or patterns in the data. This sense of patterns in the data should be further pursued in the Data Analysis phase of the project, which results in graphs or other representations that support claims about the data. The graphs or other representations follow the tables and/or maps in the Results section of the final research report, and the claims about the phenomena constitute the beginnings of the Conclusion section of the paper. In the final phases, the paper is assembled, turned in, and returned with feedback for revision; then students prepare an oral presentation for the class based on their revised paper and any additional feedback they receive from Rory.

Within the overall project activity, Rory has identified three critical steps that students often have trouble with, and need further scaffolding for: Students have to (1) "come up with a question [they] can work on," (2) "find the data," and (3) "analyze that data to get an answer."

Rory has developed a number of "question discovery scaffolds," and this is a fertile area for future research that would contribute to inquiry-based and project-based teaching. Rory had some success with whole-class brainstorming sessions such as the one described briefly here on wolves (in

a class later that day, he picked up a thread from the Period 1/2 class and discussed woolly mammoth questions). He has the students then generate lists of questions, and questions about those questions where possible, to use as props for conversations with him about potential research proposals. In the course of these conversations, he sometimes asks students what they know about their topic and what they find interesting about it (we will see this strategy in Chapter 10 in the plesiosaur project). In addition, Rory generated a list of prompts or heuristics students can use to begin research proposals, as an alternative to questions they generate solely from their background knowledge. In a note on the board, he suggested students
Think about

a. How does it work?
b. Why doesn't something work?
c. Compare "A" to "B" (alike/not alike)
d. How is "A" related to "B"?
e. Look for "patterns"
f. Look for "anomalies"

Developing further heuristics and prompts that point to some of the exemplary ways science is practiced could prove helpful for scaffolding project inquiry; other ways of encouraging students to make connections, specify and test out possible causal relationships, or build models are possibilities. Rich and Steve's case illustrates one pitfall of the comparison heuristic. Although Rory tells students that research proposals don't necessarily have to be formulated as questions, Rich and Steve's simple comparison of three moons was not adequate. When all the students did was list how the moons were alike and not alike, Rory had to repeatedly push them to answer some questions, such as why the moons are alike and not alike. Ultimately, research that offers scientific explanations answers questions of how, when, or why even if those questions aren't explicitly asked in the original formulation of the research proposal.

Rory also scaffolds question refinement and focusing. If we imagine a sliding scale from very broad to minutely focused, Rory has to help students find a productive place for scientific inquiry on the scale, since they lack experience at such inquiry. Students in Rory's class have a tendency to believe that a place on the scale nearest the broad end is most appropriate. In 1994–95, this resulted in proposed research questions such as, "Is the greenhouse effect true?" In another case, two students told me they were doing a project on "everything" about hurricanes. As indicated by students' concern with writing *six pages* on Rory's sample research question on wolves, students may lean toward the broad end of the scale out of a desire to sweep everything they find into the "reports" and "projects" they have typically done in other classes. Rory's tendency is to channel students more toward the highly focused end of the scale. In 1994–95, the student who conducted the volcano project Rory described to later classes as exemplary was worried that "the dormancy and eruption pattern of volcanoes [was] too specific." It is possible to be too focused too early, however, as illustrated by the students who scoped in on the relationship of red dwarfs and dark matter, but could find no data on either.

The pitfall of being too focused too early points to an important dependency between Rory's step 1, coming up with a question to work on, and step 2, finding the data. Students need to formulate questions that are answerable with accessible data. The projects described in this chapter illustrate particularly well how the research proposal and planning can be situated in the search for data. Dave, TJ, and Rory had settled on the idea of looking for patterns related to hurricanes over time, and when the students found data showing hurricane paths, they decided that focusing on patterns in the movement of hurricanes would be interesting to them *and* empirically investigatable. Rory has been informally encouraging groups like the hurricanes and moons groups to focus their questions based on data they think or know they can get. A perhaps beneficial refinement in the design of Rory's current activity structure for projects would be to formally incorporate in the Research Proposal milestone a delineation of data needed to answer the question and the planned source of that data. Such a design change would be akin to Rory's changing other aspects of projects from being informally *encouraged* to formally *required*. Coincidentally, this change would make the Research Proposal milestone a more complete first draft of the Method section of the final research report than it currently is (see Figure 7.2). When asked to review this chapter, Rory informed me that he thought this proposed change to the Research Proposal promising enough to incorporate it.

Finally, the projects described in this chapter point to the need for scaffolds for Rory's third crucial step in doing projects, analyzing the data to get an answer. Students in both these projects (and others not yet described) have considerable difficulty gathering their knowledge about their research topic into coherent reports with conclusions supported by data analysis. Scaffolds could be provided in the form of cognitive tools ranging from the kind of heuristics described above to computer technologies. In particular, computer tools that better help students like Steve and Rich check for particular sorts of semantic relationships among variables when they don't know where to begin could be effective scaffolds. One means for such tools to work would be by suggesting particular representations for particular kinds of relationships, such as Rory's graph in Figure 7.6 to check for covariation of two numeric variables. An example of a cognitive computer technology designed specifically to scaffold exploring the relationships between numeric variables in dynamic systems is Model-It, developed at the University of Michigan (Jackson, Stratford, Krajcik, & Soloway, in press). Such a tool could prove useful in a classroom like Rory's.

Overall, the hurricanes group and the moons group succeeded in part because they made effective use of the scaffolds and support available to them.

CHAPTER 8

Teacher's Time Limits, Students' Time Expanses

Rory is not only acting as the facilitator and guide for the hurricanes project and the moons project during the second quarter, though. Ten other student groups are conducting projects, to varying degrees of success. Barb's project on UFOs and aliens and Pete, Pamela, and Mark's project on the zodiac are two projects that run into trouble. Their problems are in part attributable to issues with time.

Time is a fundamental aspect of schooling tasks (Ball, Hull, Skelton, & Tudor, 1984; Schwab et al., 1992), just as it is of most cultural activity (e.g., Hall, 1976). Ball et al. showed how time "is the determining factor in the organization and structuring of tasks" (1984, p. 41) in schools. Schwab et al. showed how teachers' limited amount of time constrains their work during and between classes. In the previous chapter, I examined how Rory has broadly structured time in the project activity by segmenting the 11-week period of projects into phases. In this chapter, I will examine how problems with time arise in the individual class periods "between the bells," and how students' perceptions of "time passed" and "time remaining" (Ball et al., 1984) in the project also lead to difficulty.

THE UFOS & ALIENS PROJECT: FALLING THROUGH THE CRACKS

Barb is a quiet junior who enjoys alternative punk-like rock in Chicago, as Rory found out through his e-mail exchange with her. She is Asian-American, with short hair. She comes into class wearing black-rimmed glasses, four choker necklaces, and a black crewneck topped off by a baby-blue cardigan, looking somewhat like a member of the band Weezer.

During the first week of the project, Barb spends most of her time reading and writing personal e-mail during class. She tells me she is usually writing to a friend at college in Boston. For the first project, Rory requires students to work with at least one other student, but Barb gets his approval to work with a friend at another nearby high school who is not even taking earth science. After some hesitation, Rory agrees to the arrangement, largely because a similar group the previous year ended up quite successful: the partner was not taking the class, but became progressively more involved until Rory convinced him to sign up and get some credit for the work. That student was at Lakeside, however—Rory never meets Barb's partner at the other school.

Midway through the second week of the project, I ask Rory what's up with Barb. He says, "Barb's been there, but she hasn't been very [communicative] . . . let me write a note to myself here to check on her." He is unable to that day, but then at parent–teacher conferences the next day Barb's mother approaches Rory to say her daughter loves the course and the computers. Rory finds the comment ironic, because Barb is already one week late on the simplest assignment, picking a broad topic. So the next day Rory asks her to e-mail her topic to him. She spends 40 minutes reading and writing e-mail, so Rory assumes she has sent the assignment in. At the end of the period Rory asks her about it, though, and she says, "I forgot." Rory resolves to be more observant.

The next week, Barb approaches Rory and says, "Mr. Wagner, I need to talk to you about my project. I'm at square zero."

Rory reiterates some of what he has explained in the past, saying, "OK. Basically, you need to pick a topic—anything that you're interested in. Say, volcanoes. You then learn about that, and then focus down. Say, on volcano lava, or the pattern of volcano eruptions."

Dave, who is well on his way doing hurricane research, interjects, "What if the question we come up with is already answered?"

Rory answers, "Then you go do some more. I want you to explore some part of science, something that doesn't have a definite answer."

Barb continues, "I'm having trouble understanding the point of this project."

Rory reiterates his most familiar line, "I want you to *do science*."

Barb retorts, "You can just read it in a book."

Rory tries to clarify by explaining, "I want you to take it one step further, and do something new."

Barb astutely points out, "I think right now we're putting information together, not doing research."

Pleased, Rory agrees. "Right. You haven't gotten there yet. First you do the background, and then you do more. Let's go back to lava. You might be wondering about how fast lava flows. You might see in a book that there's a range of speeds. Those are some facts. But what are the factors that affect the speed? Maybe the slope. Maybe the chemistry. What exactly is the relationship between chemistry, temperature, slope, and speed? Maybe you could do an experiment on syrup. Is that a good model for lava?"

"OK," Barb says, "yeah. Now I understand. Right now we're just doing our topic. I can't think of anything. Do you have any suggestions?"

Rory tries to help Barb find "anything in Earth Science" that she's interested in from what they've talked about in the class, but they are unable to generate an idea together. So Rory goes to get the three large binders he keeps with all the previous projects students have done. He asks Barb to look through the archives for ideas. She spends close to an hour in the double period combing the reports intently, while Rory works with other students. Then Barb brings the binders back, announcing, "Mr. Wagner, I'm gonna do research on aliens . . . if they exist." Rory's crestfallen face speaks volumes.

Rory says, "That's just a real tough one. Some people say they do exist and others say they don't. Some people say that there's a coverup, and others say that there's no coverup. There are just all these accusations." Barb is undaunted, and Rory is not sure what else to suggest to her, so he decides to give her a chance to try and make it work: "Why don't you look and see if you can find anything. But be aware that you need data." Unfortunately, Barb doesn't necessarily know what "having data" entails at this point, and regardless, she ends up spending most of the rest of the week working on personal e-mail and a journal.

During the next few weeks, Rory begins to lose track of Barb again. She does not turn in her first assignment, the background information. A couple of days before the research proposal is due, Rory tells me he "really needs to find out what she's doing," but then he doesn't get to it. The next day he says, "I always plan on talking with her, but forget. There are people calling me back and forth, and then I realize at the end of class that I haven't talked with her again . . . I have no idea what she's doing."

Rory's Limited Time and Its Allocation

As I showed in Chapter 2, Rory's work supporting projects in the classroom is characterized by a high number of interactions with different students in different groups. Other teachers who have implemented project-based science instruction, such as middle school teacher Carolyn Scott (1994), have encountered and described the "trials and tribulations of time" (p. 82). As Scott put it, "there is not enough of it" even when teaching with standard methods, but the problem is compounded with project-based teaching. Scott pointed out that part of the time problem is outside of class. For example, assessing open-ended writing assignments is extremely time-consuming, and when Rory receives them from students, he feels compelled to get them back as close to the next school day as possible, since the following stages of the project are generally dependent on the previous stages. Thus, Rory tries to make milestones and papers due before a weekend at minimum, and if at all possible before a long weekend or break such as winter break.

However, Scott (1994) also pointed out that part of the time problem for project-based teaching is *during* class. In 40-minute periods, it can be difficult for Rory to spend much time with many groups discussing substantive issues around the science in their projects, especially when there are a number of other topics that frequently arise. Besides topics such as other activities in the school that are unrelated to projects, some topics are peripheral to the science in projects but important nonetheless. Some of these topics are *procedural*, such as the use of computer tools, the completion of assignments, and locating books. These procedural issues are often essential to the completion of the projects, and can result in valuable incidental learning. Finally, some project-related topics are focused on *assessment* issues such as due dates and grades received for assignments; although these are not essential in any sense, they are an aspect of most classroom tasks (Doyle, 1979).

In Philip Jackson's classic *Life in Classrooms* (1968), he pointed out that the "daily grind" in most classrooms is in part characterized by teachers doling out resources. For this reason, students experience delays and must take turns. Rory's class bears important similarities to some of the classes Jackson described—specifically, those where "students have considerable freedom to move about on their own" (p. 14). In such classes, Jackson said,

> the teacher himself often becomes the center of little groups of waiting students. One of the most typical social arrangements in such settings is that in which the teacher is chatting with one student or examining his work while two or three other stand by, books and papers in hand, waiting to have the teacher evaluate their work, give them further direction, answer their questions, or in some other fashion enable them to move along. (p. 14)

Rory's class is frequently akin to Jackson's characterization: Rory is at his table talking to one or two students who have approached him about their project. Meanwhile, six groups are scattered around the room working at the computers on the perimeter, a few are at their tables, and a few are waiting to talk to Rory. From time to time students across the room call out, "Mr. Wagner, can you help us with this?" Rory tells them, "In a minute." Once Rory is finished with the students already waiting at his table, he goes across the room to talk to the students at a computer who asked for his help. He might sit down with them and begin a more extended conversation or walk them through some procedure. If the conversation continues, Rory almost inevitably pauses to address some other students' quick questions, or, if the questions are more involved, the students wait their turn. Rory feels "the stress is higher" in project-based classes than in lecture-lab-demo classes because the teacher controls the pace more in the traditional mode, and doesn't have to respond to so many varying demands. As he put it in 1994, "I've never had so many kids *needing* me so much. And it's not like when someone has a question in a lab and they ask, 'Um, I don't get this. What's this about?' Here, they're like, 'Mr. Wagner, I need to talk to you *now!*' It matters to them much more, so more pressure is on me." In one of our interviews, Rory described a specific scenario. A student "doesn't know where he's saved stuff [on the computer], and . . . he doesn't know what to do. And to him that's a very important personal crisis . . . he's panicked, and he wants you to come over right now because his crisis is huge and immediate. And if you're doing something else, he may get very angry." Rory tries to head such problems off, but it still happens to him.

In order to better understand the dynamics and constraints related to Rory's interactions with groups, I performed a number of analyses on the 474 interactions I sampled over the 10 weeks of the project. The majority of these interactions were observed directly by me (237 recorded with written field notes, 172 from transcribed video), and a few were reported to me by Rory in debriefing conversations by phone after class (65). Figure 8.1 shows the number of interactions each project group in the class had with Rory coded by topic type (and the total at the top of each stacked bar). For Barb, the science-oriented discussions include the ones related above about what projects are and what she could do for her project; the procedural discussions include ones about having a partner at another school and Rory's request for her to send in her topic, as well as ones about problems with the printer in the classroom. Examples of assessment-oriented discussions from Dave and TJ's hurricanes project include questions about the grade they received on their paper and how much their grade will improve based on possible changes; an example of a non-project discussion was when TJ and Rory discussed lacrosse.

Figure 8.1 clearly shows that Rory has an appreciably different number of interactions with different groups in the class, and discussions focus on procedural issues (mean of 23 discussions per group) more frequently than science issues (mean of 13 discussions per group). With regard to the overall number of interactions, the hurricanes group interacted much more with Rory than the moons group or Barb (the UFOs & Aliens project in Figure

FIGURE 8.1. Observed number/topics of teacher-group discussions.

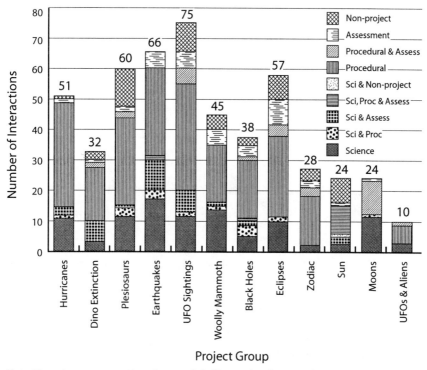

Project Group

Note: These data are not an exhaustive record of all interactions, but instead represent a sampling of days distributed across the project. The actual numbers are not as informative as the relative numbers within the sample. The total number of interactions sampled was 474, but the numbers shown here do not add up to that value because of multiple groups' involvement in some conversations.

8.1). If overall number of interactions were all that affected differential success, one would expect the moons project and Barb's UFOs & aliens project to encounter similar levels of trouble, but this is not the case. Although the taciturn moons group does not interact often with Rory, half of their interactions focus on science issues, and their project turns out quite well. The Zodiac group, on the other hand, interacts slightly more often with Rory than the moons group, but almost always around procedural issues (most often computers and Netscape). As I describe later in the chapter, the zodiac group also experiences difficulty in their project. For the admittedly small sample of 12 projects in the class, in fact, a regression model based on the number of discussions between Rory and a project

FIGURE 8.2. Variation in observed teacher-student interactions throughout project.

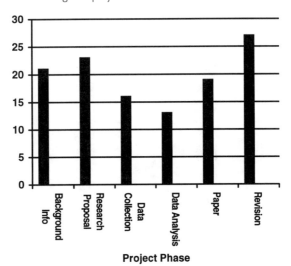

group about science issues predicts 58% of the variance in the final grade on the project (p < .01, coefficient = 2.3).

The degree to which Rory is in demand, however, varies over time. There is an ebb and flow to the overall project activity, such that Rory is stretched the thinnest at the beginning of the project and the end of the project. At the beginning students are trying to get their research started, use the tools most intensely for the first time, and get their research proposals formulated; at the end, students are trying to bring everything together. During the middle phases of data collection and analysis, Rory is not as busy (see Figure 8.2).

Rory's Reactive Stance and Reasons for It

Clearly, there are limits to the number of quality, extended discussions touching on science, procedural, and assessment issues Rory can have with students in a class period. If he were to spend the maximum daily time with each group, he would be limited to 12 discussions (the number of groups) lasting three and a half minutes on days with single periods (40 minutes), and 12 discussions lasting 7 minutes on Mondays and Wednesdays. In order to achieve this logical limit, however, Rory would have to ignore all the incidental issues and personal crises that arise naturally in the course of students' diverse work with diverse tools. As Schwab et al. (1992) have said, the perceived immediate urgency of tasks tends to determine which tasks will be fit into time constraints. In Rory's case, ignoring the incidental procedural issues would clearly deter much of students' work, especially with computer tools they are still mastering, and it could also damage students' attitudes toward those tools Rory believes can support students' work. Rory does, however, discourage students from discussions purely about grades during class, because they are deemed peripheral to the core concerns of the class, and he does not want grade discussions and disputes to deter him from supporting the conduct of projects. In practice, discussions of grades do occur during class, but Rory sometimes cuts them short to move on to other issues. In order to maximize their ability to discuss fundamental science issues with all student groups in a class, some teachers involved in CoVis choose to organize much of their time around regular meetings with students, for instance making 5-to-10-minute rounds to all project groups every other day. Rory, however, chooses to support students in a mostly *reactive* fashion during projects.

To see the degree to which Rory's support of students is reactive rather than proactive, I coded the same 474 interactions between Rory and the students by who initiated the interaction. A total of 348 of the interactions (73%) were initiated by students, and 68 (14%) were initiated by Rory (58 interactions, or 12%, were unknown because they were not noted in written field notes or reported secondhand to me by Rory). Of the 68 interactions initiated by Rory, 15 of them (3% of the total) directly followed up on discussions begun earlier in the same period (i.e., previously initiated by the students, but delayed by Rory until after he finished something else), and 53 (11% of the total) were initiated by Rory with no direct prompting from students. Figure 8.3 shows who initiated the interactions described, broken down by group.

As his experience with Barb illustrates, there is usually so much demand on Rory's time to reactively support students who have solicited his help that he never gets to students whom he would like to proactively help. The squeaky wheel does indeed appear to get the oil; in addition, the wheel that squeaks about science issues tends to earn the good grades.

Compounding Problem: Avoidance

Since he has had such trouble to this point getting to Barb during class, Rory decides to send her e-mail saying they need to talk—he knows she looks at her e-mail, after all. She sends e-mail back saying she will turn in the assignment the following week. Over half my observations from the next few weeks show Barb doing personal e-mail and other non-science

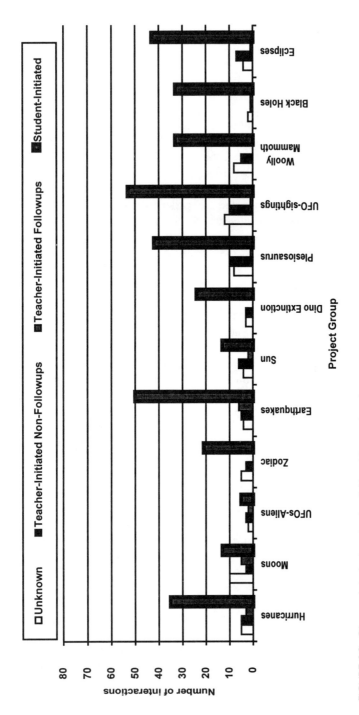

FIGURE 8.3. Observed student vs. teacher-initiated interactions by group.

TABLE 8.1. Topics of observed discussions with students initiated by Rory.

Discussion topic	Follow-ups	Non-follow-ups	TOTAL
Science	11	7	18
Procedural	7	23	30
Assessment	6	3	9
Non-project-related	0	18	18

Note. The categorization of discussion topics was non-exclusive, since one discussion could include multiple topics. Thus, the sum of the Total column is not equal to the total number of interactions, which was 68.

work, but she also begins to spend substantial time doing research on the Web related to aliens, UFOs, and the supposed government coverup of alien research in Roswell, New Mexico. Her assignments are still coming in late, though. The day before winter break, Rory sends a "low scholarship" notice home to her parents.

After Christmas break, Rory realizes that avoidance of discussing her project goes both ways. He tells me:

> There are people I don't know what to do with. Am I feeling uncomfortable with them? And them with me? The people who are really floundering are not asking for help. And I'm not offering to help. I think there's something weird in my behavior. If there's a problem I don't go over. It's often a case where I don't know *how* to help. So I avoid it.

In order to determine how and when exceptions to Rory avoiding initiating interactions with students might occur, I looked more closely at the incidence of the interactions initiated by Rory (see Table 8.1 for a summary of the topics of the observed interactions that fit this category). The follow-ups have a standard pattern: students attempt to initiate a discussion at some point in the period, but Rory is occupied with other students and tells them he will get back to them later; the students go work on something else rather than waiting in line for Rory, and Rory gets to them later in the day. These incidents, not surprisingly, tend to happen at the busier phases of the projects—at the beginning and especially the end. Such incidents obviously rely on attempts at initiating discussion by the students, which Barb is not inclined to do. Instead, these follow-ups are predominantly with the same groups who most often initiate interactions, most notably the earthquakes group—Julie and Amy—who accounted for 6 of the 11 science-related and 4 of the 5 assessment-related follow-up discussions. As Table 8.1 shows, when Rory *does* initiate discussions with students, they are also mostly procedural. This could in part be due to what is immediately visible to him. When students haven't approached Rory to initiate discussions, he tends to stand at his demonstration table in the front of the room or wander around the room. From either vantage point, he can easily notice when a computer is frozen or students appear lost in a computer program. He also initiates a relatively high number of interactions with students about non-project-related issues, even considering the fact that I usually did not record these in written notes. The non-project discussions initiated by Rory are usually short interchanges about re-entrance forms the students are required to get signed and submit after an absence, generic greetings, concerns about the students' health, and comments about students using the computers for illicit game-playing.

The few instances of discussions about science topics initiated solely by Rory, but not as follow-ups to student queries, are worth examining in more detail. Three of the seven were outgrowths of discussions that began with procedural issues during the background research phase of the project—specifically, Rory offered to help the zodiac group, the woolly mammoth group, and the plesiosaur group each on one occasion with a Web search, and it led to issues about searching for information and the group's understanding of their topic. One discussion with Debbie, who did the sun project, was an outgrowth of a non-project-related discussion initiated by Rory in response to Debbie's despondence following her friend and partner's suspension from school. One discussion with the UFO sightings group was initiated by Rory after they turned in their research proposal milestone and he had feedback for them. Similarly, the final two discussions were initiated by Rory with the moons group and the earthquakes group in the end stages of the project, after he went home and ruminated about a discussion he had had with the group the previous day. These seven instances should not be taken as an exhaustive compendium of science-related discussions initiated by Rory during this period, but they can be seen as indicative of the *ways* in which such instances occurred. Rory's tendency to avoid Barb could perhaps have been overcome had there been other doors open to begin more extended discussions, or had he been able to glean more promising seeds for ideas from her in milestones or ideas she brought to him, as many of these other groups did.

Rory makes a renewed commitment to intervene with students like Barb because, as he says, "Why wait? It'll just get worse." Over the final few weeks of the project, Rory and Barb talk slightly more often. She begins putting together her project report, and has a version ready on the due date. There is only one problem—as she tells Rory, "I have my paper, but no data yet." Rory suggests she turn it in a couple of days late with a minor debit in points, rather than turning it in without data. She meticulously glues pictures of aliens and spacecraft on sheets of paper to include with her report, but when he gets it, Rory finds that she still has no data to support a claim. Afterward, they have a good discussion about what it takes to make empirical claims. Rory says, "Your question is, 'Do aliens exist?' . . . You have to say they do or don't based on some data."

Barb replies, "You mean take sides?"

"Yeah," Rory says. "You could take a look at the Condon Report [Condon & Gillmor, 1968], like Cheryl, Bruce, and Sylvia have done . . . If you have the Condon Report, could you look at how many were identified and how many were not identified? You could show that a certain number hadn't been disproven."

Barb laments, "I picked a hard topic."

Rory says, "Yeah." There is not enough time to salvage Barb's project, and in the final draft of her paper, she writes: "Our conclusion is that there is not enough 'real' information to prove that UFOs really are flying saucers." That, of course, was Rory's fear from the beginning. But the combination of a difficult topic and avoidance of discussions with the teacher spelled trouble for the project. Not only did Barb avoid Rory's attention for much of the project; Rory also avoided her for much of the time, because of all the pulls on his attention and the fact that he wasn't sure *how* to help.

THE ZODIAC PROJECT: IT *SEEMED* LIKE PLENTY OF TIME

In addition to the problems of Rory being stretched thin on a daily basis, there are problems that arise with students' perception and resulting use of time. Rory has set up the interim milestones in the project to help push students along, but he is still not completely comfortable with the "artificiality of deadlines." His discomfort with deadlines has to do with the fact that his students are so different from one another, and the topics they choose and research projects they develop vary. Given these realities, he knows it is natural for different groups to take different amounts of time for their work, so he has tried to build in some flexibility for the milestones. Students aren't absolutely required to turn in their milestones on the due date. By offering bonus points, Rory tries to encourage those who can work faster, have a slightly easier research design, or simply have more serendipity to turn milestones in early. This works for some groups such as Dave and TJ, but at least one group last year admitted they would just as soon like to fill up the time and goof around as get the bonus points. In addition, the students can turn in milestones late with deductions for each school day after the deadline. These concessions, combined with students' beliefs about how long project work will take, can cause problems, however, as the zodiac case illustrates.

Pete is a tall, confident senior who tends to wear button-down shirts and khakis or jeans. Pamela is a razor-thin senior who likes dance but is constantly in trouble for not completing her other schoolwork. Mark is an earnest but less academically able junior (he gets Bs and Cs, as compared to Pete and Pamela's mostly Bs). He is somewhat rough-looking, and wears heavy flannel shirts and a down vest in the wintertime. The three of them sit near the back center of the room, where they can often be seen talking. They decide to team up for their project.

On the day when Rory introduces projects and discusses with the class how to do them, some of the students are concerned about the size of the assignment and the fact that it involves a big paper and presentation. Pete, in contrast, is unperturbed: he says to another student, "You've got like three months to do this." The group decides they want to do a project on the zodiac, which Rory agrees to as long as they relate it to the constellations. Since the zodiac was based on the constellations, Rory figures it should be doable as an astronomy project. In addition, in 1994–95 a student had done a moderately successful project on the scientific accuracy of astrological predictions, based on a comparison of class members' surveys with zodiac predictions. The main problem Rory had with that project was that it did not concern earth and space science, but at least it was *empirical* social science. In the case of Mark, Pete, and Pamela, Rory hopes to harness their enthusiasm for the topic, but he is a little worried about it and warns them they will need to make sure they use astronomical data. He is disturbed to find he has few books in his personal library on the constellations. So he sends them to the library. He also helps them to try using Newswatcher, and makes a suggestion to them that they search for "constellations" in Newswatcher rather than just "zodiac."

In the early weeks of the project, the group interacts little with Rory. They spend some time playing games and searching the Net for musicians such as Louis Armstrong, but also gather some information from the Web on the Zodiacs. For their Background Information assignment, which they turn in late, they assemble printouts from five Web sites on astrology. A couple of these document some of the Zodiac's development, another describes the 12 signs, yet another describes the Chinese Zodiac, and the last answers some questions about the Zodiac's relationship to the astronomical position of the sun in relation to the stars. Rory had told students they could turn in unsynthesized notes for the milestone, although it would affect their grade. He had distributed his first attempt at a rubric for the assignment in hopes of clarifying his expectations and the consequences of various possibilities. Nonetheless, a long conversation ensues with Pamela, Pete, and Mark about their grade.

After Rory turned back their Background Information, Pamela noticed Rory crossed out what was a B at the top of their paper, and changed it to a C+. She and Pete argue with Rory for the B grade, but Rory questions whether they have achieved the B level on the rubric. Pete says, "I thought you just said notes" were fine, and Pamela finds it hard to accept that even though Rory told them they didn't "*have to*" have a "detailed and complete outline," they needed that to get an A. The students were probably not used to a teacher who bothered to describe an alternative less than the ideal because he would accept it. They assumed that if they were *allowed* to turn in notes, they could get a decent grade for them. Pete is adamant that they deserve a B, because they have some good notes from a number of sources. In the end, Pete convinces Rory to bump their grade back up to a B, partly because, as Rory puts it, "this is only a small part of the project," and partly because, as Pete puts it, "it's kind of organized." This turns out to be the most in-depth conversation the group members hold with Rory during the entire project, but it is a negotiation for a grade almost completely unrelated to improving their project. At the end of the conversation, Rory reminds them, "You need lots more [data]."

In the next couple of weeks, the group continues to get little done. They do some library research and gather some useful materials, in between discussion sessions in the back of class and playing games. For their research proposal, the group suggests, "How do the fortune tellers (people that write astrological fortunes) relate the stars into the zodiac and tell people what their future holds??" Rory pushes them to focus more explicitly on astronomy related to the zodiac, so they change their proposal to "an analysis of the relationship between astronomy and astrology," specifically by comparing astrological claims about star position relative to astronomical findings. The students immediately turn in their Data Collection milestone (already one day late). Naturally, they have no astronomical data, and Rory reminds them they will need it if they intend to compare the astrological zodiac to the astronomical position of the stars. Nevertheless, they continue to focus their information-gathering on zodiacs and largely ignore constellations. In Week 4, Pete expresses interest in getting a mentor for their project, but Rory is short on astronomy mentors due to an error in his Usenet news posting requesting mentors—his post did not get distributed to the astronomy newsgroups, and he is unable to match the group with a mentor. The group continues to search for relevant resources in the library, where Rory helps Pete with a journal database, and on the Web. For their Data Collection milestone at the end of Week 5, they turn in some more summarized information on zodiacs, and Rory asks them, "Where's the astronomy?" They say they'll find some more.

Their search for astronomy data takes them to the library, and one day in Week 6 Rory goes up to check on them. He can't find them in the library, so he marks them off for not working on Earth Science (see the "Work Grades" section in Chapter 9). The following day, Mark asks about the absence, and Rory relates how he couldn't find them. Mark admits, "We went to the library, and then we went to get prom tickets."

Rory's response: "Oh, yeah. Excellent. Way to go."

Pete retorts, "Well, it's not like we weren't there."

But Rory is not going to be convinced this time, saying, "Well, how do I know? I went to check on you, and you weren't there." Mark seems chastened and agrees. Rory continues, "So that's like not being there to me. I don't know if you were there any part of the period, part of the period, none of the period, all of the period—whatever. So don't do stuff like that. OK? How can I trust you?"

Mark says contritely, "Maybe we should have told you."

The rest of the quarter, Mark works more diligently, but by Week 7 Rory is afraid they are "crashing and burning unless they pull something out of a hat." During that week, they finally look up the constellations, and that is supposed to be half of their data. They do not get their full paper in on time for the January 12 deadline, and Mark and Pamela put together their first draft the following week. Rory spends part of a period sitting with Mark and Pamela putting together their still meager materials, and they turn their first draft in on the final deadline for revisions, January 24. Their paper is a near disaster, and they get the lowest grade in the class, a 38%.

Overall, Rory let this group slide in part because they did not bring issues to him, while Pete expressed quiet confidence they would work it out every time Rory tried to push them. Pete was clearly the group leader early on, and Rory assumed he was a stronger student because he was taking the course for a higher level of credit than most of the students. Pamela and Mark had to pick up the pieces, though, and made little progress for lack of data to work with and time to locate what they needed. When Rory asked the students for feedback at the beginning of the next project, Pamela said, "You should be more specific what you want." As Rory told me in retrospect, "They didn't know what they should be doing." They had particular trouble understanding what he wanted in the Method and Results sections of their paper, but they would have had a better chance had they turned interim artifacts in. Since the zodiac group never turned in a Data Analysis milestone and didn't turn in their final paper until the due date for the revision, they only got one try at putting together a research report of the sort that Rory is trying to foster; Rory had tried to give them three—the Data Analysis milestone, the first draft of the complete research report, and the revision of the research report. By missing most of the milestones, they also avoided the natural opportunities Rory set up for students to learn about conducting empirical science inquiry—the feature that made all the difference for the moons project. But the zodiac group played it as loose and cool as they possibly could, figuring they had done reports before so they knew what he wanted, and didn't need that much time to complete it. In the final week of paper revision, the group finally began to see that they were going to be in trouble, partly through discussions with Rory. Thus, they only found out they had not done the kind of inquiry Rory was requiring when it was too late for them to salvage the project. They were unable to gather data to support any claim about the correspondence of astrological claims and astronomical reality on the position of the stars. In the end, their final report is a classic example of what Rory terms "going informational"—just synthesizing reported findings of others, with no new analysis.

As already mentioned, Rory told the students on the first day of the projects that he was not just telling them to "go out and do research" because he knows they will "procrastinate to the nth degree." So he tries to tell them as specifically as he knows how "what I want done, and when I want it done." But the flexibility Rory has retained in the deadlines works against his best intentions in a case like the zodiac project. Pete, Pamela, and Mark knew they would lose points for late or completely missed milestones, but they also knew the overall worth of the milestones paled in comparison to the worth of the final paper (one-quarter vs. one-half of the quarter grade). As long as they did fine on the final paper and the one milestone they turned in, they could get by. But they still had to learn what it took to complete an Earth Science project.

Rory knows that the necessary work to do a good, original project often takes a great deal of time and effort—"doing [projects], the stuff doesn't come just like boom boom boom." At the end of 1994–95, Rory almost decided to make projects even longer than the approximately 10 weeks they had been, because students were routinely running out of time just as they got to the interesting issues. But the bigger problem turns out to be students' *perception* that there's all the time in the world. Many students don't really get down to work until a deadline is looming. As Julie put it, "All I do is sit around except for a couple days, which is what I use to write my paper." For this reason, the time factor is a key aspect of how Rory structures projects to support students. But when students like Pete,

Pamela, and Mark don't take Rory's milestones seriously enough, they confound the primary means Rory has designed to cope with his own time constraints in supporting multiple groups working on a variety of topics.

MITIGATING TIME PROBLEMS

The projects on the zodiac and UFOs and aliens received the lowest grades in the class—38% and 40%, respectively. In part, their difficulties were due to few interactions with Rory along the way, like those that kept the hurricanes and moons projects on track. The fact that students are susceptible to falling through the cracks like this is understandable, given the extreme demands and constraints on Rory's time. In order to help prevent this from happening, Rory has set up the milestones to structure time and give the students deadlines along the way. But some of the students, like Pete, also fall into the trap of believing they have plenty of time and can get by missing a few assignments, which results in turning in milestones late or not at all. Thus, even to the extent that they ultimately realize what they *could* do to improve their project, they do so too late.

These time pitfalls could perhaps be mitigated by a number of design changes. Rory's practice of discussing the key issues in students' projects when *they* indicate they are ready (by approaching him) is successful in many cases; it also provides a degree of efficiency in Rory's use of limited time, since students who approach him are primed to take advantage of his support. But perhaps Rory should force some minimal number of discussions with groups like the zodiac and UFOs and aliens, who show signs of falling through the cracks. If students don't get a milestone in by the deadline, for instance, he could require them to meet with him to discuss where they are and how they plan on finishing. Such discussions could serve the dual purpose of encouraging the students to reflect and articulate—which would help their own monitoring of where they are—and providing Rory with seeds to think about and offer advice. I showed how Rory avoided Barb and other floundering students because he did not know how to help, but talking more with students about their projects tends to give him useful ideas. Such was the case with the moons project. When he had a conversation with Steve and Rich during class one day and at first didn't know what to suggest, Rory thought about it overnight and gave the students ideas the next day.

There is no guarantee that students will be receptive to Rory's proactive moves, however. An incident in the dinosaur extinction project is illustrative in this matter: Before class one day, Rory told me he thought Patti and Carla needed more help in coming up with promising research questions relating to dinosaur extinction. Near the end of that day's intense class, in which he had 47 separate—mostly reactive—interactions with students, Rory finally had a free moment. He sat down with Carla and Patti, who had begun playing cards with Marie and Kat. Rory then said, "OK, let's talk about your project." After a pause and no response from the students, he continued, "Do you wanna talk or play cards?"

Kat replied, "We're talking about how *cards* relate to *projects*."

With that, Rory said "OK, if you don't want to," and began heading toward the front of the room. Before he got there, he was approached by another student who wanted his input. Besides such outright rebuffs, Rory pointed out to me that students he proactively approaches may say whatever it takes to get him off their backs, with no intention of following up on his input.

Besides meetings with groups who have not turned in milestones, Rory could also regularly stress turning milestones in on time, and perhaps assign them more weight in the final grade. The subject of grades brings us to the next chapter, in which I discuss how grades and other aspects of school culture constrain and undermine project-based teaching.

CHAPTER 9

How the School Culture Affects Guided Participation

We have seen how students' ineffective use or perception of time in their projects can result in difficulty learning how to do science in Rory's class. But time is not the only cultural factor that constrains and molds project activity in Rory's classroom; other aspects of school culture play a significant role in the meaning of project activity. As Brickhouse and Bodner (1992) found with beginning science teachers, institutional expectations and students' reactions to classes impose constraints on teachers' actions. I have already described the difficulty of bootstrapping students into new practices, and some of the ways Rory's class differed from standard practices in science classes and other classes that conduct project-like activity. In Chapters 6 and 7 I described some ways Rory attempts to aid the transitions to new practices. Despite the efforts at transition, the norms of school culture color students' interpretations of Rory's class, whether he wants them to or not. For students, it can be difficult at times to even "hear" Rory's descriptions of what will happen in his class until those descriptions have consequences for their own actions. For instance, Rory mentions repeatedly that there will only be two exams in his class—one on the lectures and one on computer skills—but Katrina will still be shocked to find out they have no final exam, exclaiming, "No way! We don't have a final in here?"

In this chapter, I will describe how elements of the school's culture affect students' projects, by examining some of the action in three more project cases.

EARTHQUAKES: SHOCKS AND AFTERSHOCKS OF A GRADE FOCUS

Amy is a tall, soft-spoken senior tennis player with long brown hair. Julie is a senior friend of Amy's who joined the class a couple of weeks late, because she was out sick. Both of the group members tend to wear dressy casual sweaters or Polartec fleece. They sit in the back right corner of the room with TJ and Dave, and pair up as a group right away. They settle on earthquakes as their topic. Since they are attracted to the idea of earthquake prediction, Julie asks Rory, "Are earthquakes reliably predicted?" He tells her they are not. When she asks whether "earthquakes" is too broad a topic, he tells her they will have to focus in on specific kinds or locations or sizes. This conversation is in the midst of their Background Information, which goes well, but they are eager to focus in on a question early.

Throughout Rory's class, Julie is not shy about raising questions and concerns. Part of her misgivings about working on earthquake prediction is that she is not sure they can "discover something new." Each year, Rory has encountered this lack of confidence that "mere teenagers" can conduct original science research, as have other teachers who conduct inquiry-oriented classes. For example, Wasley reports that teachers in the Coalition of Essential Schools "discovered that [their] first task was to teach the students that they *could* use their minds well. They literally panicked when worksheets were replaced with less familiar ways of learning" (Wasley, 1994, p. 166). For this reason, on the first day of projects, Rory reassures students:

> ... I don't expect you to ... unravel the ultimate mysteries of the universe ... I'm not asking you to ... find out what happened four seconds after the creation of the universe ... we're not talking about things on that level. We're talking about exploring ... [manageable] phenomena. Things that are small enough for people to research, and get an answer to questions.

In this spirit, Rory encourages Julie to not be concerned about creating a generalizable, reliable earthquake prediction model, especially since "geoscientists have been working on [it] for years" and haven't done that well. Julie tries to tell him, "Anything I discover is new to me," and although Rory agrees, he does not want them to just learn what facts they can and regurgitate them. They do "not always [have] to answer a different question that's never been answered, but ... do something new" by putting together an original set and analysis of data that has never been done the same way before, and not simply reporting others' analyses.

After a discussion with Rory, Julie combines her interest in predictions with his suggestion about patterns to come up with the question: "Is there a pattern of earthquakes as far as when they occur and where they occur?" Their anxiety about coming up with a "doable" question that will also earn them a good grade manifests itself in repeated requests for reassurance and refinement. One day during the Research Proposal phase, Julie approaches Rory to ask, "Mr. Wagner, is this a good question?"

On her piece of paper is written, "Are there any similarities between earthquake patterns in time and patterns in magnitude on different continents?" Rory reads it and says, "Yeah."

Julie then asks, "Is it A-plus material?"

Rory wonders, "Why are you worried about the grade?"

Julie explains, "We're competitive in this class. The guys [Dave & TJ] got an A-plus and we got an A minus on the Background Information."

Rory finally tells her, "It might be too broad."

Worried, Julie mumbles "Really?"

Rory continues, "Yeah. Both the patterns in time and the magnitudes is a lot."

Julie, "The answer is no according to our research so far."

Rory thinks about it briefly and says, "I think it's a good research question. You could start with looking at the bigger earthquakes." Julie goes back to her desk.

A few minutes later, Julie returns with a possible revision. She says, "Is this good?"

Rory tells her again, "There's no need to change your question. You can leave it as it was."

After Amy and Julie begin their data collection, Julie is preoccupied by how long the paper should be: she did not believe at first that they could write five pages on the topic, and now wants to know what length of paper is optimal. Rory's answer of "whatever it takes" is discomfiting to her, so he agrees to calculate the average length of papers he's received in the past (it turns out to be 10 pages).

Increased Ambiguity and Risk in Project-Based Classes

Although Julie's pushing Rory for clarifications and reassurances may seem unnecessary, she has good reason for her actions. As Doyle (1979) has pointed out, to the degree that classroom tasks can be seen as "an exchange of performance for grades" (p. 192), classrooms, which are invariably socially complex, are "fraught with ambiguity and risk" (p. 194). Ambiguity and risk vary according to the classroom activity structure—if the activity is both familiar and rote, ambiguity and risk are low. But Rory's classroom activity structure is neither familiar to the students nor rote. As Doyle says, "Classroom tasks that require the generation of original solutions to previously unencountered problems would tend to be high in terms of both ambiguity and risk, assuming the teacher holds the students accountable for the quality of their solutions" (p. 194). Doyle goes on to point out that many student strategies in classrooms may be directed toward reducing ambiguity and risk, just as Julie's actions do. But the teacher may try to help out as well, as Rory does here and elsewhere. Like the moons and hurricanes groups, the earthquakes group has difficulty with data analysis: Julie and Amy fall into the pitfall Rory has identified of data analysis "by inspection." The fact that they manage to get the milestones in on time, though, allows them to get feedback from Rory on what graphs could help their analysis. Initially, they make scatter plots of earthquake size versus years for each continent, and Rory suggests combining all the continents on one graph to directly compare them.

All along the way, Julie and Amy seek frequent feedback and reassurance from Rory that they are on the right track, and they interact more with him than every group in the class except the UFO sightings group. All goes smoothly until they turn in their completed research report and get it back with a 60% mark the following Monday. Rory does not look forward to class that day, and begins it by saying, "I'm giving this stuff back to you. *Please* read the comments. Please . . . Whether you like them or not is irrelevant, but I tried to make suggestions . . . I didn't do this just to blast everybody." The students reassure Rory, but he continues, " . . . I just *fear* this day, because I give these back and everybody goes, 'Oh, I can't believe this. I got an F . . . and my project's terrible.' And they're not." The students say they get it, but the complaints begin immediately.

Even though the grades students get on the first draft of the report are only temporary and everyone in the class has a chance to rewrite for full credit, many students, including Julie and Amy, question the grading. They have to wait a while to talk to Rory, but eventually do so for an extended period. First Amy points out that Rory did not include the Method section in his first reminder on the board about the "parts of a paper." Rory tells them he knows he forgot on Monday of the previous week, but corrected it the day after that. They think otherwise, but he tells them it was on the handout he gave them a while back anyway, and copies are always available if they lose them. Julie is outraged that they "only got three out of five [on the title page] for not having a *date*." Rory tries to explain that the title page only has three parts, so that's how it works out. It does not matter at that moment that they know how to get the other two points— simply add the date to the title page—and will get full credit for them when they revise the paper.

Next, Julie moves on to more substantive parts of the paper, but still focuses on the points, saying, "Listen, the Conclusion . . . I mean, we wrote something down. How can you give us a zero, if we were writing something down?"

Rory replies, "Well, because you didn't analyze the data, and so those two are connected."

Amy retorts, "It's not all [missing]. The analysis. We have a lot. It's right there."

Rory tries to clarify, saying, "Yeah, but you didn't do it. I know what it says, but you didn't do it." Ironically, Rory's reason for giving the students 0 out of 20 for the Conclusion, and for the Method when it is not adequate, is directly related to students' tendency—exhibited here by Julie and Amy—to nitpick about points. Julie tells Rory that she thinks "you should get extra credit for *doing* it" at all, but Rory's experience has taught him that could backfire. Too often, calculating students given a chance to revise settle for leaving problems they acknowledge if they can get a decent grade without doing the work to fix them—and Rory knows that many changes Julie and Amy need will take thought and time. Rory explains to them and other groups later that he is just trying to let them know that the changes they need to make are important, and make it difficult for them to ignore his comments. Outside of class, Rory explained to me that one reason he was trying this strategy was that a similar strategy worked in pushing students to assemble data the previous year. He said he decided to "really go to an all-or-nothing kind of . . . grading system." When he started giving students a zero on their Results section if they didn't have adequate data, he found that students took his comments seriously and turned in revisions of much higher quality. He knows "it seems harsh, but it worked, so why not try it again?" So he is not trying to say that what the students have done is worth nothing, or that he thinks it represents no effort; instead, he is trying to encourage students to take his comments seriously, to greatly improve their paper and their grade.

Ulterior Motives for Seeking Guidance

After looking at Rory's written comments some more, Julie says, "Change our graphs? After you sat with us on the computer while we did our graphs, and now you want us to change them all!" She is referring to the fact that Rory spent the better part of a class and the free period afterward helping them put together graphs. She figures since he was there, he already had a chance to tell them what should be changed and had implicitly indicated they were good enough.

Rory replies, "Well, I got smarter, what do you want me to do?"

This turn in the interaction brings up another complication. Barbara Rogoff (1990) has pointed out that in situations of "guided participation" with a more experienced adult and a child learner, *children guide adults' guidance*. What this means is that "assistance is likely to be requested for just those aspects of the task that [children] are not quite able to complete independently" (p. 109). Julie's effort to appeal to Rory's work with them on their graph points out how grading in classroom situations complicates Rogoff's normal dynamic of guided participation. Students will not only recruit teachers' help to aid in completing a task they could not complete alone; they might recruit the teachers' help to increase the likelihood that the teacher will buy in to the students' tactics and approve their actions with a high grade, simply because the teacher did not correct students earlier. In other cases, students who are having trouble may avoid teachers to keep the teachers unaware of their deficiencies, as happened with the plesiosaur group.

Learning the Science Research Article Genre

Amy then asks what is wrong with the picture they have included on the final page of their report, of a car crushed in the San Francisco earthquake of 1989. Rory tells them they "didn't need it." The inclusion of pictures to which they never refer in their text is a common mistake by students, and Rory explains that such pictures are not included in scientific research articles. Pictures that are interesting but not substantive may be included in a "popular science article," but not in a formal article such as they are writing in his class, he says. In this case, he tells Amy, "It's like a tattoo on your forehead to make yourself look better—if you don't need it, don't put it there." Over the next couple of days, they will hash out quite a few ways in which the scientific research article genre differs from standard essay writing: the actual numbers behind the graphs may seem boring, but they should be included; the abstract may seem to cause repetition with later sections, but it is useful nonetheless; a method section is needed so that others can attempt to confirm or falsify your work; and above all, the writing and line of reasoning must be explicit and logical (see O'Neill, 1998, for a more complete discussion of appropriation of the research article genre). This last point is summarized by Julie when she explains to the even more exasperated Debbie, "You have to write the paper out like you're writing it to a kindergarten." Cheryl chimes in that she's "been writing papers where it's assumed your audience . . . already had some prior knowledge of the subject . . . like, if you're writing the paper on . . . *Hamlet*, you don't have to *retell* the story of Hamlet, because you're assuming they already know the story of Hamlet."

Rory thinks "the reality is someplace in between writing for a kindergarten, and writing for a very enlightened audience, because . . . what you're trying to do is convince the reader . . . that there's a logical, step-by-step process . . . from the data . . . to the conclusion." Just as O.J. Simpson's lawyers have to do more than "throw all [their evidence] on Ito's desk," students have to "laboriously go step by step and prove this, and disprove this, and . . . dissect like that."

Julie points out that "This *is* only for writing." Rory cannot change the fact that the stakes are not analogous to a murder trial. Not only that, but the research report is only going to be turned in to him and not read by a wider audience (unless the students send it to mentors, which Rory encourages later in the year). Other research on writing instruction has indicated that writing that has a communicative function beyond demonstrating competence to the teacher is more motivating to students. For example, Bruce and Rubin (1993) have shown how correspondence by electronic mail among students in different geographic locations results in the students having authentic reasons for trying to make themselves clear. In addition, scientists who use the scientific research report genre have different motivations for working within the cultural norms of science: they want to get published and advance their careers in their chosen field. The situation of the students is different, but Rory cannot make it the same. So he says simply, "But this is the way science is done! It's the same idea." Julie concedes the point, but Rory continues, "You don't have to have . . . four thousand pages, but just show me, logically, how you get from step one to step two to step three." Julie assents.

The Impossibility of Providing Crystal-Clear Instructions

Since producing documents written in an unfamiliar genre falls into Doyle's (1979) characterization of "generation of original solutions to previously unencountered problems" (p. 194), the activity tends to be high in terms of both ambiguity and risk for students. Doyle described how research shows that students in such situations argue "that they had a right to be told explicitly what they were expected to do," out of a sense of fairness. From my first year of presence in Rory's classroom, I can recall students entreating him, "Just tell me what to do and I'll do it!" Like those of the teachers mentioned by Doyle, Rory's curriculum changes generate efforts on students' parts to reduce the high ambiguity and risk. One form such efforts take is students simply trying to convince Rory that what they already did was good enough, when seen in a certain light. Julie may be following this strategy during one of the long conversations after getting their paper back, but she explicitly denies it, saying, "I'm not trying to say that we don't want to do anything else, you know? . . . It's just like I want to know what I can *do* to make it better." A few minutes later, though, Julie belies her statement to Rory in a conversation with Dave and TJ out of Rory's earshot. TJ and Dave think Julie and most other students complain too much, but Julie indignantly tells them, "We might not have to do our report . . . over again."

TJ asks Julie, "Why not have to do it?"

Julie answers, "Because he didn't understand our report."

Another form efforts at reducing ambiguity and risk about grades take in Rory's class is treating Rory's commentary on returned papers as explicit instructions and a kind of contract for a good grade. Amy and Julie, as well as the dinosaur extinction group, follow this strategy. After receiving their first draft back with extensive commentary and discussing their changes and revisions with Rory in extensive discussions over the next week, they turn in a revised paper. They ask Rory if he wants their old version with the new one, and he says no. When they get the paper back, they are outraged that their changes were not sufficient. They say, "We made all these changes that you told us to, and now you're telling us other things." Julie doesn't think it is fair, and also thinks it shows he is inconsistent. Rory tells me after class, "I told them I don't want to compare the papers line for line . . . plus, I see new things when I get a new one . . . But I hate to tell them something and not follow that." So he looks at what he said previously and gives them more credit for addressing it, just as he does with other students.

Afterward, Rory tells me, "There's no fix [for this problem] except to give it to them and let them argue . . . today was for arguing, two periods worth." He sits down and tries to fix his inconsistencies when the students challenge him. In this way, Rory "gives the students a voice," encouraging them to break out of their passive roles and take some control. As Wasley (1994) has pointed out, giving the students such voice can be powerful. Rory also indicates that he respects their well-reasoned arguments. But in the case of producing such ill-specified and organic documents as scientific research reports, the notion that Rory's commentary on a draft can serve as a detailed contract specifying the necessary and sufficient conditions for a quality revision is absurd. Within the new whole created by a revision, new issues that are virtually impossible to predict and plan exhaustively for will arise; as Lucy Suchman (1987) has argued, attempts at exhaustive instructions for situated actions will fail to account for all contingencies, because "coherence [is] based on local interactions" (p. 28). For Julie, however, the strategy of holding Rory to "the terms" laid out in his original markup proves a fruitful strategy for raising her group's grade—with a curve, they receive the highest grade in the class, 102%. Julie's expectations for clarity from Rory are expressed at the end of the year in a survey response to the question, "If you could change the way grading is done in this class, is there anything you would change about it? If so, what would you change?" Julie writes: "My teacher is unclear on what he wants from these projects. He gives us a low grade for things that we did, that he asked for . . . After we explain that we did what he told us, he gives us an absurd grade, like 107%, on a project" (for more on this survey and assessment in Rory's project-based classroom and two others, see D'Amico, 1999).

Despite the important concerns their case highlights, Julie and Amy make progress throughout their project, perhaps in part because their extended conversations with Rory shuffle consistently between arguments for assessment points and sense-making conversations about science. Through such conversations, they find that determining "what constitutes a pattern" is not as straightforward as they had once thought. They begin to learn to write in the unfamiliar genre of scientific research reports. And they learn some analysis strategies they adjust and apply in a later project on lightning strikes. But as my analysis of time problems showed, the proportion of Rory's time demanded by the earthquake group is considerable, and it may contribute to problems encountered by the less proactive groups considered next.

THE SUN PROJECT: FROM COOPERATION TO EXPLOSION

In Rory's most extreme period of discussions with and challenges from Julie, he says to me, "This is difficult . . . what makes it bearable is this is not like Debbie. It's sort of playful . . . Even Julie, who has the angriest edge, is OK . . . It's a discussion, not an argument." With Debbie, in contrast, conversations frequently degenerate into arguments.

The Seeds for Anger

Debbie is an opinionated junior who has a tendency to wear rumpled layers of clothes. She chooses as her project partner her boyfriend Jason, a student from another period of Rory's class. Debbie expresses interest in doing a project on the geomorphology of the Bermuda Triangle, but eventually she and Jason settle on investigating a topic Jason is interested in: what will happen to the Earth when our sun "explodes" and our solar system "ends." After researching background information and learning more about the topic, Debbie becomes disheartened. She approaches Rory and says, "We have to talk. Our project sucks. It's about what happens when the sun explodes. And we found out it won't."

Rory reminds her the sun will expand into a red giant, as they have reported. He suggests that they could look at how far it will go, how hot it will be, and where the Earth will be. She has been trying to begin her Data Collection, so says, "I haven't been able to find any information, just books with equations." They sit down and work on what they need to know: the temperature of the Earth, the range of what would happen, the temperatures and sizes of the sun at various stages, the size of the Earth's orbit, and probably records of what happens to other stars. At the end, Debbie simply says "OK" and leaves. Like Barb and the zodiac group, Debbie and Jason are not getting their work done in a very timely fashion, and then their problems escalate when Jason gets suspended from school, for misusing his extensive knowledge of computer networks to pilfer a list of student passwords during Rory's class (not his first offense). Although Jason and Debbie maintain it was all an "accident," Jason is suspended for some time and cannot complete the project for credit. After the incident, Debbie becomes more hostile toward Rory, whom she blames for Jason's problems, and more despondent about their project.

Rory approaches Debbie about these issues, and they begin by talking about Jason. Debbie says, "You screwed up my project, and you suspended my boyfriend." Rory tries to discuss this with her, and stresses that people have to take responsibility for their own actions. Eventually, Debbie agrees that it is not really Rory's fault, but she says, "I don't care. I'm angry."

Efforts to Fix Problems

The conversation turns to what to do about the "screwed-up project." Debbie tells Rory, "I found the answer in a book, so it's pointless to even do the project."

Rory asks, "What's the answer in the book?"

Debbie replies, "The answer in the book said exactly what's going to happen. The sun's going to expand. It's going to swallow up all the planets to Earth. All the other planets are going to get very hot. Everything's gonna suck. Everybody on Earth is going to die. All the water's going to dry up. Earth is going to melt."

The syndrome of "finding the answer in a book" is a recurring problem in Rory's class. He says often "somebody will tell them . . . somebody's already figured it out." The students respond by saying, "OK, we're done, we can't do this" or "It's already been figured out" or "Now what do we do?"

Instead of abandoning the project altogether, as Debbie suggests, Rory takes his usual tack of looking for ways to salvage it. He tries again to suggest data she could locate to make an empirical case for *how far* the sun will expand, *how hot* the temperature will get, and how the components of different planets will *react* to that heat. As an example, Rory says she could look at "What happens to the atmosphere in Jupiter when you heat it up to, you know, certain temperatures?"

Exasperated, Debbie says, "That is *impossible* to find."

Debbie's response exhibits her lack of understanding of the process Rory is trying to get her to participate in. He doesn't want her to *find the answer*; he wants her to *make a claim* based on an empirical argument. She is only familiar with finding the answer, as synthetic library research projects require. So Rory says, "Well, yeah, it's impossible to *find*, 'cause if you could find it, then you would have the answer again, and you would be right back where you are now."

Debbie replies, "But I don't have anything even remotely like that."

Rory tries to encourage her, saying,

Then, well, you have to think about it. Think about it. You have to analyze the situation. How hot is the sun gonna get? How far away is it gonna be away from Jupiter? What happens? You know what the clouds are, you know what Jupiter's made out of [i.e., its constit-uent elements, which she has reported]. What happens when you heat those materials to such and such a temperature? Well, it's what's gonna happen to that planet then . . .

Still discouraged, Debbie says, "Well, that's impossible."

Rory counters, "I didn't say it was gonna be *easy*."

Debbie Explodes, Not the Sun

Debbie goes off, Rory presumes to work on some of these ideas, but she turns in her first draft of the complete research report with no data analysis. Her grade is an abysmal 45%. Once again despondent and angry, Debbie comes up to Rory saying, "You made me do this topic." He points out that he of-fered suggestions, but explicitly left the choice up to her. Referring to the lack of data analysis, Debbie says, "There *was* no data analysis to do . . . What is there to analyze, if I find the answer [in a book]? It says right [in the report] what the sun is going to do: get very big, and then it'll fade to red then white then blue, and then it'll get a little bit smaller and turn into a white dwarf, and then it'll get smaller and smaller until it fades out."

Rory tries to clarify, saying, "Somebody *says* this is what's gonna hap-pen. What your job to do is . . . is to go in and look at [some] *data*, and *reconstruct* it, and see if you agree."

Debbie claims, "But I do, because," and gestures mutely at her paper.

Rory elaborates further, saying, "No, you don't. You just say, 'Here's what happens.' And that's it . . . You don't *show* me anything about how big . . . the sun get[s]. How hot will it be?"

Rory persists in elaborating these possibilities, but Debbie's anger is insurmountable. Eventually she shouts, "Have you ever tried looking up this topic?" When Rory says no, Debbie yells, "Fine! You try! You find it!" She slams her paper down, and storms out of the room.

This incident, and some with Julie, recall Jay Lemke's (1990) assertion that students have an absolute veto power with which to threaten teachers. Lemke says such "uncooperative behavior" keeps many teachers from attempting innovations. But when teachers like Rory *do* conduct their class differently, they inevitably meet with some resistance. Based on his experiences in the past, Rory is aware of the danger of students refusing to cooperate. However, he is also aware from his experience that "the anger generated when the students [feel] 'cast adrift' from the 'traditional' style of education they worked hard to master for success" can be difficult to shake. Some of the students in his first year "felt betrayed and were appropriately angry, even if they proved successful in the new system—the anger hung on with them." Henceforth, he could not gain any level of cooperation with the angry students. Consequently, Rory is wary of student anger, and he treats students' complaints with respect. He sees himself as having to promote his teaching practices, "to convince them to play the game— that this is new, and this is better, and this is good, because . . . it's a switch from learning facts to learning how to think creatively." Inevitably, he expects criticism, but "it seems to [him] that the kids you get those criticisms from the most are the kids who are having the most trouble doing it, and so they're angry, and so it's your fault that they don't get it." They may be good students, but "they really . . . wanna be told what to do . . . It's like 'Fill me up, tell me what to do, and I can do it, but don't let me think about what I have to do, because that's too hard for me.'"

End Result: A Wholly Adversarial Relationship

As Debbie's project continues, the arguments and anger escalate. The next day, Debbie returns with her paper and approaches Rory. He asks what her question is, and she says:

> Nothing. My question is that I think this grade blows, because I did exactly what you told me to do, in the Method. Everything here [in the report] is *exactly* what you said to do here [in the handout; see Appendix B]. I gave you the process I did to do my research. I gave you why I was looking for it. Why I needed it. How I went about trying to find it. I was very specific, and I don't think it was fair for you to give me [less than the full] twenty points, not to mention *zero* out of twenty points.

She showed the paper to her advisor as well, and tells Rory the advisor agreed that "that grade really sucked." Rory goes on to explain about the grade and how it can be improved. At one point, Julie enters the conversation and says, "You have to redo it. I mean, why argue over the points?"

Debbie points out, "But I don't *want* to redo it."

Julie just says, "Oh."

Debbie continues, "The point is that I worked so hard on this, and I think it's absolutely ridiculous that I had an A in the class and then he gives me a 39% on the paper . . . I should get more credit than that just for handing it in." The fact that the difficulty of achieving a high grade in Rory's class increases significantly from the first quarter of the year (when introductory activities are done and most students, like Debbie, had As) and subsequent quarters (when projects are done) is another recurring complaint of students. For instance, Sylvia—who got the highest grade in the class first quarter but whose group struggled at the beginning of the second quarter—asked Rory, "How can I get the same grade I did last quarter this time around?" Rory has to tell Debbie, Sylvia, and other students that the nature of the work is completely different in these quarters, so the means of achieving high marks must change as well. Debbie continues to vent, but Rory wants to focus on how to fix things, and she just wants to get a better grade.

Returning to Rogoff's (1990) characterization of guided participation, the kind of adversarial relationship Rory and Debbie have developed appears problematic. Rogoff points out that guided participation relies on a degree of "intersubjectivity" between the teacher and the learner. For the correct level of intersubjectivity, "both common ground and differences in perspectives and ideas are needed . . . Otherwise, communication would not be necessary or interesting, and there would be little C– impetus for partners to develop greater understanding or to stretch to develop a bridge between alternative views" (p. 202). A primary difference between Julie's and Debbie's situations is that Rory was able to maintain a cooperative relationship with Julie that allowed for some intersubjectivity along with challenging differences in perspective, while by the end he and Debbie had trouble reaching *any* common ground. Even though he is suspended, Jason ends up salvaging the project to a C- level by performing some of Rory's suggested analyses. Near the very end, Rory tries to discuss an interesting scientific issue from one of their analyses, but Debbie rebuffs him, saying, "Never mind."

THE DINOSAUR EXTINCTION PROJECT: JUST TRYING TO GET BY

I have showed how some contentiousness in instituting scientific inquiry activities is inevitable. If the contentiousness spins out of control or time creates problems, projects can encounter difficulties and may fail. Even when those pitfalls are avoided, however, some students' work may prove disappointing because they choose to do as little as possible to get by. The dinosaur extinction project provides an example.

Patti and Carla are two juniors who sit in the far corner of the room. Patti wears an outfit of dark beat-up clothes and often provides the class with witty, ironic commentary. Carla has frizzy, shoulder-length brown hair and wears earth-toned, worn clothes that announce her affinity for the Grateful Dead.

Although Patti has little interest in "dead animals," as she puts it, Carla's interest in dinosaurs leads the pair to choose dinosaur extinction as a topic. They are both more interested in English than science and math, and thus it is not surprising that their Background Information milestone is well written. In addition, they put more effort into it than they would have had they not "misunderstood what [Rory] wanted"—they thought they had to give him the final form of the Introduction to their paper. After this first milestone, however, things don't go as well. On the advice of the mentor Rory assigns them (an expert on dinosaurs and ice ages working at a university), their Research Proposal is to choose two of the theories for the dinosaurs' extinction and show how one theory is superior. They have trouble finding any more information beyond "the basic overview of the theories," but they are not overly concerned. During the Data Collection phase of their project, they send e-mail to their mentor looking for library or Internet references, but keep forgetting to look for responses. Rory's suspicion that "maybe [they] aren't taking advantage of the resources they have" turns out to be correct when it comes to their mentor, who is willing to help, but they'd just as soon try to quietly get by doing as little work as possible.

Student Responsibility for Work

During the four weeks between their Background Information report and beginning to put their final report together, Patti and Carla spend the better part of their time in the back corner of the room socializing. Rory sees their project going in the wrong direction—specifically by "going informational" and just relying on reporting what others have said—and also sees them getting little done, so he tries to push them. His efforts to interrupt one of their card games are rebuffed, however.

Exploring Patti's perspective as related to me in interviews outside of class is enlightening. She tells me she prefers a project-based class like Rory's to traditional classes with lectures, labs, and tests (like her Biology class was), because

if someone's like lecturing me, and making me do experiments, and
testing me, I don't do well. 'Cause I get annoyed, and then I'm like,
"Well, this is boring." I mean, like, "I don't need this." . . . But . . . if
there aren't tests and stuff, and basically your grade's on . . . in class
work and stuff . . . I have no problem with it. 'Cause I'll actually do
it. I'll own up to what I have to do. . . . But, if they're constantly testing me and stuff, it's just like, "Oh, I don't care."

Patti also likes the fact that "it's a very lenient class." She says they "completely just get away [with] sitting around class talking about whatever
. . . And it'll detract from our grade, but not that much. . . . I think that's
good, because it makes us responsible for what we do and don't do." She
says she is "willing to take the responsibility that [she was] blowing off
part of the time." She prefers a class that is "more laid back . . . 'cause you
don't have someone breathing down your neck constantly, like. 'You gotta
make this deadline, what are you doing?' . . . Like, freaking out at you."
    Despite the fact that Rory is not "freaking out at" students like Patti
and Carla who are not working hard during his class, he is not indifferent.
He just feels firmly that students must take the initiative themselves, and
take responsibility for their own actions. As Patti points out, she is willing
to take the responsibility, but she is only willing to take as much initiative
as is necessary to get what she considers a good enough grade. She tells me
that she is "not the person striving for straight As . . . [she sees] how *little*
[she has] to do to get a relatively good grade." She knows she could work
harder to move from a C+ to a B–, but doesn't want to. She says, "I figure
if you can make the grade, and still . . . screw off as much [as you want],
then it doesn't matter really. But if you're getting like a D or an F, then
yeah, it *does* matter, 'cause obviously you can't pull it off."
    Patti's comments make clear why David Cohen (1988b) has described
teaching as one of the "impossible professions"—because the success of
teachers' work depends ultimately on students' actions, which only the students themselves can control. The prototypical example Cohen discusses is
psychotherapists, whose complete success is impossible because their clients
must ultimately take the actions that define their therapists' success—
psychological health for the client. Cohen further described the allocation
of responsibility for success as a possible resource for the practices of professionals. In the teaching profession, what that means is that expecting
hard work and quality work from the students is a rich resource. But to
the extent that teaching practitioners bear responsibility for the positive
results of practice, high expectations become a poor resource. In other
words, if the outcome that matters—here, student learning—is judged un-
acceptable, most often by some measure such as test scores or grades, the

teacher will be given the blame. In such cases, practitioners may try to redefine success in terms acceptable to the clients on whom they depend for success. In a teacher's case, this means they try to adjust the grading system so that students can pass.

Rory was faced with this dilemma when he first instituted projects and many students were not producing quality work. He did not want to compromise the terms of quality and success he'd established for projects as scientific inquiry—he wanted to demand that students have data, analysis of that data, and conclusions supported by that analysis in order to have reports judged to be good. But in the first year, most of the class was not getting to that point. He told me that when he realized a large portion of that class was failing according to his standards,

> I sat there and I went, "I can't, I can't give them all F's." I mean, maybe I can give them like *half* points for data . . . but . . . how could I give them credit for something that wasn't there? . . . I didn't want to kill them, because I knew as soon as I do that, that I'm gonna get killed, because they're gonna explode . . . and they're gonna . . . complain to their parents . . . complain to my boss, and then I'm in trouble. Like, "What the hell are you doing here? You're failing everybody." But I thought . . . at some point the poop has to hit the fan, and I'm gonna have to start guiding this in the direction that I want it to go, and so that's what I did. And they all exploded, and they did all the things that I thought they were gonna do.

That was the year when he developed an adversarial relationship like the one with Debbie with a significant portion of the class, and Rory was not pleased with the results. Besides creating risks for him as a teacher, Rory was well aware that projects are an intersubjective achievement of the student groups combined with his own guidance. Ever since, he has been improving his support and guidance, for instance by introducing and refining the milestones. Still, it is possible for projects to end up with poor-quality products despite good efforts. Since Rory does not want to compromise the terms of quality and success he's established for projects as scientific inquiry, he must take some other tactic besides making paper grading more lenient.

Work Grades: A Tactic for Decreasing Teacher and Student Risk

As Powell, Farrar, and Cohen (1985) have pointed out, teachers and students are used to "treaties" that allow them to be more passive, such as "Don't ask me to work too hard and I won't cut up in your class." To address the problem I have been discussing, Rory has instituted a treaty with the students, something like, "Come to class and work while you are here to a decent degree, and you are unlikely to fail." He puts this treaty into practice with what he calls "work grades." These are one way Patti knew she could raise her grade. Twenty-five percent of students' grades for each quarter while conducting projects are made up of the work grade. Students will get all the points at stake for the work grade if they come to class every day and work on their project. If students are absent, they can make up the work day outside of class. Rory adapted this idea from another teacher after the anger and adversarial relationships of his first project, and before he began having the students turn in milestones. He told me he had often heard kids say, "Geez, you know, I worked my butt off in this class and I got a crummy grade." He figures, "As long as you work as hard as you can in the class, that's a big chunk of your grade, and everything else probably will take care of itself." The main thing he is asking of kids is that they do their best. As he says, "What else can you ask somebody to do? Walk on water? You know, treading water would probably be good enough. You don't have to walk on it."

Problems with Work Grades: Time and Affordances of Assessment Practices

So the work grades are meant to help students succeed in what Rory recognizes is a difficult class. But work grades have been difficult to implement, and have brought along some unintended consequences. Along with the positive implications for students' grades come some negative ones as well, and Rory has tried to improve the way he does work grades in some way in almost every project cycle over the past 4 years. One issue is that students who like to socialize at school, like Patti and Carla, may be unwilling to take advantage of the opportunity to raise their grade by working on their project. In addition, as students like Julie have argued, students who work well at home but not during class will be punished. Also, students need to monitor themselves, although they are not accustomed to doing so. As Patti points out, high school students have learned to *depend* on teachers to hassle them when they are not working: "You're given all of this free time, with no teacher being, like, 'Work!' And all of a sudden [when your grade suffers] you're like, 'Great! Crap!'" She added, "I mean, we're high school students, we're naturally going to screw up; you know, if you give us that much freedom, we're gonna take advantage of it. We just have to learn not to." The final negative consequence is that Rory has to have evidence to back up claims that students do not deserve credit for working on a given day. As Rory said, "I couldn't [just] say well, so-and-so worked, I think, [and] got an A for work, and so-and-so got a B for work."

In order to maintain evidence of students' work, Rory has instituted the practice of keeping a notebook with a work log for each group. On each day, Rory makes notes of what he observes the students doing and gives them an overall plus, half, or no credit for a work day. That way the whole thing can be added up and more objectively judged. Rory told me the system "kind of goes back to [his] quantitative beginnings." Especially early in his career, "everything was based on numbers so [he] could justify it," by saying, "Well, you had a 97.259, so you get this."

The practice of keeping such exhaustive records is unfortunately time-consuming, and Rory still admits it is imperfect. It is often difficult to tell whether students working on a computer are doing their projects or something for fun. Even more importantly, we know from the previous chapter that Rory's time is already at a premium. Given the fact that grades are a reality that is not going away in Rory's school and therefore his classroom, I want to consider them as a design constraint with certain affordances. In particular, I think it is important to realize that assessment can afford both *judgment* and *guidance*. The time Rory spends discussing students' ongoing work with them or marking up milestones or papers they have turned in serves *both* a guiding function *and* a judgment function. The work grades Rory marks in his book, on the other hand, serve *only* a judgment function. There are times during class when Rory wanders around the room looking over students' shoulders to see what they're up to, and the only result is a mark in his work grade book. Such assessment for judgment does not help students accomplish scientific activity in any direct way, and in fact contributes to Rory's lack of time to do assessment for guidance. In addition, the judgment aspect of the work grades may overemphasize the "performance-grade exchange" nature of classroom tasks (Doyle, 1979) in students' minds, again to the detriment of the scientific nature of classroom tasks. In the zodiac project, for instance, Mark, Peter, and Pamela made sure to come in and make up days they had missed getting work credit for, but blatantly ignored turning in some of the milestones. In the earthquakes and hurricanes projects, on the other hand, Julie, Amy, TJ, and Dave were luckily more concerned about turning in milestones than in monitoring their work grade; in fact, Julie actively resisted working every day, and took as much opportunity as she could to socialize with Amy and her other friends in the class while still getting the milestones done. Even though Julie and Amy were somewhat preoccupied with the performance-grade exchange, their focus on the milestones helped them.

Given this distinction between assessment for judgment and assessment for guidance, it becomes clear that teachers should try to maximize opportunities for assessment for guidance. Part of the problem for Rory is that students' entire grade can't be based on the end products of projects (paper and presentation), or else the situation is just too risky for both the students and Rory, and the opportunity to "assess for guidance" is only retrospective. To show that "the product [isn't] everything," Rory has tried to "accentuate the process" with his daily work grade system. But since work grades afford judgment whereas milestone assignments afford guidance, the latter might be a better feature to accentuate. Rory has considered replacing the current work grades, which I have argued afford only assessment for judgment, with increased grading emphasis on the milestone assignments. My analysis suggests that this design change would be helpful.

Seeking Teacher Buy-In over Scientific Disagreements

Patti and Carla turn in the first draft of their complete research paper in time to get some guidance from Rory, however. After they get their paper back with extensive commentary from Rory, they have several discussions of some length about it. One portion of the discussion is particularly interesting:

Patti: I think we had miscommunication here [gesturing to paper] . . . the seas were flooded.
Rory: Where?
Patti: Everywhere.
Rory: I'm digging deeper because maybe where it was mattered.
Patti: It's not clear in the book.
Rory: Since it's your paper and you know more about it than I do, you can make some decisions. Once I make these comments, just ignore them if they don't matter. Researchers can have different opinions, and it's OK.
Patti: But you're grading it.
Rory: We have different opinions. It's my job to get at those . . . I'm just trying to bring more stuff out that maybe we should know. But if you can't, that's OK.

The first important aspect of this discussion is Patti's statement that "you're grading it." This recalls Julie and Amy's earlier attempts to get approval from Rory on the graphs they made. Even though Rory says students should ignore comments he makes on drafts if they know they don't matter, such actions *will* likely affect their grade negatively if they don't discuss the issues with him. This is not necessarily a problem, because such discussions afford opportunities for important scientific sense-making, as I have previously mentioned. But the importance of students bringing such issues to Rory is not explicitly mentioned by Rory, so students who have less "interactional competence" (Mehan, 1980) with Rory than Patti or Julie may miss such opportunities.

Opposing Epistemologies of Teaching and Learning

Rory's statement that "it's your paper and you know more about it than I do" relates to an epistemological conflict that sometimes causes problems in Rory's classroom. David Cohen (1988a) characterizes the dominant epistemology with the phrases "teaching as telling" and "learning as accumulation [or absorption] of facts" (p. 257). I will refer to this as the "transmission epistemology" because it implies that knowledge is transmitted directly from the teacher's mind to the students' minds (Pea, 1994). Many of Rory's students espouse transmission, and it can be used to accuse Rory, most often with the claim, "You haven't taught us anything." Rory's epistemology of teaching and learning, on the other hand, is in line with Cohen's characterization of the roots of inquiry-oriented instruction: teaching is facilitating or guiding, and learning is constructing knowledge and solving problems. Rory recognizes that the disparity between his beliefs about teaching and those of more traditionally minded students and parents can lead to problems. He told me that such "traditionalists" are likely to say to him, "Well, if you're not *teaching* them anything, then how are they supposed to *learn* anything?" He responds, "I'm not teaching them to memorize facts, [but] I am teaching them how to do other things. Facts you can always find."

The transmission epistemology has several corollaries. One corollary, which Patti seems to espouse, is that teachers should have all the knowledge of their field stored in their heads, in order to be deemed knowledgeable and competent. During an interview outside of class, Patti mentions to me in hushed tones one shortcoming she feels Rory has:

> I think occasionally he needs to know his information better, 'cause there are times when he'll be like, "Oh, this." And then a couple days later, he'll be like, "Nope, I was wrong. I was off by like five." Or something like that [when] talking about the stars . . . he'll just be like, "Whoops, I was wrong, looked it up again. This is the right thing." . . . And you're just like, "OK, whatever."

In the "knowledge as problem-solving" view espoused by Rory, it is only natural that he look up such random facts rather than memorize them all, and that he cannot know everything about all the students' projects. As the teacher, the key is that he has considerably more expertise in sound scientific practices than the students, and a clear understanding of the major conceptual knowledge within earth and space sciences—not necessarily every minor detail. Not coincidentally, the transmission epistemology meshes more smoothly with traditional teaching practices such as lectures and exams, which Patti emphatically rejects as ineffective, but she does not recognize the conflict. Patti also finds it questionable that Rory is a learner as a teacher; specifically, that he is constantly trying to learn how to teach his class better. She says to me, "It seems like he's learning at all times, like, how to do his class better . . . I just think it's frustrating, 'cause . . . he's learning . . . He doesn't even really know, *completely*, how to do this class."

The belief that teachers should have all knowledge has already led to problems in Rory's experience. Rory says when some students "lost some of that faith that the teachers know everything . . . then that became, 'Well, you're not doing anything, so you must be really stupid.'" For instance, Debbie is a student whose anger, and perhaps discomfort with being asked to move away from a more passive role, pushes her to confront and at times accuse Rory. Similarly, when Julie states that Rory may not have understood their report and she had to clarify it for him, the implication is that Rory's knowledge is lacking. On another occasion, when Rory does not immediately know the answer to one of her questions about how to make a particular change to a graph in a software program, Julie says, "If you don't know how to do it, how can we do it?"

A second corollary of the transmission epistemology is the belief that doing science inquiry is much less valuable than telling and memorizing science facts. Thus, in 1994–95 Rory mentioned at the end of the first project that some students who were disappointed with the results of their project could do something better the next semester. One student then asked, "Are we doing this again next semester?"

Rory replied, "Hopefully you'll do a different project."

She clarified, "No, I mean when are we going to *learn* something about Earth Science?" Despite the fact that they had begun to learn how to research and perform empirical analysis, the student did not recognize this form of learning as valuable. Later in the year, she confessed she thought, "We don't learn anything in this class." When I pressed her, she conceded, "Well, we learn something, of course." Similarly, later in 1995–96, I ask Cindy what she thinks of projects. Her response is:

> I don't like it. I wish we just had a normal class like with taking notes from the board, and using the textbook, and taking tests. I would have liked that better . . . Like I was in here one day during second period . . . and I wish I was in the other class . . . 'Cause they

do more things, like they really *learn* in class. They do labs and take notes and take tests and everything.

Another corollary of the transmission epistemology is the idea that Rory must not have told the students what he wanted in his assignments if they didn't *understand* what he wanted. Patti said to me, "Sometimes you just want like, proper explanation. I mean, that's what we're here for, to like, learn exactly how to do things." And she felt he wasn't telling them exactly how. Like Julie, she did not recognize that instructions on how to do open-ended projects cannot be exhaustively complete, because there are too many contingencies. But Patti *did* recognize that she knew what she was doing the second time they did projects, although she did not attribute the change to her own learning. She believed Rory gave them a new handout with "exactly . . . what he expects." *But the handout was the same.* The difference was that her understanding of his instructions was more complete, because she had participated in one round of projects. To reiterate the point from Chapter 5, the activity of guided participation in projects provided the opportunity to bootstrap her understanding of scientific research. They had learned something to build on, despite the fact that Patti and Carla's final report "was just basically just taking information out of a book, like, and tossing it around." Because of her epistemology of learning, Patti told me, "I didn't learn anything" in the dinosaur extinction project, except possibly "the asteroid theory is the theory that is most, like, acceptable, [and] a few details about it, like where the craters are and possibly how big they are."

Looking at learning from an epistemology that values problem-solving and participation in scientific practices, I see Patti learning more in Rory's class than she herself does. For her second project, she works with Diane and Tom (two other students who have difficulty during round one) on a project about tornadoes. They gather data on tornadoes and deaths caused by tornadoes, and construct graphs that provide evidence that although the number of tornadoes appears to have increased over the past 50 years, the number of deaths caused by tornadoes has decreased. In an interview, she tells me they have developed a "theory on it," that "we're technologically more advanced, so we have all these tracking devices, to track tornadoes, and give warnings and stuff. When back then, they didn't, so if a tornado hit, it was completely out of surprise, and so they just died." In conversations in class, Rory discusses with Patti's group how they could try to support their theory with the data they have or with other data, but the students do not get to the point of establishing causal evidence in the time they have. Instead, their analysis only goes so far as to demonstrate the trends in tornadoes and deaths. Nonetheless, Patti's ability to contribute to a scientific inquiry shows signs of increasing over time.

THE CULTURE OF SCHOOL AND THE PROBLEM OF PROJECTS

In this chapter I have described and illustrated a number of implications that the culture of schooling has for project-based science. Both students and teachers experience increased ambiguity and risk. The ambiguity manifests itself in the impossibility of teachers giving clear and exhaustive instructions to students for inherently complex and open-ended tasks, including writing research reports in the unfamiliar scientific genre. When grading is a part of schooling (as it is in most schools in this country), classroom tasks involve to some degree an exchange of performance for grades. The inherent ambiguity of project-based instruction means that students' risk of getting poor grades is increased. At the same time, teachers' risk of giving large numbers of poor grades due to poor-quality products— which reflects negatively on their teaching practice and effectiveness— increases.

The increases in risk for both teacher and student have a number of implications, some of which are positive, and more negative. Students' angling for grades can push them to seek Rory out for guidance on how to conduct scientific inquiry effectively. The ensuing discussions can involve valuable scientific sense-making when they involve students and teacher coming to new understandings from different perspectives. But they can also be tilted so far toward students sycophantically seeking buy-in from the teacher that opportunities for learning are compromised. In addition, students may become so angry and frustrated at the ambiguity and the difficulty of accomplishing a project, as happened with Debbie, that they are no longer able to reach any common ground with Rory. Although learning will not take place if student and teacher already have *complete* agreement, some common ground is necessary for interaction to succeed.

Typical school culture is not characterized by students having as much responsibility for their actions and consequences as they are given in Rory's class, and they may try to return the responsibility to him to reduce their risk of failure. Thus, students like Debbie may accuse him of "making them do" something. They may also accept only as much responsibility as is absolutely necessary. Thus, students like Patti may choose to do only as much as they have to do to get by in his system. To encourage student responsibility and decrease the risk that students will fail, Rory has tried instituting a system of work grades. Giving students daily grades for working or not has proved difficult due to the ubiquitous time constraints on

Rory; the work grade system also affords only a judgment function, without providing any guidance for the students. Since the milestone assignments afford both a judgment and a guidance function, I suggest they could ultimately prove more productive without the system of work grades.

Finally, students espousing the transmission epistemology of teaching and learning may have difficulty accepting the pedagogy of project-based science. Students who believe that "teaching is telling" and "learning is accumulation of facts" may find fault with Rory because he is open about not having all Earth Science facts stored in his head, but instead knows how to find needed information and use it in inquiry. Notably, Rory's position is supported by such luminaries as Herbert Simon, a Nobel laureate in Economics. In *The Sciences of the Artificial*, Simon (1981) proclaimed that knowing in the information age has been redefined as "knowing how to find" rather than just "remembering." The same students who find fault with Rory's knowledge of science may judge scientific inquiry as less valuable than being told science facts; in this way, they may not see the value in the inquiry skills they themselves gain, because they perceive that they don't *recall* the kinds of broad but shallow *facts* they value more highly in school.

CHAPTER 10

Coaching Active Students Through Transformative Communication and Encouragement of Student Voice

Educational reform efforts directed at fostering project-based learning have a tendency to substitute entirely teacher-directed pedagogy for entirely student-directed pedagogy (Rogoff, 1994). As Rogoff describes, *lecture-based* classrooms depend on transmission of knowledge from an active teacher to a passive learner. In contrast, *unguided discovery* depends on acquisition of knowledge by an active learner with the teacher remaining passive. However, the model of *"community of learners"* is based on the premise that "learning occurs as people participate in shared endeavors with others, with all playing active but asymmetrical roles" (p. 209). Teachers like Rory interested in fostering inquiry learning in their classes need to try to create a community of learners atmosphere. This implies that they must play a unique role of structuring and guiding student activities in the classroom without taking away the students' active role. Some researchers refer to this middle ground as "guided discovery" or "guided learning." As Ann Brown (1992) says,

> Guided learning is easier to talk about than do. It takes clinical judgment to know when to intervene. Successful teachers must engage continually in on-line diagnosis of student understanding. They must be sensitive to overlapping zones of proximal development, where students are ripe for new learning. Guided discovery places a great deal of responsibility in the hands of teachers, who must model, foster, and guide the "discovery" process into forms of disciplined inquiry that would not be reached without expert guidance. (p. 169)

The projects described thus far make clear the complexity of structuring and guiding students in their project work. Some of the students, such as Dave, TJ, Steve, and Rich, respond easily and agreeably to the supports

Rory has devised. Some, such as Julie, Amy, and Patti, seem to be reluctantly aided by Rory's supports. And a few, such as Barb, Pete, and Debbie, do not seem to have received the kind of support they needed (either because of time constraints or because they rejected it). Different students in the class *need* and also end up *getting* different levels and kinds of support. Matching the kind and level of support students *need* with what Rory *gives* them is a difficult balance to maintain, though. Consequently, as Rory put it, he can "feel sort of like a tree swaying between two extremes of providing students with structure and allowing them to do it all themselves." One way to conceptualize teachers' new role in such classrooms is by *scaffolding* student work (Collins et al., 1989). In addition to the modeling and structuring of activity I have already described, scaffolding can be provided through coaching—supporting and guiding students' work along the way. In this chapter, I will consider some of the coaching strategies Rory uses, and how he strives to balance between the extremes of providing too much scaffolding of this sort and providing too little.

PLESIOSAURS: COACHING AND CO-OWNERSHIP

Three juniors who sit at the middle table of Rory's classroom during the first quarter of the year team up for their first project. Beth and Laura are both gregarious, and have participated frequently in class discussions during lectures. Cindy, on the other hand, is usually quiet and somewhat mousy; she was the student who watched many others complete the computer competency test before getting the courage to try it herself.

After toying with a couple of different topics for their project, like volcanic islands, Cindy and Laura settle on dinosaurs, and then focus in specifically on the plesiosaur. Beth is absent the day they make the choice, but is quickly just as enamored of the creature as the others, saying, "Isn't he cute?" when she sees a picture. They can be heard to repeat its name slowly, relishing its sound, and they show anyone willing to look pictures of the dinosaur, which lives in the sea. It has a long neck somewhat like a brontosaurus. In fact, it looks like the fabled Loch Ness monster, which some legends say is descended from the plesiosaur.

Cognitive Apprenticeship into Search Strategies

During the first week of the project, their search for background information on the plesiosaur is not fruitful. They find a couple of books with nice pictures but only sketchy material on the plesiosaur. After the week of difficulty, Rory sits down with them for most of a double period to help them search the World Wide Web, since he feels information on a major type like plesiosaur must be out there. They try searching for the word *plesiosaur* and don't turn up much that looks promising. But Rory points out that "sometimes you just have to go to those [unlikely looking] things, and see what's there." Then they look through a number of linked pages related to dinosaurs, discussing the type of dinosaur and the time period in order to make decisions about where information on their dinosaur might be. Along the way, they end up discussing how the Mesozoic period is subdivided into the Triassic, Jurassic, and Cretaceous periods. This session is interesting in that it provides a significant degree of opportunities for incidental learning both about science topics and the Web.

The session also illustrates students' difficulties searching for information. As Rory found out when he first started projects, assuming that students' search methods will be sophisticated—either using traditional means such as the library or new means such as the Web—is a mistake. In fact, the introduction of the often overhyped Web can bring problems as well as provide solutions. Rory says many students figure they can "just plug in a key word and a worldwide search [will] bring all the information [they] need right to [their] computer within seconds. Too bad it doesn't work that way." Students often fall into the extremes of being too broad or too specific, like the student who typed "hurricane" into a Web search and was overwhelmed by the thousands of hits returned, since she did not know how to refine her search. At the other extreme, some students type all or part of their research questions directly into a Web search, and expect "every piece of information that can be useful for their project." For instance, Amy searched for the exact phrase "pattern of earthquakes," but did not find answers or useful data sources.

People often view the Web as a "superlibrary," but the basic information students need for their background research is often more difficult to locate on the Web (at least with late 1990s state of the art) than in textbooks or library books. Rory therefore asks students to exhaust printed sources before moving to the Web. Once they do move to the Web, as the plesiosaur group has done at his urging, they may not be willing to "take the time to look" and "collect bits and pieces" of useful information unless Rory encourages them. It is often helpful for him to sit down with them and say, "Well, let's try this," as he does with Beth, Cindy, and Laura. One problem, again, may be their experience from other classes, where they are often told, in effect, "Here's all the stuff you need in this little box, here's the recipe, just follow this list, write stuff down, and when you get to the end, you're done."

In the course of searching the Web, Rory has a brief discussion with the students about the credibility of the information they find there. Their search turns up some pages of abstract art with "plesiosaur" in the title, and Cindy asks, "Is this just information that people put on?" Rory tells her it is, to which she replies, "Really? . . . So if we get it from here it might not be true?" Cindy can barely believe it is "legal" to put "made-up stuff" on the Web, but it slowly becomes clear to her and Laura that "if you like print something fake in here, it doesn't matter." As Cindy perceives, this implies that they could do a report based on the information, "and it could be wrong." The same problem, of course, holds for some print sources, as Rory points out to students from time to time. As Rory points out, the best remedy is using multiple sources, both on and off the Web, to corroborate one another.

Cindy continues venting frustration: "Don't you hate the fact that it might be someplace here, but you can't find it, 'cause it's so complicated?" The group's search with Rory on the Web that day does not turn up much, except for a couple of promising library references. Over the next week, they are able to use the information from library books to inform their Background Information report, which describes the age of dinosaurs; unique features of the plesiosaurs, including its long neck and arms used for swimming; and theories of dinosaur extinction. They seem genuinely excited when Rory tells them their report is "great" and gives them an A+.

In order to find more information on plesiosaurs, Rory has suggested they post to Usenet newsgroups concerned with paleontology. As with Netscape, though, they have to learn how to use the tool, and which newsgroups discuss dinosaurs. As Cindy put it, "To find stuff you have to know all this stuff we don't know." Rory responds, "Right, which is why we have to talk." When they talk to him, it creates the kinds of opportunity for learning on demand that he is trying to foster. After the group has completed their background research, Rory helps Laura and Cindy compose and post a message entitled "research project on plesiosaurs" to sci.geo.geology. He coaches them by giving them some suggestions on the general gist, urges them to make it clear what they have already done, and then leaves them to work on it themselves. Later, he approves their final message before they send it out to the world:

> We are students at [Lakeside] High School doing an Earth Science project. We have been searching for information on the Plesiosaur throughout the Internet and librarys [sic]. So far we have found general information on the appearance and habits of the Plesiosaur but we need additional general information so that we can come up with a specific research question. We would appreciate any information

you could send us, or places we could search on the Internet about our topic. Thank you very much, we will appreciate greatly any help you give us.

This request is much better than the student who posted a message a year earlier saying, "I need to know everything on volcanoes in one week." Such inappropriate and ineffective usage prompted Rory to institute a policy of asking students to show him messages before posting to Usenet. In this way, he retains the metacognitive role of monitoring for well-formulated requests, which students can later do for themselves after gaining experience. In the Plesiosaur group's Usenet news post, we thus see examples of several strategies recommended by the cognitive apprenticeship literature (e.g., Collins et al., 1989): learning on demand, coaching, and monitoring.

Despite the fact that Laura and Cindy's posting is less directed than is ideal, they receive several responses by e-mail, including one from a paleontology graduate student who agrees to be their mentor. He gives them some references, and they write him e-mail asking for more. After they begin to focus in on a research question, however, Beth tells me they do not find their mentor's suggestions as helpful as Rory's, and stop corresponding. As Rory told me in an interview that fall, he has higher hopes for a richer relationship with the mentors, "where people are kind of like working together to find an answer," but "kids just don't quite get it" yet. In this first project cycle of 1995–96, student interaction with mentors is focused on the kind of searching for references Rory finds problematic, although one student the previous year continued to exchange e-mail with her mentor about science-related issues even after the project was over. Rory continues to work on ways of fostering such richer relationships with mentors throughout the 1995–96 school year (for a more complete discussion of lessons from these "telementoring" efforts see O'Neill, 1998; O'Neill et al., 1996).

Negotiating a Research Proposal Co-Owned by Students

During the following week, the group has to come up with a focused research proposal. After the whole-class brainstorming session on research questions, students begin working in their own groups generating questions about their topics. The next day, Beth and Cindy approach Rory, announcing they have a research question. It is, "Are accumulations of plesiosaurs associated with areas of high marine productivity?" Rory sees a number of problems with the question. Although it suggests a "doable" empirical analysis—comparing the number of plesiosaur skeleton findings in locations to fossil records that indicate high marine productivity—the results would most likely be dubious because the fossil record is spotty. The problem is, the number and location of plesiosaur fossils found may not reliably indicate the relative numbers of plesiosaurs living at those locations in prehistoric ages. Fossils do not form as easily in some locations as others, regardless of how many animals lived in the locations, and fossils are not as easily found in all locations. To avoid these pitfalls, Rory asks them to step back, saying, "What drew you to plesiosaurs in the first place?"

Cindy talks about their long necks, and Beth about how they swim. That reminds Rory of a comment Beth had made while looking at library books two weeks earlier. She had announced, "This [book] says they flew through the water like sea turtles, and sea turtles swim very quickly . . . This [book] says they didn't swim very quickly." Rory had only said "hmm" at the time. The group had not mentioned swimming speed in their background report, but Rory had apparently filed it away.

Rory asks Beth, "Didn't you read a debate about whether they were fast or slow swimmers?"

Beth says, "Yeah. Some of them said they were fast and some said slow."

Rory suggests, "Maybe you could do an analysis of swimming motion. Like how fast they go. You would need to know how animals move and how they swim."

Rory stresses that they need not follow his suggestion. Besides opportunity for learning through a greater level of student participation, Rory's policy of not forcing students to follow his recommendations is part of a general policy of leaving a large amount of responsibility with the students. If he *makes* students follow his recommendations, students are likely to claim he alone is responsible if their efforts do not turn out well, as a way of weaseling out of making improvements. But if students work together *with* him in earlier stages and have a strong voice in decision-making, they can establish *co-ownership* (Pea, 1997). With co-ownership of the project, students are more likely to be willing to work together with Rory to figure out productive alternatives if they encounter difficulties. Since Rory is "not driving the direction of anything, other than [laying] the framework," dialogue with the students becomes much more important.

Rory's policy of leaving final decisions up to students does have its pitfalls, however. Most notably, students sometimes choose against a course that Rory sees as particularly promising. Despite Rory's input, other students have chosen not to pursue questions such as, "What color was dinosaur skin?" and "Why do elephants and woolly mammoths occupy similar ecological niches, despite unrelated evolutionary lines?" In this case, however, Beth and the other members of her group like the idea, and decide to run with it. As Beth says, "It reminds me of the reanalysis of dinosaurs that they did, and whether they were slow or fast—*Jurassic Park* was more accurate than the old picture of lumbering dinosaurs."

Following the discussion where they decide to focus on the swimming motion of plesiosaurs, the group members go off to review the relevant sections in the library books they have gathered, and Beth returns a few days later saying incredulously, "Mr. Wagner! Do you know whether the plesiosaur moved by rowing its flippers or flapping them like wings?" One of her library books states that plesiosaurs swam with a rowing motion, and another book states that they swam by underwater flight, flapping their flippers like wings straight up and down in the water. Neither book mentions a controversy. As Beth tells me later, "I thought he was like all-knowing. That he like knew there was this controversy. But he didn't." In approaching her teacher, Beth is looking for the *answer*, the kind needed for a library research project. She tells me she "had never done a project where there hasn't been really an answer, or someone who's already found the answer." Rory shows Beth that her question about the swimming method can be *the* question in *their* research project—*they* can assemble evidence and figure out which swimming motion they think it is.

INTERLUDE: TRANSFORMATIVE COMMUNICATION IN ACTION

This exchange between Rory and Beth provides an example of a key strategy for supporting students in accomplishing unfamiliar activities, which Pea (1994) terms "transformative communication" (or "TC"). Pea's notion of transformative communication helps explain how learning and activity in Vygotsky's (1978) "zone of proximal development" (ZPD) can be accomplished. Vygotsky's model of learning holds that learners accomplish activities with the help of more expert others in a social setting (on what Wertsch, 1991, terms the "intermental" plane between minds) that the learners could not achieve on their own. This social activity helps learners advance their own understanding on what Wertsch terms the "intramental" plane within an individual's mind. Applying the model of the ZPD to teaching can prove elusive, however. How do teachers know where students are? And what do students' contributions look like? For instance, when he is trying to help students formulate research questions, Rory says, "I need to negotiate with them without taking over. I don't want to give them the question. I want them to generate a question. But how do I help them to do that? There's no clear path." But an interactive process allowing students to be active inquirers and the teacher to be an active guide would help. Transformative communication is one such process, and it has played a key role in the success of some projects.

TABLE 10.1. Dialogue sequence for transformative communication.

1.	Students make a move in the research process with certain intentions, guided as well as limited by their current knowledge.
2.	The teacher does not expect the students' move, given a sense of their competencies, but understands how the move, if pursued, can have additional implications in the research process that the students may not have intended.
3.	The teacher reinterprets the students' move, and together students and teacher reach mutual insights about the students' research project through questions, suggestions, and/or reference to artifacts.
4.	The meaning of the original action is transformed, and learning takes place in the students' zone of proximal development, as the teacher's interpretation and reappraisal (i.e., appropriation) of the students' move is taken up by the student.

Pea contrasts his view of communication as transformative with views of communication as transmission and as ritual. Again, the view of communication as transmission tends to encourage either an active role for the teacher and a passive role for the learner, or vice versa. The view of communication as ritual tends to encourage active participation by all parties, but in activities with already shared meanings—the generativity needed for education is lacking. So Pea suggests the transformative view of communication. According to this view,

> the initiate in new ways of thinking and knowing in education and learning practices is transformed by the process of communication with the cultural messages of others, but so, too, is the other (whether teacher or peer) in what is learned about the unique voice and understanding of the initiate. Each participant potentially provides creative resources for transforming existing practice . . . (1994, p. 288)

Transformative communication is achieved through mutual "appropriation" (Newman, Griffin, & Cole, 1984; Pea, 1992) by participants in social interaction to create meanings that neither participant alone brought to the interaction. In Rory's project-based science classroom, designed to support students in carrying out their own original research, crucial episodes of transformative communication have followed the dialogue sequence shown in Table 10.1.

In the above interaction between Beth and Rory, we can see a concrete enactment of the four-stage dialogue sequence shown in Table 10.1: (1) Beth approaches Rory looking for *the answer* to a fact-based question, which she expected her "all-knowing" teacher to provide: did plesiosaurs swim by the underwater flight or rowing motion? If she could get the answer, she would include it in her report on plesiosaurs, which she may have been seeing as like research projects in other classes synthesizing established facts; (2) Rory does not know the fact Beth was looking for, nor does he even know there was a debate about plesiosaur swimming motion; but he knows that part of the game of science involves marshaling evidence to support one of several competing claims such as the ones in the books Beth had found; (3) Rory reinterprets Beth's move, saying, "I don't know. Why don't you have that be your research question?" They talk about how she and the other group members could contribute new evidence to a scientific debate rather than just report others' findings; and (4) Beth's fact question has been transformed into a research question, as evidenced in her subsequent practice.

TC as Most Helpful in Difficult Phases of Project

Rory's three key phases of projects—formulating the research question/proposal, finding the data, and using data analysis to reach an empirically supported conclusion—are candidates for transformative communication. Of these, I have identified key episodes of transformative communication at the first and third phases, which Rory has found the most difficult for students. The plesiosaur project and the UFO sightings project to be described later in this chapter provide examples of transformative communication during research question formulation. The moons and hurricanes projects provide examples of transformative communication at the data analysis phase.

TC in the Moons and Hurricanes Data Analysis

In the moons project, recall how Rory found a claim dangling at the end of Rich and Steve's conclusion unsupported by data analysis: "We have come [to] the conclusion that both Titan and Earth's moon [have] a much greater mass and density than Miranda, and that this could be why both Titan and Earth's moon have longer orbiting time periods." This was the first time the students had attempted to answer *why* the moons behaved the way they did, but the claim was not supported. In this case, Rory appropriated what the students had done—put together separate graphs of orbital period, density, and mass, and made a claim related to the same data elsewhere—and showed them how it could be transformed into graphs more conducive to checking the relationships the students mentioned. Steve and Rich had constructed a line graph of the orbital period for the three moons, a horizontal bar graph of the moons' density, and a vertical three-dimensional graph of the moons' mass. The students knew they could make graphs to represent single data variables, and after working with the data for several weeks had generated their intuitive claim about relationships between variables, but Rory helped them to see *how* they could directly check the relationships with a graph of two variables at a time, using the existing data. Rory sketched example graphs, and the students used their own versions to support claims they later made.

In the hurricanes project, recall how Rory asked Dave what patterns the hurricane paths in the data set they had constructed generally followed. Dave was able to articulate the idea that most of the hurricanes followed a C-shaped path, but did not know what to do with this idea in the data they had. By looking at the spaghetti bowl map, Rory saw that not *all* the hurricane paths were shaped that way, and suggested that Dave and TJ categorize the different shapes and code all the hurricanes to determine the percentage that fit the C shape. The boys did not take advantage of the suggestion after that discussion, and turned in their report with no numerical counts of the shapes to support their claim that "most of the recorded storms . . . made a C-like shape." So Rory suggested to them again, in his written comments, that they needed to "show/prove" the statement true, by determining what percentage of the total number fit the shape. Dave and TJ understood the suggestion the second time, and performed the coding to create a table and an associated pie chart to support their claim.

TC Provides Mutual Insights to Participants

In these interactions, Rory helps the students transform the moves they make in the research process with limited understanding into more sophisticated moves that neither he nor the students would have originally predicted, thus leading to *mutual insights*. The interactions can take place over an extended period of time, in real-time or written discussions, but the important things is that *both* teacher and student participation contributes. To borrow a phrase from Donald Schön (1982), the process of transformative communication enables both Rory and his students to "engage in a conversation with the situation which they are shaping" (p. 103), but in this case it also allows them to engage in a conversation with each other. Whereas Schön was talking about reflective practitioners of design, such as architects, working alone, the process is remarkably analogous in these social interactions between teacher and student. Architects are "likely to find new and unexpected meanings in the changes they produce [in their drawings] and to redirect their moves in response to such discoveries" (p. 103), but Rory and his students are likely to find new and unexpected meanings in the changes they produce *in one another's interpretations and the situation.* As Rory tries to tell the students, they *do* know important and useful things about their topic and data as they get further into their topic, but he often needs to help them *see* how what they know can be used to accomplish scientific inquiry. Rory and the students "come to appreciate and then to develop the implications of a whole new idea" (p. 95).

Project Activity Structure Supports TC

In these cases, the activity structure that Rory has designed for conducting projects helps him to support students through transformative communication. The activity structure sets up the students' desire to formulate a researchable question or an analysis strategy that will help them to answer their question, and Rory makes suggestions that help students see how the work they have done and the knowledge they have gained can help them get to the next stage. As Rory found in his frustrated attempts at model projects, students learn on a need-to-know basis—"they won't care [about data analysis strategies] until they have to do it." But when they do have to do it, they can more readily recognize how the strategies Rory is trying to teach them are helpful.

TC Related to Learning

Although the focus of my research is not individual learning per se, I would like to point out some evidence of how transformative communication can result in individual learning. Again, the Vygotskian notion of the ZPD suggests that the activity which Beth and Rory accomplished on the intermental or social plane could result in learning on the intramental or individual cognitive plane. Rory helped Beth see that claims about the phenomenon of plesiosaur swimming motion need not be accepted as simple "fact" or "fiction," and together they figured out strategies for independently confirming or refuting the claims by assembling independent data. In her next project, Beth chooses underground nuclear testing as her topic, and encounters claims from environmental organizations that such testing causes geologic damage. She is still working with an activity structure that supports her in important ways, such as prompting for research questions and data to address the questions. But there is one aspect of action that had been performed by Rory in the first project, in dialogue with Beth, that she performs without the benefit of social support later. After further research on underground nuclear testing, she suggests, with no prompting from Rory, that the environmental organizations are making catastrophic claims without supporting data. She has, in an important sense, learned the need for and nature of adequate evidence to support scientific claims. With this peek into the future, I conclude this interlude, and return to the action of the plesiosaur project after the formulation of the research question.

DIGGING UP PLESIOSAURS SUCCESSFULLY: DEVELOPING FLUENCY WITH A VARIETY OF TOOLS AND RESOURCES

With a strong research question grounded in what turns out to be a heated debate among paleontologists about how plesiosaurs swim, the plesiosaur project is headed in the right direction. After some more trouble finding information on the swimming motion, the group, spearheaded by Beth, finally begins having more success tracking down useful references and experts. Laura had talked for weeks about visiting the local natural history museum, but it closes too early on weekdays. One day after school Beth telephones the museum, and is told their plesiosaur expert is on sabbatical in Cairo. They refer her to another expert on the East Coast, whom Beth eventually tracks to a dig in Montana. Rory says, "This person was delighted [Beth] called, and excited to talk with her . . . She gave some references to her, in magazines like *Nature*." The paleontologist confirms the controversy surrounding their research question. The articles eventually lead to more useful references, including a book entitled *Dynamics of Dinosaurs and Other Extinct Giants* by R. McNeil Alexander (1989). Beth decides to try to contact other experts, including Alexander. She finds his university affiliation in the "About the Author" section of his book. She then searches the Web for the University of Leeds and finds Alexander's e-mail address. She writes him e-mail, and he writes from Leeds several weeks later. With the help of her father, Beth conducts a real-time chat on the Internet with the expert, who tells her she "sounds very knowledgeable." Needless to say, Beth is thrilled.

This series of events is remarkable, considering the fact that Beth told me in her first interview she was "not a computer person" and she "learned how to use the computer" for the first time in Rory's class. She found what she was able to do after a few weeks in her project particularly pleasing, since she "never was on the Internet before, *ever*." Clearly, the introductory activities in Rory's class, along with those frustrating sessions searching for plesiosaur information, paid dividends in terms of developing familiarity, as Rory had hoped. Reformers such as Resnick and Rusk (1996) have pointed out the importance of helping children develop fluency in new technological media; through her successful search efforts, Beth demonstrates fluency not only with new media, but with combinations of new and old media such as books and the telephone. Rory has said he hopes to "get students to think for themselves and give them basic instruction in how to find the answer to any question they might have sometime in the future" using the Internet. This goal has clearly been met to a significant degree with Beth, who says in her final interview, "My research for the [project] helped me in my other classes, 'cause . . . I think I really learned . . . *figuring it out*. And *thinking* and . . . not stopping your research at the library. And talking to people . . . who are experts. Who've written the books that are in the library."

Finding information on the Internet and the Web can be difficult, however, and it is worth pointing out that heuristic strategies such as Beth's location of the author in a print literature review have proven useful to Rory and his students over time. Another strategy that one of Rory's students suggested is finding promising contacts' e-mail addresses on the bottom of useful Web pages you encounter. By following such a lead, one student located a plate tectonics expert at the Ocean Research Institute in Tokyo, Japan, and corresponded with him. Rory suggests this strategy to Dave and TJ in their second project of the year, when they are searching for avalanche data; they send e-mail to addresses on ski resort Web pages, and eventually track down archived avalanche data. In addition, just knowing which universities, research centers, and museums have expertise in a given area of science can be helpful, because you can search for their Web sites and then use them as a base for beginning to browse. Beth adopts this strategy in one of her searches when she seeks out the British Museum of Paleontology's Web site, because "they're supposed to have a great plesiosaur skeleton."

Beth's episodes of search success also illustrate how Rory encourages the use of diverse resources to aid in project work and problem-solving. His principle of accomplishing the project "by whatever means necessary" frees the students to work with any resources of "distributed intelligence" (Pea, 1993b) that they can locate or create. The resources Rory encourages students to tap range from artifacts such as traditional print media, videotapes, and networked hypermedia to tools such as search engines, graphing programs, and presentation programs to people such as scientists who read Usenet news or work on projects related to students' chosen topics of study. This change in orientation from isolated cognition to using any resources that will aid thinking was begun with the open-notes exams. This is in stark contrast to science teaching environments where students must work primarily on their own, with only their teacher, their assigned textbook, and whatever lab handouts and equipment they receive as resources. As with other aspects of Rory's teaching, openness to such distributed resources, especially other people who provide valuable expertise, can be a difficult change for teachers who are used to greater control and thus a greater degree of the credit for success. Importantly, Rory's allowing students to access a wide variety of resources and people does *not* guarantee success or "delivery" of the needed support; but helping students learn how to access these resources and other sources of expertise allows a teacher like Rory who is spread thin to make a project-based class work better. Paradoxically, Rory himself has to find ways to facilitate students' learning how to use and access such external resources so that he can become less essential to their later success. But Rory's time spent early on helping Beth and her group paid off when Beth was able to take some of the lessons and accomplish impressive research digging without Rory's direct support.

THE PROMISE AND PITFALLS OF GROUP WORK

At the same time as Beth's successes in finding information, problems begin to arise in the project group. Beth has been the clear leader all along, with Laura making efforts to contribute. But Cindy frequently hangs back in class when the others go to the library searching for information. Beth and Laura decide to "make Cindy do something," specifically find data on sea turtles to compare to the plesiosaur, and write up the group's Data Analysis section. The data analysis plan that Beth and Rory work out relies on a comparison of plesiosaur fin anatomy with the similar flippers of sea turtles. Since some sea turtles use a rowing motion and some use underwater flight, determining which turtles have the most similar fin anatomy will act as evidence for which motion plesiosaurs used. Rory warns Beth and Laura against leaving it up to Cindy, but they insist.

Cindy writes up an attempt at data analysis, but it turns out to include no data on sea turtles to compare to the plesiosaur. With the complete research report looming, Beth reaches a low point and is extremely upset with Cindy. That night, though, Beth has her chat with the expert in Leeds. Reenergized, she finishes two drafts of the paper over two successive late nights. The next morning she comes in before class and announces that she had a dream in which she "was swimming with a plesiosaur [in] this really warm and peaceful blue water."

Rory asks, "And how was it swimming?"

Beth grins, saying, "It was flapping its flippers like wings!" That is, of course, how she will claim the plesiosaur swam, concurring with Alexander.

Their paper is impressive in its explication of the debate and the types of motions, but the claim about plesiosaurs swimming with underwater flight is simply a recapitulation of Alexander's line of reasoning. They have not added anything. As Rory writes in his comments, they are "just agreeing with an 'expert,' and *not* doing science." Thus, the group's preliminary grade is low. After Rory's reassurance that they have a chance to rewrite the report and improve their final grade, Beth is not worried, but Cindy nearly hyperventilates, afraid she will fail the class. Given their recent clashes, it is an interesting turnabout that Beth comforts Cindy.

Beth begins by making the minor changes needed on the paper. The next day, Cindy continues her "errant" ways, as Laura describes them. She arrives at class when first period is almost over, and misses the others at the library. Several days later, she is supposed to bring in a book with sea turtle information. She has forgotten it, but assures Beth she will have it the next day. Cindy never brings the book in, and Beth turns in the paper without the comparison, because she was "just at the end."

Rory is faced with a dilemma when he grades the paper and finds the group's grade just below a B; he feels Beth's excellent work especially warrants a better grade. He ends up slightly boosting their grade to a B on the report. As with other groups, all the group members benefit from the grade on the report, even though Beth did the majority of the work. In the group's self-evaluations, however, Beth and Laura both assess Cindy's contribution as minimal, and thus her individual grade suffers.

Research on cooperative learning and group work in other classrooms sheds some light on the problems encountered by Beth, Cindy, and Laura. Rory's strategy of rewarding the group as a whole for good work, combined with an effort to make all individuals accountable for contributions, is supported by other researchers (e.g., Cohen, 1994). Other means besides group self-evaluations have been used to try to foster individual accountability, such as individual performance on a learning assessment. This could be accomplished by asking each student in the group to extemporaneously summarize what they have learned at the end of their project, or asking each student to be prepared to give the group's oral presentation at the end and then randomly choosing one. The problem with the latter strategy is that it prevents the students from dividing up the work and making presentations in tandem with others, which is a complex and useful skill.

Elizabeth Cohen (1994) also points out that "status factors" can affect interaction and performance in small groups. Beth and Cindy's differential contributions make sense in light of the distinctions in status Cohen describes, where "low status students interact less frequently and have less influence than high status students," and status is defined as "an agreed-on rank order where it is generally felt to be better to be high than low rank" (p. 23). Cindy is a student of lower status than Beth in terms of both academic confidence and performance. The differences cause considerable problems. One means of addressing the problem of differential participation, and thus differential opportunities for learning in a group work setting, is by assigning students *roles* and tasks within the group. For example, in Complex Instruction (Cohen, 1994) and reciprocal teaching (e.g., Palincsar & Brown, 1984), students are given roles, such as "learning leader" and "learning listener," and trained in performing the tasks associated with good reading, such as summarizing the text, asking clarifying questions, and predicting what comes next. Such efforts increase low-status students' contributions and also their opportunities for learning. As a practical matter of implementation in the classroom, the problem with the role assignation strategy is that it, too, must be designed and facilitated by the teacher.

Despite the difficulties often encountered fostering group work, Rory thinks it is worthwhile. One of the reasons he was attracted to group work in the first place was that students can help one another. Research in other settings (e.g., Mehan, 1989; Roschelle, 1992) has shown that sense-making conversations among peers fosters learning, and students like TJ and Dave experience these benefits. Dave says he "really like[s] working in groups" because "a lot of times . . . you think your natural opinion is good, and then . . . you'll get another idea from someone else that's just as good . . . [plus] it's just nice to have a bunch of people in the same boat."

Even when students' skills working in a group are not as well-developed as Dave and TJ's, Rory feels some struggle to improve is warranted. When asked why, he said, "Because we live in a collaborative society . . . we all have to interact with people, and [some] people are better at it than others . . . it'd be better if everybody were better at it." Rory thinks Cindy and Beth *both* need to work on their collaborative skills, and Beth agrees. I asked her afterward what the most frustrating part of doing projects was, and unhesitatingly she said, "My group." She also said she "want[s] things done [her] way" and needs to get better at working in a group.

USING A SAMPLE WRITE-UP AS A MODEL

Beth *is* able to improve the plesiosaur research report to some degree, and she tells me that Rory's distribution of a sample research report from another project "really helped [her] see what he wanted." This was crucial, since she'd "never done a project like this." Rather than a complete report, however, the sample paper Rory distributed is just the beginning sections. Thus, Beth does not have any model for the problematic Data Analysis section. When Rory asks the students for feedback about how he can help them accomplish projects more successfully, Beth suggests it "would be a good idea to give an example paper." Rory tells her he was "worried about wasting paper, and wasn't sure people would use it." Someone like Beth clearly would, however. Beth's suggestion reminded Rory of his own master's thesis. His advisor gave him a copy of a similar thesis, and "the whole time I used it as a blueprint for what I was doing, just changing words and terms where it made sense." Beyond just giving an example, Rory considers annotating it to provide more context and make explicit the goals that are being met with the text in each section. The annotated example report is a promising addition for the future, because it would help the students use case-based reasoning (Schank, 1990) to generalize the lessons of the specific example paper to their own writing.

After the rewrite of the report is done, the group still has to prepare a presentation to the class. The strained relationship between Beth and Cindy comes to a head in a shouting match one day after Beth and Laura return from the library and again find Cindy doing nothing. Beth complains that Cindy hasn't done anything, while Cindy complains the group doesn't talk. Laura tries to moderate. They are able to divide up the work for the presentation and get through it, however.

SCIENTIFIC INTEREST AND PROFESSIONAL COLLABORATION FOR THE TEACHER

Beth told me that one of the things she really liked about Rory as a teacher was that he "got as excited as I got" about the plesiosaur project. Rory's excitement about the project is relevant in light of the fact that teaching may become routinized and teachers lose interest in the material intellectually. Sarason (1971) refers to a survey of experienced teachers in which "without exception those who have been teaching for five or more years admitted that they no longer experienced their work with the enthusiasm, excitement, sense of mission, and challenge that they once did" (p. 163). He goes on to point out that "teaching is *giving*," and "to sustain the giving at a high level requires that the teacher experience *getting*" (p. 163). One reward teachers can get is involvement in intellectually stimulating problems. To sustain teachers, Sarason calls for making schools more interesting places for *teachers* as well as for students. Rory experiences the rewards of thinking about intellectually stimulating problems in the plesiosaurs project. In fact, during the following quarter, Rory convinces another group to work more on the plesiosaur, and begins to become involved with the wider intellectual community studying this aspect of paleontology. Rory's access to e-mail, combined with working on diverse and unexpectedly interesting questions such as plesiosaur locomotion, helps overcome another common problem with schools pointed out by Sarason (and others, e.g., Schwab et al., 1992): teachers are generally isolated from interaction with other adults. Rory has an ongoing exchange with paleontologists involved in the plesiosaur debate during the third quarter.

UFO SIGHTINGS: BALANCING STUDENT
VOICE WITH TEACHER ADVICE

The table to Rory's right and the adjoining computer are where Bruce, Cheryl, and Sylvia spend most of their time. Bruce is a quiet and somewhat rumpled junior. Cheryl is an outgoing senior who is dramatic in her manner, which is not surprising, as she is involved in theater. Sylvia is a senior who is graduating early in December. Like many students over the three years Rory has been allowing students to choose their own research topics, Bruce, Cheryl, and Sylvia express an interest in UFOs and aliens. Rory had been frustrated at all of the previous efforts, because the students had been unable to design a research project on UFOs that relied on empirical data and argumentation. Despite his misgivings, he decides to let the students run with their topic, since he maintains that he cannot predict all the promising avenues students might uncover or generate.

Motivational Benefits and Pitfalls of Openness to Student Ideas

Researchers on tutoring and project-based learning have pointed out that motivational benefits can be reaped when students are given *control* over decisions about what they do—as Rory is trying to give Bruce, Cheryl, and Sylvia—and when they are given the opportunity to work on problems and projects that *interest* them (Blumenfeld et al., 1991; Lepper, Woolverton, Mumme, & Gurtner, 1993).

But, as usual, there are tradeoffs involved in the design decision to give students a high level of control over the decisions in their projects; specifically, resource management, poor choices, and misunderstandings. If Rory weren't so open to students working on different topics, it would be easier for him to manage resources. If a teacher decides that everyone is going to do a project on the same topic, students can share resources like books and Web sites and also share ideas, while the teacher can more easily develop content expertise on the topic. In addition, giving the students real choice on matters that are fundamental to their work, as Lepper et al. (1993) mention, means that they are free to make decisions the teacher does not think will be best in the long run. This happened in Barb's UFOs and aliens project, but in the case of the UFO sightings project a dubious idea results in a successful project. Finally, students who are unaccustomed to being given key choices may not realize that their teacher would actually *let* them pursue a course that might not work out well. In a close-ended curriculum or lab, it is clear beforehand what will fit the recipe, but in open-ended projects, it is impossible to tell. Thus, students may once again fail to "hear" Rory's recommendations about topics to the degree he intends. Sylvia is horrified to find later in the UFO sightings project that Rory discouraged the group from choosing the topic they did. This happens in part because the students don't really know what they are getting into at the beginning, and can't until they understand the context better.

As the mixed success of projects indicates, the problem, as Rory points out, with starting from students' interests and letting them have a voice is that it is "awful hard" in many cases "to transform something you are really interested in to something you can do" as scientific research. Involving students in decision-making, rather than telling them what to do, can be time-consuming and difficult. The pitfalls of student participation in the *whole* process of research has been recognized by a number of student–scientist collaborative efforts, but even though it is often messy from scientists' perspective to have students involved in the whole process, it is educationally significant (Pea et al., 1997). Transformative communication can prove useful in maintaining this balance between student ownership and the teacher finding ways to guide students in potentially promising directions, since *both* parties make crucial contributions. As Rory described it,

> Sometimes [students] come up with things that are really creative that I would have never thought about, which then lead me to think of other things that might be doable. And sometimes . . . they get real close to something, or have a neat idea, but it's not doable, so then, how do you turn that into something that is doable? Sometimes they do it, sometimes I can do it.

An example is provided by the way Bruce, Sylvia, and Cheryl's project moves from being a project about "whether UFOs are alien spaceships" (just as Barb's started out *and* ended up) to a project about confirming or supporting natural explanations of UFO sightings.

Transforming Background Information into a Research Question

Along with the other groups, the UFO sightings group begins the project by collecting and synthesizing background research on the topic before deciding on a specific research question. In their interim report of background research, they mention the so-called Condon report (Condon & Gillmor, 1968), the only official study of UFO sightings put out by the U.S. government. Condon and his colleagues claimed UFO sightings could be explained by meteor showers, rocket launches, and other known phenomena.

Two days after he gets the milestone background information reports from students, Rory says to me before class, "I should watch out for groups that need support instead of just waiting for it to become a problem. I think I'm trying to back off because I don't want to give them a topic and make it *my* project." Given the problematic nature of UFO projects in the past, Cheryl, Bruce, and Sylvia are obvious candidates to provide with extra support, and Rory is intrigued with the group's description of the Condon report. In his brief meeting with me before class, he discusses the fact that Condon's analysis took an empirical approach based on supportable or refutable claims about alternate explanations for UFO sightings—essentially taking a scientific approach to a problem usually approached through mere hearsay. So during class that day, Rory initiates a discussion with the UFO sightings group about potential research questions. The interaction with the UFO sightings group proves pivotal in formulating a specific research question, and is another example of transformative communication.

Shortly after completing attendance and answering some procedural questions from various students about the research proposal assignment, Rory says, "OK, you guys," to Cheryl, Bruce, and Sylvia, and sits down with them. The following interaction takes place:

Rory: OK, what do you want to do?
Bruce: We want to show UFOs are alien spaceships.
Rory: [doubtfully] Any ideas on how?
Bruce: I don't think there's any way to prove it unless they saw the alien in there and they waved at them. That's the only evidence there is.
Rory: Right. That's the problem . . . You know, Joe and I were talking about the analysis Condon did that you wrote about in your Background Information. It was interesting because Condon claimed to have explained the sightings with known phenomena. [For your project] you could verify what somebody like Condon has done. That's another thing people do in science . . .

He gives them the example of the cold fusion debate a few years ago, and then points to how this could be applied in their project:

. . . these guys said they had created cold fusion in the lab. But when other people tried it, they couldn't duplicate what they said . . . In science, once someone says they've proved something, others check it . . . The idea [here] is to verify the government's explanations. Say they said it was a meteor shower. You could look at the date, where the meteor shower was, and when and where people saw the UFO. Does it match the same spot? If the sighting was here [points one direction] and the meteor shower there [points another direction], the government's explanation could be wrong.

The students decide to run with the idea. In this example, the students originally present the Condon report as relevant to the history of the UFO debate, and thus something to be cited. Through their interaction, Rory and the students create a new meaning for the citation: the seeds of a study intended to provide independent confirmation or falsification. Thus, this sequence of interactions, starting with the submission of the report by the students and continuing with the discussion in class, can be seen as another instance of transformative communication.

I will not describe the rest of the UFO sightings project in much detail. I will note, however, that this research formulation succeeds despite the fact that the group is dysfunctional in terms of attendance. In addition, none of the group members pick up on the technology as quickly as Beth. In frustration near the end of the project when they are assembling their paper on a word processor, Cheryl comments "I think I'm gonna turn Amish—I hate computers." Instead of high-tech resources, the group almost exclusively uses local libraries. For their final paper, the group chooses four UFO sightings from the 1960s described in the Condon report, and tries to independently confirm or falsify the report's explanation. The independent confirmation is based on printed data sources found in library searches, such as NASA launch records that confirmed a scheduled reentry of satellite Agena into the Earth's atmosphere occurred at the time an airplane crew reported a UFO over Mexico, and could have been seen in that location.

REPETITION LEADS TO IMPROVEMENT

Despite Rory's best efforts to support projects through the activity structure punctuated by milestones and to guide students' work through transformative communication, some projects don't turn out well. Although I did not carry out detailed observations on the second-semester project cycles of 1995–96, the data I have suggests that the repetition of the project cycles allows some students to improve who have trouble the first time around. For example, one student in 1994–95 told me that "the second project is going better because we understand Rory's expectations better." During the same year, two students did an abysmal project on UFOs during the fall, but made significant improvements in research formulation and data analysis later when they did a project on geyser eruption patterns. Later in 1995–96, Mark, who worked on the zodiac project, and Tom and Fred, who worked on the woolly mammoth project, teamed up. The group members chose geysers as their topic and built on some of the ideas the group the previous year did not finish. Surprising both Rory and myself, "the strongest guy" in the group was Mark. He worked very consistently, and they gathered data and did an analysis of dormancy patterns in geyser basins that lay adjacent to one another. For the final project, Beth, who had such trouble finding a partner who she felt was contributing well, and had told me she would probably work alone, asked Mark to work with her since he had done such an impressive job. The two of them did a project on why Saturn has more prominent rings than the other big planets. Also later in the year, Patti, Diane, and Marie, who worked on three different projects that ran into trouble the first time around, did an interesting project about the relationship between the number of tornadoes and the number of deaths caused by tornadoes per year. Patti saw the second project as much more manageable than the first one, because they "pretty much [knew] what he expect[ed]." At the beginning of the project in the third quarter, Rory asks the students for feedback on how they think projects could be improved, and Pamela asks him to "be more specific" on what he wants. Rory tries to, but for many students, the simple repetition may help more than the *way* he explains what he wants.

IDENTIFYING AND HELPING STUDENTS WHO NEED MORE SUPPORT

Nonetheless, as it stands, some kids just don't have much chance to succeed in Rory's class. Two prime examples from this class are Cindy and Barb. Both of them could use more structure and guidance than they receive in Rory's class. In the middle of her volcanoes project, Cindy has "collected all kinds of information," but when I ask her whether she has any data or numbers of eruptions, she says "sort of . . . mostly I've got this information that I have to put together." She continues to have procrastination problems, and does not seem to understand that projects involve more than synthesizing known facts. She would rather "do labs and take notes and take tests and everything." She also feels "like this class is a waste of time . . . I feel like I don't learn anything. *I don't know how to do things this way* . . . Some people like it better [this way], but I wish it was more like a normal class" (emphasis added).

The question this begs is: what can be done to address the needs of kids like Cindy? One possible design change is to adjust the level of structure available for students on their second or third time around. This could involve offering such students project ideas, for instance from the list of promising questions Rory has been accumulating for several years. Even more support could be provided if Rory were to recommend that such students work on questions for which he knows data resources are available, as another CoVis teacher does. Such a strategy could undoubtedly introduce or exacerbate other problems in the system, such as questions of fairness given the deliberate differences in difficulty of such projects. But to the extent that this strategy could be made workable, it would provide a leg up for a student like Cindy, who is uncomfortable with new practices. When she was confronted with the computer skills exam, she had an opportunity to get more comfortable by watching others perform successfully; she had much less opportunity to become accustomed to new practices without failure in project work.

MAINTAINING THE EQUILIBRIUM BETWEEN EXTREMES

Project-based science teaching and learning involve complex role changes for teachers and students. I have described some of the complex work performed by Rory to try to maintain a balance between the extremes of highly structuring student activity and leaving it too open. Since each student and group requires a different level of structure and guidance to maintain equilibrium, the "impossible task" of teaching becomes more difficult. Moving too far in one direction or the other compromises both motivation and learning. If we imagine Rory's image of a tree swaying between these two extremes, the goal is to maintain *equilibrium*, so that the tree does not fall over and students remain challenged with maximal opportunities to learn. The cases detailed here show how it is possible to guide student work just enough to maintain that equilibrium.

Too often, the complex work teachers perform as facilitators and guides attempting to maintain this equilibrium for project-based student work is left mysterious. The dialogue sequence for transformative communication may shed both *descriptive* and *prescriptive* light on the situation. It describes important features of dialogue that have proved transformative in teaching-learning episodes, and it provides a discourse strategy which other teachers may productively use as a "cultural tool" in future episodes facilitating their students.

Several particular directions toward which teachers can steer transformative communication became apparent through the examples detailed here. In particular, teachers can steer the difficult task of research question formulation toward independent confirmation or refutation. This is a potentially important leg up for students having trouble formulating research either because their topic is difficult or because they lack confidence. To aid in this process, Rory could ask students to *look* for scientific claims during their Background Information research that they might like to question or see if they can independently support during the later phases. In addition, students could look for scientific debates like the plesiosaur locomotion controversy or the explanations of UFO sightings (and also the question of whether a new object identified in space is a black hole and the debate about whether Pluto is a "proper" planet, both of which Adam pursued). Such debates may spark student interest and sense of ownership, and demonstrate to students that science involves research and argumentation that they as thinking persons can participate in. As Beth said, the most interesting part of her project was that "it was sort of just like a mystery . . . that I had to like figure out." Obviously, latching onto scientific debates is not a foolproof recipe for success, as the dinosaur extinction and UFOs and aliens cases exemplify. Students need to find debates for which they can get and use empirical evidence, and even so, they may still encounter other pitfalls along the way. Nonetheless, the results can be unexpectedly impressive when Rory and the students are able to maintain a balance between openness and guidance.

CHAPTER 11

Designing Project-Based Learning Environments

As is only fitting, I will start this concluding chapter with a story from Rory. One day near the end of my time in his class, we were reminiscing about the territory he'd covered when he compared his experience with project-based teaching to mowing his lawn. When he first got a riding mower, he said,

> I was really nervous and a little embarrassed . . . because I'd never [mowed] before, and everybody could see me doing it, and they'd see if I did a crappy job. Then I imagined all the people in the neighborhood thinking what an idiot I was. So anyway, I got out there and just started mowing it. I sort of went around in these different patterns, and tried to figure out the best way to do it . . . I try and make it as efficient as I can. And I try to do it differently every time, because I read somewhere it's better for the grass . . . Recently, when we were going out of town, I asked one of the neighbor kids to mow the lawn. Before he would agree, he said to me, "Mr. Wagner, I can do it. But I can't do all those fancy patterns you do" . . . So . . . I was afraid they'd think I was an idiot . . . and the whole time they thought I was an expert.

Rory says, "Doing projects has been sort of like doing that for me. It's hard and risky when you first start, and you're a little embarrassed. But if you keep working on it, it gets better." This is true of any change from familiar practices, teaching or otherwise. I have conducted this study and assembled these tales in hopes of giving teachers and others interested in reform places to start.

THE CALL FOR MODELS

One reason I hope this case study can prove useful to others interested in project-oriented teaching is that some teachers have requested models. In interviews conducted as part of an evaluation of the CoVis project's expansion (Shrader & Gomez, 1997), one experienced teacher talked about the problem of implementing a project on global warming. She found it "so open-ended" that she didn't know how to get students started. As I have argued, this teacher felt that in our society, teachers have been trained to be "traditionalists," just as students have. When asked for ideas on how to help people get started with project-oriented pedagogy, she said,

> I think I needed to run through a good model . . . [to see] how teachers are directing the kids and how are they keeping them on task in the classroom . . . You have to give them some kind of direction . . . walking me through a project I think would help me. Most of us teachers, once we've done it once or twice I think from there we can pick it up.

This work is intended to provide a model to help other teachers see what a teacher *does* to support and guide project-based activity.

THE NEED TO CUSTOMIZE THESE IDEAS FOR OTHER SITUATIONS

Rory, too, believes that other teachers can implement some form of project-oriented instruction, based on particular aspects of their situation. But other teachers would do well to remember that they will have more success if they explicitly situate their designs for their classroom learning environments based on particularities of their class, teaching style, available resources, goals, and administrative situation. Thinking about what other teachers can gain by looking at what he's done, Rory suggests they think about two things: the "time dilemma"—how much can you and are you willing to devote to projects?—and "what will your administrators . . . and parents in the community *think* about doing science a different way?" To address the latter issue, Rory makes an effort to convert parents and administrators at open houses and inservices. When he shows and describes what he is doing, most parents say, "Wow, this is really cool, I wish I had done this when I was in high school, and I wish I could come back and take this class so I could do all this neat stuff." Even taking such things into account, Rory warns other teachers that there "is no guarantee that it's going to work for you." Just as there is no recipe to tell kids exactly what to do, "there's no recipe for this, either."

Rather than a step-by-step recipe for how to implement projects, I have tried to present Rory's work as a set of strategies he has implemented and used successfully in certain cases, offset by a set of constraints he has to face based on certain universals such as time and common cultural norms such as students who have been enculturated into traditional schooling. Donald Schön (1982) makes the point that *outsiders* cannot *solve* the situation in which practitioners find themselves. Instead, they can *enable* local practitioners to design their own interventions. In this case, my explication of Rory's work cannot solve other teachers' challenges in implementing project-based pedagogy, but I hope that the strategies and experiences described here can enable others to design their own local solutions.

Rory believes that many teachers potentially interested in trying these strategies will already have the most important qualities for "what it takes" to put project-based science teaching into practice in technology-rich classrooms. He refers to those qualities as "PFC," which stands for *patient, flexible,* and *creative.* To do project-based science,

> You have to be *patient* with yourself and the kids, because this takes time and is not easy. You have to be *flexible,* because things go wrong with the technology and so on . . . And you have to be *creative,* because you have to be able to come up with new ideas, and adjust to the situation, and work with what you have in interesting ways.

Since good teachers "are already patient, flexible, and creative . . . they just have to learn how to use it in a new realm, in a new way."

ADAPT AND IMPROVISE: IMPROVEMENTS
THROUGH ITERATIVE DESIGN

Throughout the years he has been practicing project-based teaching, Rory has made an effort to follow the example his grandfather and father set him as "practical tinkerers." As in the Clint Eastwood line from the movie *Heartbreak Ridge,* Rory has continually made an effort to "adapt and improvise" his guidance to better support students. He told me,

> You know, in the beginning when we started doing this, it was basically . . . just trying to get them to do work. And then . . . it was too open. And then it was giving them more structure, and then it's like,

fiddling around with it, it's fine-tuning. So it still is fine-tuning, and again, with experience, then you start recognizing the patterns like I've started to do. So that's helpful. You just get better at what you're doing all the time, I guess. You should.

In Rory's case, he at first had trouble helping kids get far at all on their projects. To solve this problem, he instituted a system of milestones to help structure students' work. Then in 1994–95 he began helping students refine research questions, by making sure they focused in on doable questions *after* learning about their chosen topic and using examples of successes students had had the previous year as models. He also made improvements in helping students *find* relevant empirical data, by learning how to use Internet resources such as Usenet news and the Web; and in helping students to understand what empirical data *is* by requiring them to turn in tables or images that show the data. And finally, in 1995–96, he made further progress in helping kids learn to perform data analysis by requiring that they turn in graphs. Throughout his efforts, Rory has tried to live by the maxim from Teddy Roosevelt, "Do the best you can, with what you have, where you are."

THE CHALLENGE: "TUTORING" MANY STUDENTS AT ONCE

Wood, Bruner, and Ross (1976; cited in Rogoff, 1990) identified six functions tutors fulfill in scaffolding a child's performance, typically in one-on-one interaction. The role that Rory plays as a project-based teacher is remarkably similar to their description of tutoring, but he is performing it for more than 20 students. Rory tries to recruit students' interest (Wood et al.'s Function 1) by allowing them to work on any topic in Earth and Space Science they choose. He has reduced the number of steps (Function 2) by putting a system of interim milestones into place, and refining the milestones when they don't function well. He maintains pursuit of the goal (Function 3) by providing coaching feedback in the form of transformative communication, which helps motivate the students by giving them a voice and helping them see how their ideas can be built upon and improved. He highlights critical features of what students produce (Function 4) through having the milestone assignments that feed into the research report, and literally marks discrepancies between the reports that students produce and more ideal science research reports in writing and in discussions. He tries to control frustration and risk (Function 5) in students' project work by giving students an opportunity to revise their work and by respecting both their complaints and suggestions about how he could better help them.

And finally, he demonstrates an idealized version of projects (Function 6) by verbally describing examples of successful project ideas and giving an example presentation to the class; he plans on providing an ideal project report for students to use in the future.

CONSTRAINTS ON PROJECT-BASED LEARNING ENVIRONMENTS

In order to better enable others to use this case study as a model for thinking about other project-based learning environments (PBLEs), I will provide an overview of Rory's design. In doing so, I will first focus on elements of Rory's environment that primarily serve as *constraints* on successful accomplishment of projects, elements that are *mixed*, and elements that tend to be *resources* that afford accomplishment of projects. As stressed in Chapter 2, however, each element can manifest itself as a constraint that *dis*ables certain functions and a resource that *en*ables other functions. The elements range from personal motivational factors to cultural beliefs to practices.

Time

The constraints continually influence activity in Rory's class, and occasionally spur crises. Time can cause problems in two ways. Some students, like the zodiac group, can become complacent because they perceive an abundance of time. They mistakenly believe in the early stages that doing a project is not much different from other reports they have done in school, and they inevitably figure out at the end of their project that they should have put in more work earlier. At that late date the time is too short to salvage much, though. Conversely, Rory's time is clearly limited, especially in terms of the number and length of interactions he can have with students during class. Thus, it's not surprising that some students like Barb, can get shortchanged when other students, like Julie and Amy, manage to command a great deal of Rory's time.

Risk and Grades

Since open-ended projects increase the ambiguity and risk of classroom practice, especially for students like Rory's who have little experience with comparable learning activities, grades become a salient concern for both the teacher and students. Students can try to reduce their risk and optimize their grades by trying to turn Rory's written and oral comments into contracts which, if fulfilled according to the letter, should guarantee a high grade. Treating Rory's feedback as such a contract, however, subverts the organic nature of research and reporting. In order to reduce student risk of failure, Rory has instituted a system of work grades, which guarantees students points for time on task and punishes them for time off task. This system inevitably causes conflicts and arguments with students that hinge on nitpicking for points; the system also exacerbates Rory's lack of time, because keeping the necessary records consumes considerable time. For these reasons, it appears that placing more value and attention on Rory's system of milestones might be preferable to focusing on work grades. Finally, the ambiguity and risk associated with learning how to do projects while being graded on them can lead students like Debbie to explode after encountering difficulties. Such explosions can result in the development of an adversarial relationship between teacher and student, and the degree of common ground necessary to accomplish guided participation is lost.

Conflicting Beliefs About Teaching and Learning

The transmission epistemology that many students espouse constrains Rory's ability to successfully institute project teaching, which is rooted in the social constructivist tradition. Seeing teaching as telling and learning as accumulation can lead students like Patti to conclude that Rory lacks the knowledge he should have—memorized facts about minor details in Earth Science—and also to devalue their own learning because they have not accumulated that same kind of facts. The practices Patti learned of figuring out ways to empirically examine questions about the phenomenon of deaths associated with tornadoes, as well as theorize about their causality, are valued more highly in the opposing epistemology. The transmission view is also associated with students not recognizing certain limits on communication involved in Rory's teaching of new practices; specifically, they do not make any distinction between Rory's *telling* them about assignments and their *understanding*, even though the interpretation of meaning by student and teacher can and frequently does widely differ. When students don't recognize the possibility of a gap between what they are told and what they understand, they are likely to accuse Rory of being unfair. In addition, students who espouse the transmission view cannot recognize or accept the need for projects to be somewhat unpredictable and improvisational, even for an accomplished teacher like Rory—he should know where every project should be going, or he is deemed lacking in expertise.

MIXED CONSTRAINTS AND RESOURCES FOR PBLEs

Some elements of Rory's design for project-based science are mixed in that they serve in some ways as resources that aid accomplishment of projects, and at the same time serve as constraints that hinder projects.

Transitional Activities

Rather than starting the year with activities wholly unfamiliar to his students, Rory starts with familiar activities, such as a lecture tour and teacher-directed assignments to introduce technology. He encourages transitional practices such as student questioning dialogues during the lecture tour. He has students conduct standard library research and *then* build off that foundation into new areas. The negative aspect of these transitional activities and the positive aspect are two sides of the same coin: their affinity to traditional modes of teaching and learning can mute or hinder Rory's attempts to move students toward new practices, but they can provide a helpful way station on the path.

Teacher's Personal Beliefs and Proclivities

Rory's personal beliefs and proclivities can also both constrain and afford opportunities for supporting student project work. His preference for a reactive stance during class makes it more likely that some students he knows need support will fall through the cracks, but it also makes him eminently receptive to students' unexpected problems and nurturing of their excitement. His openness to student feedback about how to conduct the class and support them, as well as his willingness to hear students' complaints and arguments about their projects, helps to maintain an atmosphere where students feel valued and respected; but it also creates time drains and distractions from substantive issues.

Models

Model projects have been used both successfully and unsuccessfully in their many incarnations within Rory's class. The complete model projects managed by Rory were subject to the pitfall of allowing students to disengage from critical thought, but summarized example projects do allow Rory to make the crucial decision processes of research design, data collection, and analysis explicit. These examples can help students gain a conceptual understanding of what they are trying to accomplish. In situ modeling of alternate ways of thinking about problems—genuine thinking aloud and discussion of research decision-making—is part of what Rory does in transformative communication. Finally, written models in the form of archives have helped students to generate ideas, both of the variety Rory would like to encourage—like the earthquakes project—and the sort that he would like to discourage—like the UFOs and aliens project. A partial sample of an exemplary research report helped some students like Beth as a model for their own research report writing. Annotation could help both of these kinds of written models be more useful to students.

RESOURCES FOR PBLEs

Finally, a number of elements in Rory's design for project-based science serve primarily as resources which enable students' successful accomplishment of projects.

Student Ownership and Interest

Rory's policy of giving students ownership of their projects and the final say in strategic decisions affords giving the students a real voice in the classroom and its practices and in maintaining a high level of interest and motivation in students such as the hurricanes group and the plesiosaurs group. Overall, student ownership tends to have positive results, but it does constrain Rory's ability to control action in the classroom; thus, some students—like Barb in the UFOs and aliens project—make choices against Rory's recommendation and his fears are realized. On the other hand, Rory knows there are some students who make choices against his recommendation—like the UFO sightings group—that open up unexpectedly successful avenues.

Technological Tools

Technological tools also play a generally supportive role in Rory's design. Electronic mail and Usenet enable access to experts working in various capacities in Earth Science. Some experts provide feedback and information for students, most commonly data relevant to an inquiry. Experts who agree to act as mentors can provide more in-depth and ongoing support. The World Wide Web has proven useful for data search and gathering by groups such as the hurricanes group. Computer applications such as spreadsheets enable students to do graphing as part of their analysis. Although the technologies have these many affordances, they do not necessarily reduce pressure on Rory as teacher because they engender a significant need to support and train students in their use. Thus, some of Rory's class time is taken up with procedural issues related to the technology. Although such sessions can result in valuable incidental learning, the problems and stumbling blocks with the technology can at times distract from the core mission of accomplishing science inquiry. As Rory's expertise with technology has grown, this has become less of a problem. But for teachers working at the edge of technology development, adapting to change will always remain an issue.

Activity Structure with Accompanying Artifacts

The activity structure Rory has developed and refined for projects, with a system of milestones associated with artifacts, affords students a crucial scaffold for accomplishing inquiry. The activity structure breaks down the long and complex project into subgoals, and the association of artifacts with the subgoals engenders an intermediate need to know among students about how to do such crucial issues as how to formulate a research question on UFO sightings or how to carry out an analysis of hurricane path shapes. The need to know and the need to turn something in encourages students to approach Rory with any confusions they have. The ensuing conversations afford Rory an opportunity to provide guidance that is likely to be taken seriously and appropriated. The interim artifacts that students produce serve as externalizations of students' knowledge and current thinking, which Rory can provide written feedback on. Since the activity structure is designed to correspond to portions of the science research article genre, the feedback that Rory provides on interim artifacts is not just retrospective. Unlike a set of isolated assignments, students' milestones build upon one another *and* some form of each early milestone is plugged into the final research report. Thus, students can iterate their ideas and writing in the Background Information assignment when they are preparing the Introduction of their final paper, and they can do the same for the Data Analysis milestone for their Results section.

Transformative Communication

On those occasions when students are putting their milestones together, transformative communication among Rory and the students may take place. The presence of the activity structure, as well as student ownership and interest in their projects, help engender occasions for transformative communication. In such conversations, Rory can get insights about the students' current thinking and about the possibilities for the students' projects; he can also provide students with insights about how they could expand on and use what they have begun to know in the next stages of their inquiry. These conversations with one another and the situation are a powerful way for teachers with expertise in inquiry to guide students.

TRADEOFFS OF PROJECT-BASED SCIENCE IN SCHOOLS

Some historians of education have remarked that the 20th century has seen the pendulum of reform efforts swing back and forth between traditional goals of education and progressive goals (e.g., Cuban, 1990; Ravitch, 1982). One possible explanation for these pendulum swings is that maximizing a traditional goal often severely compromises a related progressive goal, when in fact both goals are laudable. If a teaching strategy associated with progressive education has a tendency to undermine a reasonable traditional goal, it may lead to calls for "back to basics." Conversely, if a teaching strategy associated with traditional didactic instruction has a tendency to undermine reasonable progressive goals, it may lead to calls for child-centered reform.

Rory's design of a learning environment for project-based science can be seen as an attempt to find a workable equilibrium between such tradeoffs. For the design elements described above to help rather than hinder Rory's efforts, he must maintain a balance along a number of dimensions. As mentioned in Chapter 9, reaching and maintaining the equilibrium point for different students and groups can be difficult.

Familiarity versus Growth

To optimize the balance of familiarity versus growth, Rory has to find a way to "change the game" from traditional schooling and also change the rules *without* casting students adrift. Students may naturally resist such changes, because they are associated with increased risk. As a teacher changing the game, he is prepared to explain, defend, and even "sell" his reasons for the changes he would like students to make, and also to *acknowledge* students' increased risk. In addition, the changes in practices may result in students' misconstruing their teachers' intentions. Rory thus needs to be concerned with *recognizing* when students are getting off track; the milestones in the activity structure serve this purpose. In addition to the milestone artifacts, which to some degree externalize student thinking, the mere presence of looming milestones results in many students making their confusions and needs known to Rory. For the students who don't do as well at getting milestones in, perhaps Rory could more directly encourage students to make their needs known by proactively approaching the teacher for support. Finally, the changes in the game may result in students beginning to flounder. In order to help, Rory tries to connect to practices students already understand; Rory does this through transitional activities in the first quarter and at the beginning of projects, and by building later phases of projects on the foundation laid in the previous phase. To solidify student learning of research design, data search and organization, and analysis, Rory also repeats the project cycle three times during the year. Along the way, Rory also needs to support students bridging from their current knowledge and practices to new practices. Thus, Rory frequently asks students what they know or have done so far, and may build on that knowledge through transformative communication.

Structure versus Exploration

To optimize this dimension, Rory provides students with a basic framework for their activity, but the interim deliverables require students to actively think and participate in the research design and analysis decisions. As we saw in the UFOs and aliens and zodiacs projects, some students still need more structure than they are getting. I have made some suggestions on how to address the needs of students who need more structure; for instance, Rory could provide students who experience trouble the first time around more scaffolding by giving them a list of promising topics for which he has a number of well-developed ideas. For each topic, he can think ahead of time about ways to address the three key phases of projects: research question formulation, data collection, and analysis. In this way, he could provide extra scaffolding as needed while still maintaining as much challenge for the students as possible while the project develops. One key pitfall to watch out for with this strategy would be becoming too rigid in a possible path students could take, and missing opportunities for challenging them to think instead of providing them canned solutions.

Predictability of Coverage versus Student Interest/Commitment

To optimize this dimension, Rory makes recommendations and gives the students nudges, but leaves the final say resting in their hands. When the pendulum swings too far toward traditional predictability, the teacher alone has decision-making power, whereas swinging to the other extreme leaves students unguided. In episodes of transformative communication, Rory is able to establish co-ownership with the students and optimize this dimension by coaching without taking over, as we saw in the research proposal phase for the plesiosaur project and the analysis phase for the hurricanes project. Rory has become more effective at this kind of support with increasing experience in project-based teaching. His effectiveness is partly due to exposure to a range of project cases, which provides him a sense of the pitfalls and promise different paths may hold; this is one purpose for sharing Rory's experiences with others in a case study like this one.

Consistency versus Customization

Optimizing balance along this dimension is important, because greater consistency reduces the risk of failure due to falling through the cracks, but greater customization maximizes teachable moments. Rory tries to customize the amount and kind of support provided in the form of verbal and written feedback, but still guarantee a minimum level to prevent students from falling through the cracks. During class, he lets students make their needs known, and responds to those needs. Since all students are not likely to approach Rory without some prodding, it is helpful that interim milestones provide more occasions for feedback and support. Since occasions for discussion around substantive science topics appear to be so important, instituting some means of ensuring a level of minimum interaction with students—for instance, by increasing the assessment worth of milestones—could increase some students' chances for success.

Isolated Cognition versus Situated, Collaborative Cognition

Traditional schooling is associated with students being asked to think in isolation from their peers, and without the help of any tools such as calculators (Resnick, 1987), whereas progressive schooling routinely stresses peers working together with authentic tools. Rory leans more toward the progressive extreme along this dimension, by requiring students to work together, encouraging communication with people who can offer directed expertise, and encouraging students to use any and all tools at their disposal. When students work in groups, however, problems can develop like the one we saw with Cindy and Beth: the more confident and able student learned more and the less confident and able student fell further behind. Rory tries to help students manage troubles with work division that can feed into problems such as the plesiosaur group's, and also makes the students to some degree individually accountable; but more concerted measures would undoubtedly make a difference. The problem with instituting such measures is balancing them with all the other kinds of support and guidance Rory is trying out.

Interrelations in the Tradeoff Space

Finally, there are important interrelations between the dimensions described above. For instance, when more student interest and commitment are fostered, students are more likely to initiate interactions at the most teachable moments. The students in the plesiosaurs project shared their enthusiasm for the dinosaur with Rory from the beginning, resulting in discussions with guidance from Rory, and also gained vital practice with search tools they used themselves later. As the project continued, Beth's growing commitment and interest in plesiosaurs made her eager to share triumphs and difficulties with her teacher. Also, Rory's design of an activity structure that requires a high degree of exploration and thought within it increases the likelihood that students will seek him out for needed guidance at teachable moments. For students who are slower starters, maintaining sufficient levels of consistency helps maintain their commitment.

CONTINUED CHANGE AS INEVITABLE AND REVITALIZING

Even with all the effort and refinement Rory has put into his project-based teaching, he has still not been able to make everything work to his satisfaction. In an e-mail message he once said to me, "You know what, I'm starting to become convinced that the [reworking] is an endless process. Seemed a little depressing at first, but on the other hand it's not all that surprising considering the kids are always changing." And since teaching is an "impossible profession" (Cohen, 1988b, p. 55) it can never be done perfectly.

Over the years, continually recognizing needs for improvement can become frustrating and tiring for educators. But in some ways the educators who believe they have reached a stable solution may be the ones who are worse off, because they are fooling themselves. As Zilversmit (1993) said, "Essential for the health of education is the *process* of change. Questioning accepted ways is essential to the health of change [and] schools . . . therefore, the reiterated demands for change are not signs of failure; they are part of a process that is essential to keeping education vital" (p. 182). Zilversmit goes on to point out that change can be *revitalizing*. It has certainly provided a great deal of excitement and interest for Rory in his teaching, along with the frustration of difficulties.

RESOURCES FOR GUIDING EXPEDITIONS INTO SCIENCE

I return now to our metaphor of expeditions in the mountains from Chapter 2. I would like to stress some of the lessons for teachers and others interested in supporting learning environments for expeditions, like Rory's and his students', into the world of science.

For teachers, making the expeditions more successful involves *creating, fostering, and recognizing footholds for transformative communication*. Some of the footholds can be built into the activity structure with milestones beforehand. Once students step into these footholds and take some steps, more footholds may become available. In assignments students turn in and comments students make during class, more crevices that can be used as footholds may become apparent, as long as the teacher recognizes them as something that can be transformed into a productive move in scientific inquiry. This is knowledge-intensive and thought-intensive work for teachers. It may involve making mundane connections between experiences in one volcano project and another volcano project, but it may also benefit from creative and surprising connections, such as Rory's idea of making a grid and performing counts to analyze hurricane paths, based on his own experience of performing mineral content analysis. At the very least, it involves rumination on students' projects outside of class, such as Rory did in the UFO sightings project; or poring over students' cryptic writing, as Rory did with the moons project.

For teachers and others interested in designing and creating supportive resources for learning environments, making science expeditions more successful involves organizing and if necessary creating *elements of the landscape* that can be pointed out. Like the feldspar on Rory's original expedition years ago, materials that can be pointed out, and perhaps picked up, can be helpful to supporting projects. Such "distributed intelligence" in the environment can allow the teacher to offload some of the supporting. In this way, items such as a set of Time-Life books Rory thought he would never have use for have become a resource for students beginning their background research on their topics. Additionally, collections of data resources such as the hurricane Web site Dave and TJ used and a book of volcano eruption data Rory has acquired serve as valuable sources of empirical data. There are many opportunities for creating and finding useful and usable collections of data resources to support project-based science teaching and learning. Especially useful are materials that relate to topics that especially appeal to students. In this Earth Science class, popular topics often involve disaster and destruction (e.g., lightning, hurricanes, and earthquakes), aliens or space exploration, and the environment (e.g., global warming, water quality, and energy). As more resources about these topics become available, kids can seize them and build off their interests. In addition, the work of students from year to year can become a growing activity base (similar to a knowledge base) for future projects, in that they both supply ideas *and* potentially supply data collections that can be reanalyzed and refuted or refined, or combined with other data collections for completely new inquiries.

THE PROMISE OF EXPEDITIONS INTO SCIENCE

To the degree that Rory and the students are able to maintain the delicate balance of motivation and support, students can be inspired in unexpected ways, just as they were on his summer trip to the Rockies. Beth and Cheryl, who worked on the plesiosaur and UFO sightings projects, respectively, provide two examples of such unexpected inspiration. Neither Beth nor Cheryl considered themselves "science" people coming into Rory's class. Beth started the class saying, "I like science . . . but I'm not good at it." Cheryl signed up for Earth Science because it looked like the easiest science credit available to her.

Through their participation in Rory's class, however, their perspectives have changed. Through her work on the UFO sightings project, Cheryl says she "learned the way scientists speak—I'd never really written a scientific paper before." She also learned that science is "not like math where there's one answer . . . I used to think [science] was 'this is how this is' and 'this is how this is.'" Although math educators would surely be displeased with her opinion of their subject, Cheryl's perspective on science as inquiry rather than memorization is heartening.

Through her work on the plesiosaurs project and afterward, Beth becomes interested in and capable of engaging in scientific debates such as the geologic implications of underwater nuclear testing; she also becomes virtually obsessed with a reptile she had never heard of before she arrived in class. She gets excited to find the image of a plesiosaur image on a juice box one day, and tells me, "I have all this plesiosaur paraphernalia. I'm gonna order . . . a skeleton of a plesiosaur." She says, "I grew academically" and "figured out that I could really . . . learn things with my mind." Along with McNeil Alexander, she says, "I would say that I'm one of the leading experts on the plesiosaur . . . Like how many people in this world know about the plesiosaur?" This young woman has clearly come a long way from thinking she is "not good at science," even though her beliefs may be a bit grandiose. In her expeditions into science, she will surely find that unseen peaks become visible around the next bend in the trail. But the view is glorious from her current vantage point. And that can't hurt as Rory guides her on new expeditions into science.

And as the year goes on, Rory will continue to explore the paths students' projects can take in their ascents to such heights. And like the trusty Sherpa guide he tries to be for his students, he will return to the foothills at the beginning of each new year, and invite more students on new adventures to the peaks.

Methodological Biography: Walking Around in Other People's Shoes

I will always remember a comment I heard Tracy Kidder make at a talk (1995). Kidder was asked by an audience member what difference he thought his presence made researching books like *Among Schoolchildren* (1989). The audience member wondered whether and how the situation changed when the author wasn't there. Seeming exasperated by a question he probably hears often, Kidder replied, "I don't know what happened when I wasn't there! I wasn't *there* when I wasn't there!" The lesson I took from his comment is: Don't try to get rid of yourself; admit your presence and try to make good use of it.

A question that qualitative researchers are commonly asked is, "How do you plan to manage the *problem* of subjectivity?" This question implies that objectivity is ideal and subjectivity represents only negative bias. I disagree with the idea that subjectivity should be minimized, and instead agree with those researchers who believe that subjectivity should be taken advantage of because of the interpersonal richness and entry into meaning it offers (Ayers, 1989; Lightfoot, 1983). Bill Ayers put it eloquently: "Subjectivity is not a dirty word when *subjects* are the objects of study" (1989, p. 16, emphasis added). Since I admit that my personal perspective has played an important role in the conduct of this research, it is only fitting to describe that perspective to readers. I have modeled my effort after Bill Ayers's (1989) and Pierre Bourdieu's (1990). As they did, I will try to reveal dispositions that my background and experiences have helped foster.

BORN A MEDIATOR

I was born in South Bend, Indiana, in 1965 and spent what I have often considered a sheltered childhood there. I was the third of five children, all of whom my parents had after getting married in their thirties. Our family was close and lived a relatively self-contained life—having waited so long, my parents told me, they were content to focus on raising their children, and we kids were often content to play with our brothers and sisters. From an early age, I took on the role of mediator. Fights took place between almost every pair of siblings, except no one fought with me. I often joke that I was born a pacifist—I just refused to fight, so no one was interested in fighting with me. When someone got in trouble or angry, I invariably tried to find common ground or appeasement. From my current vantage point, I see the mediation skills I developed as quite useful, but know that I at times feared justifiable anger.

DEVELOPING A SENSE OF SECURITY AND CONFIDENCE

I recall my childhood as a time of warmth and security, highlighted by holiday celebrations with my immediate family and grandmother. Along with many others in our community in the shadow of the University of Notre Dame, we were Roman Catholic. The community was conservative on the whole and not very culturally or racially diverse. The comfort and security of this background may have increased my self-confidence at the same time that it fostered my curiosity about people and experiences different from my own.

My mom and dad were an interesting pair—she a registered nurse with a master's degree and he a plumber and pipe-fitter with postsecondary apprentice's training. He dropped out of college after his football career was ended by a knee injury. I knew that we were not well off financially, and that Dad had to work a great deal of overtime to help make ends meet. Nonetheless, he would come home from work in his stained blue shirt and play and laugh with us. Mom took several years off work to stay at home raising us, and became active in school and later church activities. Both of my parents always seemed to have complete confidence in me. In my mind, the greatest gift they gave me was the belief that I could accomplish just about anything if I put my mind to it and worked at it. Luckily, my experiences in school and sports seemed to back up their confidence in me.

SCHOOLING SUCCESS

I was lucky enough to have a disposition well suited to traditional, highly structured teaching. Much like Cindy, described in this study, I would not necessarily have been comfortable with open-ended projects in those days. I remember an independent project I had to do in physics class my senior

year in high school—we had weeks to do it (along with our more traditional labs and tests), but I put it off until two days before it was due and
had a difficult time finishing. Unlike Cindy, though, I managed to pull it
off, as I did most of my schoolwork. I have always found it ironic that
many of us who talk about changing traditional schooling so much were
successful in that same system. But in my case I feel that more challenges
to think for myself and participate in the framing of problems would have
benefited me at an earlier age. I had to learn these things eventually—as an
undergraduate to some degree, but even more so at work and graduate
school. I have found that the adult work world (or at least the kind of
professional work I have been involved with) rarely provides answers to
the request, "Just tell me what I should do." Like Rory's students, I have
had to build those answers for myself, albeit with the support and guidance
of others.

OPENING NEW WORLDS THROUGH SCHOOL EXPERIENCES

The teachers I remember most vividly were the ones who challenged me or
opened my mind to new worlds. My 7th grade history teacher started a
reading club and helped me see the tension of the Cuban missile crisis by
reading and discussing Kennedy's *Thirteen Days*. My high school German
teacher opened up a whole new culture for me. Most of all, though, I recall
my high school English teachers, who introduced me to books that began
to expand my world.

In 9th grade, we read *To Kill a Mockingbird* (Lee, 1960), and it had a
profound effect on me. At the end of the book, Scout stood on Boo Radley's porch and imagined what the events of the summer recounted in the
book must have looked like from his perspective. She said, "Atticus was
right. One time he said you never really know a man until you stand in his
shoes and walk around in them. Just standing on the Radley porch was
enough" (pp. 278–279). The sentiment of standing in someone else's shoes
has been expressed by many, but *that novel* made it *real* to me. The novel
took me to that place, and showed me in some small way what it must
have been like to walk around in some other people's shoes. Given my
already mentioned propensity for being a mediator, I began to see how
many conflicts and misunderstandings are caused by people being unable
or unwilling to see another's perspective, and tried to figure out what might
explain their actions, no matter how odd they seemed to me at first.

At the end of high school, I decided to attend Brown University on the
East Coast even though I had never left the Midwest, let alone visited the
school. In part I wanted to see a wider world and other perspectives first-

hand. College did indeed open up new perspectives for me, and I ultimately dropped the idea of completing premedical requirements and instead focused on my stronger interest in language and literature. In regard to science education reforms, I would note that although I always had an interest in biological and physical sciences, one reason I decided against a career in them was that I never became as engaged in them as students like Cheryl and Beth did in Rory's class; literature and culture were what came to life for me. I completed a concentration in Comparative Literature, with a focus on 20th-century novels from the U.S. and East Germany.

MEETING CULTURAL COMPLEXITY IN STUDY ABROAD

Brown had an exchange program with a university in the German Democratic Republic, a nation known only as "East Germany" to most people in this country. I remember in high school German class constantly confusing the *Deutsche Demokratische Republik* and the *Bundesrepublik Deutschland*. The "Democratic Republic" was the name of the East German state, while the *Bundesrepublik* or "Federal Republic" was the name of the West German state. We used to ask: How could East Germany call itself democratic when they were *really* communist?

In the spring of 1987 I found myself flying across the Atlantic toward this same distant land, however, and taking a train to Berlin, across the border at Friedrichstrasse, and north to Rostock on the Baltic coast. Studying abroad in the GDR was undoubtedly the most profound learning experience in my life. Part of the learning was about the language, through participation in the daily life of a city where speaking English was not enough; when I went to grocers, restaurants, train stations, and many other places, I had to figure out how to get my point across in German. Most times there was simply no other choice, and besides, I *wanted* to learn it so I could follow everything and participate more fully in whatever was going on around me. When I first arrived, more than five years of German classes did not help much.

I remember the first day, arriving at the student dorm, and talking with my German roommate and some of his friends as we looked down at the city of Rostock. They kept saying this phrase, "*Guck mal*," which sounds like "kook moll," as they talked about their city and pointed out things in the distance. They said, "*Guck mal*, there's the train station," and "*Guck mal*, the Russian military base is over there" and "*Guck mal*, we'll be going to classes over there in the pedestrian mall." I had never heard the phrase, presumably because it was a colloquialism irrelevant to formal classes. When I got upstairs to my room, I pulled out my big dictionary and couldn't find the word because I didn't know how to spell it. Finally, I had to ask someone, and they told me it meant to "look" or "see." As in English, the phrase could either mean to literally cast your eye in a direction, or to consider what someone is saying. I had a great deal to learn about how to "see" life in the GDR as my new friends were asking me to consider it. It did not take long to figure out that the simple view of a people oppressed by an evil state did not begin to capture the complexity of the culture I was walking around in.

It did, however, take me a while to figure out how to accept or get my mind around all that complexity; so much so that the four-month trip in my junior year was not enough. I returned for a year to the GDR to teach English and study the educational system after I graduated from Brown. Eventually, I had to admit there were innumerable contradictions about the place and the people. I found that this nation, reviled where I grew up, did a much better job recycling than communities back home, although they allowed dangerous levels of industrial pollution. I found that GDR citizens had universal child care, where no such thing was available in the U.S., but that many citizens had to at least feign loyalty to socialism and the Party to get a promotion. I found that people in the GDR had time to spend with each other and they used it to truly talk with one another, perhaps more so than many in the U.S. trying to get ahead or even just get by. I felt that I began to *understand* some of my friends in addition to growing fond of them.

Nonetheless, I was still walking around in a Westerner's shoes, both literally and figuratively. In fact, some of my friends in the GDR told me that I could pass for a German from a distant region—thank God I eventually shed the notorious American accent—*except for my shoes*. You see, shoes made in the West just looked different from shoes made in the East. Similarly, I knew that my experience, no matter how empathetic, did not allow me to fully see the world as GDR citizens did. For one thing, I had special privileges, like being able to buy Yoplait yogurt in the Western store with U.S. dollars, even though I refused to (that wasn't hard, since the local dairy products available at the grocer were much better anyway!). Far more importantly, I could always cross the border to West Berlin, Lübeck, or Denmark with my U.S. passport. The soldiers with automatic rifles and large dogs might look menacing to me, but they would not jail me as they did my friend Ingmar when he tried to cross.

EMBRACING COMPLEXITY

Experiences such as study abroad, as well as the loss of both my parents to cancer, have led me to conclude that embracing complexity is necessary in life. This is related to my reluctance to rely on statistical research techniques alone to examine classrooms, which I felt would oversimplify the social world of the class more than qualitative methods. One danger in my belief system is that I might be *reluctant* to reach conclusions even if they are valid or useful, for fear of oversimplifying.

But my experiences have also helped me to see *how* to reach more complicated conclusions. Seeing life in the GDR obviously contributed to my belief that social life is inherently complex, for instance, but I began to develop ideas about how people's actions can relate to multiple levels of meaning and culture. Looking at different levels of meaning and intersecting cultures and subcultures can often help to explain seeming contradictions between actions or events on personal and societal levels. For instance, people act in some ways to fulfill roles assigned to them by the wider society, but find their own means of expressing personal and interpersonal idiosyncrasy within those bounds. Some of my friends in the GDR were publicly allegiant to the socialist party but privately critical of its actions, and also privately expressed a great deal of "illicit"—from their party's perspective—interest in Western culture and society.

BECOMING A RESEARCHER

After returning from the GDR, I eventually began working for a software development firm. I learned a great deal about software, business, and leadership, but was ultimately dissatisfied with the bottom line being quarterly profits. In college my interest in computing had grown out of an educational project with a German professor, and I decided to go back to graduate school in education so I could work on finding ways for using computing well in education. My search brought me to Northwestern in fall 1992 and within a semester to the just-beginning CoVis project.

As mentioned in Chapter 1, I became a research assistant in January 1993 and worked on the project while taking classes. My role on the project varied. I helped to develop some software for aiding scientific visualization of climate and weather; helped plan and staff workshops about technology and pedagogy for teachers, including Rory Wagner; was a technical aide and observer in the classroom of Rory and two other teachers; and helped plan, carry out, and analyze surveys of CoVis students.

In June 1994, I passed my qualifying exam. A few days later I married Katie Plax and my work as a research assistant necessarily shifted. Since Katie was in medical school at the University of Rochester, I moved quite a distance from Northwestern. I also began developing the ideas for the study described here. I became increasingly interested in a classroom observational study despite the need to travel from my new home in order to observe CoVis classes. It would have been easier to do survey research, but it would not have provided as many answers to the complex questions that most interested me. I cannot thank Roy Pea enough for encouraging me along this path, and referring me to Bill Ayers for direction on making it work.

I had always admired Rory Wagner's courage and work in the classroom, and had spent some time in his class along with a few other teachers in my first two years. That fall, from our attic in Rochester, I began to correspond by e-mail with Rory about his project-based science teaching. Eventually I proposed this study to him on a visit to his class later that fall, and we were on our way.

In the course of my graduate studies, I learned a great deal about educational theory, history, and practices, and of course about research methods. One of my discoveries was that formal research methods had been developed for "walking around in other people's shoes" that I could adapt for my own.

METHODS FOR CARRYING OUT THE STUDY

Numerous methods have been developed over the years to ensure the rigorous conduct of interpretive research, and I have appropriated many of these for the study. According to Geertz (e.g., 1973, 1988), the primary means of achieving and demonstrating rigor in social and cultural research is by "being there" in the research setting for extended periods. Time in the setting is the best antidote to addressing the problem of *bounded rationality* (Simon, 1957)—the limits of human information-processing capability. For this reason, I have conducted this research in the tradition of deliberative inquiry described by Erickson (1986). In the deliberative inquiry approach, the researcher admits to questions coming into the field, and conceptualizations that shape his or her understandings. Fieldwork is viewed as progressive problem-solving, where assertions and characterizations of patterns are repeatedly checked against ongoing observation of the setting and probing of informants, and refined based on further findings.

Prior to the conception of this study, I was present in Rory Wagner's classroom as a technical aide for one period every day during 1993–94. My relationship with Rory was solidified at that time, and maintained at CoVis meetings throughout that year. I created an initial formulation of research questions and methods for this study in the summer of 1994. After Rory Wagner agreed to participate, I began participant observation in one of his classes to refine the focus of the study and begin the process of progressive problem-solving. The main questions I zeroed in on are:

- What is the teacher trying to teach through his course, and how do students understand his intentions?
- How does the teacher structure project activity for students, and how do students interpret and use that structure?
- How do the teacher and students interactively accomplish projects?

My fieldwork primarily took the form of participant observation in one of Rory Wagner's three Earth Science classes during 1994–95 and 1995–96. Along the participant–observation continuum discussed by Glesne and Peshkin (1992), my role can be characterized as "observer as participant." Thus, I acted "primarily as an observer but [had] some interaction with study participants" (p. 40). In 1994–95, I was present on average one to two days per week from October through May in a Period 7/8 class. The most complete and intensive work, which makes up Section II of the book, was from the first half of the 1995–96 school year. During that year, I was present for approximately half of the meetings of Rory's Period 1/2 class from the beginning of school through the end of the first round of student presentations (52 of 95 classes). In addition, I conducted debriefing interviews by phone with Rory after class about the day's events on as many of the days when I could not attend as possible (another 20 of the 95 classes). This leaves 23 days where I did not gather field notes. Following this period, I made spot checks that allowed me to gain a sense of development throughout the rest of the year and the students' remaining two projects—a total of 10 days' classroom observation and 6 phone interviews with Rory.

This extended time in the research setting allowed me as a participant-observer to apprehend more and more of the complex structure of events. By being there and developing rapport through personal interaction with participants in the setting, I have attempted to reach ever-closer approximations of understanding Rory's and his students' perspectives. One example of this progression can be seen in the difference between the primary questions as laid out in early conceptions and those laid out above. Early on, I had a strong focus on the use of technological tools, but through interaction with Rory came to understand that *his* focus was on the accomplishment of science projects—technological tools were primarily interesting to him insofar as they helped accomplish projects. Thus, he appropriated those technological tools he thought could provide significant gains in accomplishing projects, and rejected those he thought provided little gain relative to their costs.

Like Lightfoot (1983), I believe the development of rapport through personal interactions allowed my subjective personality to be used as a tool to better the research, rather than something to be avoided. Interpretive researchers also attempt to critically assess throughout the research process how their own subjectivity may bias the work, and reveal that subjectivity to the reader (Ayers, 1989; Glesne & Peshkin, 1992). For this reason, and following Bill Ayers's (1989) example, I have included earlier in this section a brief autobiography focusing on issues related to the conduct of this research.

I have used a number of mindful means to assess the adequacy of specific assertions or hypotheses in the course of fieldwork and analysis. Deliberate sampling for a variety of evidence types can increase the discipline of inquiry (Patton, 1990). The sources of data I have used to develop an understanding of the meaning perspectives of the various participants, and to triangulate the testing of assertions, are written field notes of classroom observations and "debriefing" discussions with Rory directly after that class; videotapes of selected classes during each major stage of the activity cycles in the class (the introductory phase described in Chapter 6 and all phases of projects described in Chapter 7); four formal audiotaped interviews with Rory Wagner on his history of project work, running a project-based classroom, and supporting specific projects; interviews with four individual students and one pair of students during and after their first projects in 1995–96; handouts passed out by the teacher and project assignments turned in by students during the period studied; and e-mail discussions between myself and Rory Wagner about projects and his class.

I have checked the adequacy of my interpretations with informants, to see whether the interpretations ring true to lived experience (e.g., Ayers, 1989; Brickhouse & Bodner, 1992) and thus that my perspective as a researcher and that of participants was converging (Mehan, 1978). At various stages in the development of this work, I asked for Rory Wagner's reactions and feedback, and incorporated them.

Like most interpretive research, mine has involved a process of "coding"—typifying or categorizing data and events—to aid the formulation and testing of assertions about what is going on. I transcribed all interviews with Rory and his students and classroom observation (from handwritten field notes and videotapes for the days available) from the 1995–96 school year, and coded them in a software package. The process of typification produces important threats to the validity of research findings (Phillips, 1990)—undue influence by early experiences in the setting and by positive instances (i.e., ones that confirm researchers' assertions) over negative instances. I have followed Erickson's (1986) two recommendations for addressing these threats to validity—machine recording and forming tentative assertions while still conducting fieldwork. Since I had used machine-recording techniques and transcribed verbatim, I was able to return to the different observation periods for further analysis with an eye to questions unformulated at the time. By forming assertions while still conducting field-work, I was able to deliberately search for negative instances or disconfirming evidence in the research setting, and use that evidence to refine my assertions.

ETHICAL PRINCIPLES GUIDING THIS WORK

In my time with Rory and his classes, I tried to maintain several principles, including *reciprocity, respect,* and *privacy.*

Rory and I received different rewards from my work and presence in his classroom, but I hope some degree of reciprocity was retained. Clearly, he does not share in some rewards, such as my Ph.D. Rory and I shared two important goals, however: improving project-based teaching and learning in classrooms. One way I try to contribute to these goals is through the research that I produce, which I share with him and others. But that was not the only way. I also became a resource for supporting him and his students more directly. Thus, my role in the school was not strictly limited to observation. During class, I helped the students with technology and project-related problems, but Rory and I both recognized I had additional responsibilities such as note-taking that I could not neglect. I sometimes had to remind the students that I needed to do other work even if their technical problems were not solved. When substantive issues about projects arose, I often repeated that I had no authority on procedures or grades, and my knowledge of Earth Science was abysmal compared to Rory's. After class, I provided a sounding board for Rory to reflect and share ideas with. I did not just absorb such comments, but at times also shared a different perspective or just the fruits of an extra set of eyes on classroom activities. Over time, Rory began to combine *his* primary work of teaching and planning the class with *my* primary work of research more and more. For example, he updated his own work grade sheet while updating me on groups' activities over the phone, and also planned future activities and made notes for himself on new ideas that grew out of our conversations.

Regarding respect, I viewed my primary job as *understanding* what Rory and his students were doing in relation to projects, *why* they were doing so, and what *consequences* their actions had. I admitted to having opinions about classroom activity, but did not presume to have all the answers. Therefore, when something "negative" or problematic occurred, I tried to figure out *why* it happened before judging the incident negatively. This usually led to uncovering either (1) some constraints or tradeoffs I had not recognized, (2) alternative motivations and goals for the actions, or (3) previous events that informed the actions of which I was unaware.

This often led me to change an initial opinion about what appeared at first to be a mistake, although alternative choices sometimes still appeared attractive. This is similar to the idea Schön (1982) relates about teachers "giving students reason" rather than assuming they simply make uninformed mistakes. When you walk in someone else's shoes, you can usually find a reasonable reason from their perspective. Considering alternative choices and their implications was part of what Rory and I were both trying to do, to inform practice and research. So this kind of discussion also served to uncover and flesh out strategies to take that one or both of us had not previously considered.

Since Rory was not accountable to me and I felt the strategy usually fruitless, I did not generally tell Rory what I thought he should do. This relates to a vivid memory I have of my dad talking about the "educated" engineers coming in to the Bendix plant, where he worked as a pipe-fitter, and making pronouncements about the way things should be done. Dad talked about how they knew nothing about the way things *really* worked, yet they came in and thought they could tell everybody how they could fix things and make them better. Inevitably, the educated engineers' suggestions caused all kinds of other problems that the people there every day could have told them about, if only they had listened. Now I was in the position of possibly becoming the know-it-all with all the formal training and no respect for the people *really* doing the hard work. I didn't want to make the mistake those engineers did—I wanted to listen and try to make sense of the way things worked in this setting.

So instead of giving pat solutions that probably wouldn't work, I tried to ask probing questions about why Rory did what he did. Sometimes I reminded Rory of an alternative that *he* had mentioned to me before, and asked whether he thought about doing that in another situation. I also mentioned some ideas I knew other teachers had tried or researchers had suggested, but I tried hard to present these as possible alternatives, not the *only* alternatives. I also reminded Rory frequently that I think project-based science teaching in a classroom is both complex and difficult.

One value behind this kind of attitude was simply respect for Rory's professional work and choices. This attitude was concordant with my belief that there is not any one fully specifiable way to do projects well. In other words, I don't believe there is such a thing as *the* ideal realization of project teaching, but rather many possible valuable realizations that are different in many ways. This has to do with teachers working in many different contexts, but also with the reality that each teacher (such as Rory) and class of students can *take* actions to *change* the context in which they are working, and thus change what future courses of action might work.

Of course, there were logical limits to my not expressing outright disapproval. If Rory had acted abusive toward students, I would have been forced to confront him, but he of course did not do so. On those occasions when Rory left the classroom and I was the only remaining adult, I did not pretend I would let the students do whatever they would like, and I never had any problems.

Regarding privacy, students' real names were never used in materials read by outsiders. Rory was given the option of being anonymous in written work, but chose not to take it. I have tried to keep the high school anonymous. Rory and his students could request that any comment or action be off the record and not reported in the research. I assumed that any negative comments students made about Rory were not intended for his ears; if such comments led me to discuss an issue with Rory outside class, I did not identify the student to Rory until after the end of the school year (I took this step because Rory was in a position of authority over the students, and his grades could be subjectively affected). All conversations between myself and Rory contributed to my understanding of what he was doing, and thus became potential research data even when our meetings were mostly social. This fact eventually became a burden I was able to shake after realizing I needed no more data.

Recently, the courage that it took for Rory to open up his classroom and his work was literally brought home to me. Katie had had a session where she was videotaped doing a history with a pediatric patient's mother, for teaching purposes. I was reminded of how nerve-wracking it is to be videotaped with the knowledge that no matter how laudable the intentions of the taping, it can and will be used in some sense to judge what you've done professionally. Like her, Rory put a great deal of effort and time into his professional identity, and it is admirable that he was willing to repeatedly endure that kind of scrutiny. I only hope I retain reason to have gained that trust.

Class Handouts

Rory Wagner distributed these handouts to students during the projects described in Part II. These are "living documents," so they have undoubtedly been revised since.

HOW TO DO AN EARTH SCIENCE PROJECT

Scientists try to understand the world around them. They do this by trying to figure out "how things work." To do this they usually have to make measurements and observations. The more careful they are, the better their "data" is. Then they try to figure out what the measurements and observations mean, keeping in mind the "laws of nature" that control everything around us.

You are going to act as scientists, and "explore" the workings of Earth Science "phenomena." You are not being asked to solve all the world's problems, or unravel the Ultimate Mysteries of the Universe. But your research will be "original" to some extent, because if somebody already knows the answer to your "question," you don't really have a question. Basically, you're going to be looking at how do things work? What proof (data) can you find? Can you "convince" your classmates that you have really "figured it out?"

How do we go about this process? Scientists start in many different ways. Some of them have questions that "pop up in their heads" so to speak. Things they have "always" seemed to want to know about. They want to know "why" things happen. Sometimes, however, the opposite happens. Some scientists see what is "usually" happening, and notice that it doesn't "always" happen. They try to figure out "why doesn't it always happen?" Sometimes scientists stumble upon new things while looking for something entirely different. Or, they might be given an area of research by their "boss," to see what they can find out. All of these are ways to do science.

The important parts of doing a project are:

- *The Question*, which is what you are trying to find out about some phenomena;
- *The Method*, which is what you actually do; this could be an experiment, or it could just be a description of how you collected and analyzed your data to answer your question;
- *The Data*, which is the information you collect, usually information in numerical or visual form, from which a conclusion can be drawn. This can either be data which you would collect by observation or experimentation, or by collecting and using someone else's data;
- *The Conclusion* you come to, based on the data you collect.

Here are the steps we will use to do our projects, with time "guidelines" for each step of the process. These time guidelines are not entirely "set in stone."

1. Find a *broad topic* in Earth Science that you are interested in. (1–2 days)
   a. Is there an Earth Science topic that interests you? (Volcanoes? Floods?)
   b. Can you use any available information sources to discover "anomalies?"—things that are different from the usual.
   c. What are your own interests in life? (sports, photography, music?)
      - can you find a way to combine your interests with Earth Science?
2. Find a research partner or partners. *Group Maximum Size = 3* (1–2 days)
   a. It could be someone in your class, any of the other Earth Science classes here at [Lakeside], or any of the CoVis classes at schools across the U.S.
   b. Your partner(s) should really want to explore the same topic that you do.
      - remember, you don't need an "anchor" you need a "partner."
      - use e-mail, personal conversations, CoVis newsgroups to find them.
3. Do background material research. (2 weeks)
   a. You need to find out the way things work. For example, if you were interested in "caves," you need to find out how they are formed, where they form, what rocks do they form in, how long does it take for them to form?
   b. You need to know enough about the topic to be able to explain it to someone else, so that they understand the basics too.
   c. You have to do some reading in Earth Science or other specialized

science books, encyclopedias, etc., to get this background information. Some may be available on the Internet.

4. Narrow your broad topic into a research proposal. (1 week)
   a. You don't have to actually find data in this part, just come up with
      an idea for something to explore.
   b. What is it about your broad topic that is most interesting to you?
      Maybe you're fascinated by the fact that caves only form in certain
      states, or maybe there is one near your vacation home in Wisconsin.
   c. Be sure that your research idea is "do-able." No trips to the end of
      the galaxy to collect data!
   d. You need to find an idea that you can "test," "measure," "experi-
      ment on" (this is called "collecting data"), or be able to find existing
      data to "support" or "prove" your research idea. It basically has to
      be *small enough to do.* Finding the "cure for acid rain" or "how to
      stop planetary greenhouse warming" might be topics that are a little
      too large to handle. You don't have to collect all the data yourself!
      There are hundreds of scientists in the world working on lots of
      different research projects. Somewhere there might be someone col-
      lecting (or has already collected) the data that you need. This is
      where the library, telephone, and CoVis communication tools come
      into play.

5. Figure out how you are going to try to answer your question.
   a. What do you already know about the topic?
   b. What other questions about the topic come up?
   c. What information do you need to find the answer to the "question"
      you have asked?
   d. Where do you find the information you need?

6. Collect Data. (2 weeks)
   a. Use all the resources available to you.
      • Library books, periodicals, journals, personal conversations, data
        bases, images, whatever it takes, whatever you can find.
   b. This might also be experimental data your group collects.

7. Analyze your data to see what you have discovered. (1 week)
   a. Graph your data to make any patterns/connections more "visible."
   b. What does your data tell you?
   c. Does your data "support" what you started out to "prove"?
   d. Does the data "explain" the phenomena you were exploring?
   e. If the data shows something "different" than what you expected,
      why?
      • this might be the "real" project!!!

8. Write a paper explaining your project. (2 weeks)
   • See the separate handout.

9. Prepare a presentation to the class. (1 week)
   - there will be more information about this later.

PROJECT MILESTONES AND DUE DATES

In order to keep the work going at a steady pace, you will be required to turn in documents, on or by the following dates, as proof that you have completed each of the different steps. Points will be given at each "Milestone" for the work satisfactorily completed. The Milestones grade will be part of your semester grade. The "point values" below are the number of points that you get when you meet the deadline, you lose a point a day (5-4-3-2-1-0, or 10-9- . . . -2-1-0) until you are out of points for that "section." Five (5) "Bonus Points" will be given for Research Proposals, Data Collection, Data Analysis and Papers that are completed and accepted BEFORE the due date.

The First Deadline is Friday!

Friday November 10th
THE BROAD TOPIC (5 Points) and A LIST OF GROUP MEMBERS (5 points)
REMEMBER, ONLY 2–3 PEOPLE IN A GROUP
You can "package" these first two things together, and *send them to me by e-mail.*

Wednesday November 22nd
BACKGROUND INFORMATION on your topic (10 points)

- Start with your text book or any of the Esci texts in the lab.
- Read the chapter/section that relates to your topic.
- Take notes or make an outline. *Show me* the notes/outline.
- *Everyone in the group should be doing this* in order to become familiar with the topic.
- If you need more information than your text can provide (which SHOULD be the case) *see me for additional resource* books located in the "office" next door. AFTER these resources have been exhausted, the Library may be used, *but you need my permission to go.* DON'T just walk out!!! The Internet is not usually a good place to look for this information.

Friday December 1st
The RESEARCH PROPOSAL (10 Points)
This MUST BE APPROVED by me before you can go any further.
Send me a copy by e-mail.

Friday December 15th
DATA COLLECTION is due to be finished. (10 Points)
Send/give me a COPY. *This does not have to be electronic*, but it could be.

Friday December 22nd
DATA ANALYSIS should be done. (10 Points)
Send me a copy by e-mail.

Friday January 12th
The PAPER is due. (10 Points)
I need both a good *paper copy*, and an *electronic copy*.

Friday January 19th
CLASS PRESENTATIONS should be finished.[1]
Presentations will be January 22nd and 23rd (before finals) and January 29th after finals. More about this later.

Questions? See me.

PROJECT REPORTS

The following reports are required from each GROUP:

1. *Written report.*
   Length: as long as you need it to be to inform the class about your project. Typed, double spaced. 10 point type.
   Graphs, diagrams, and charts: each report *must have* one or more *Data Tables* to logically/neatly present your data. Each report *must have* one or more *Graphs/Charts* to help you visually present the findings of your data analysis. The spreadsheet program Excel will aid you with tables and graphs/charts. *Diagrams* may be included in the paper if they help to illustrate a point or explain a process. If possible, all of these items should be placed in the "body" of the report along with the text (like a book or a newpaper), instead of on a separate sheet of paper. If it isn't

possible to include the tables, charts or diagrams directly *in* the paper, they should be as close to the text that refers to them as possible, and not at the end of the paper. Be sure to *label them* ("Table 1," or "Graph 1," or "Diagram 1," etc.) and *include a descriptive caption* ("Graph showing the relationship between . . . "). All diagrams/tables/charts should be typed, computer generated, or copies from reference materials. If copied from another source be sure to quote the source in, or immediately after, the caption ("Graph from Press, 1987"). If you have to attach an illustration to a page, it should be glued neatly (*rubber cement preferred*), not taped or stapled.
Format: This report should follow the format below.
2. *Class presentation.*
This presentation allows you to share your research with the class. Basically, it should include: 1) your original proposal/question, 2) the information from your "Introduction," 3) your "Method," 4) your "Results," and 5) your "Conclusion." You need to describe your project goals, tell how you did your research or collected your data, and an analysis of your data (your results). Visuals are encouraged. Computer images, or overhead transparencies would be best. Posterboards will be allowed, but every item on them must be clearly visible to everyone in the audience. No drawings on the chalkboard, except during the questions and answers.
Time: Each presentation will be limited to 15 min, followed by a question/answer period.

RESEARCH PAPER FORMAT

Each paper must have each of the parts listed below. Each section, *excluding* the "Title page," must be *clearly labeled* in your paper. There may be more than one section on each page.

1. *Title page.*
This page should include the title of your project, names of the authors, and date submitted.
2. *Abstract.*
This section is a brief summary of your work. Be brief. It includes: 1) your Proposal (project idea/question), 2) a description of your Method (what you did), and 3) your Conclusion. This should not be more than 200 words long. The abstract gives the reader a quick overview of your project, so that he/she can decide from the abstract if he/she needs to read the rest of the paper.

3. *Introduction (Background material/information).*
   This section is for the background information that you collected. You should include enough information here to provide the reader with enough general background information to 1) understand your research, 2) show them that you really know what you are talking about. This section should summarize the important findings that have preceded your work, the work of researchers or scientists that studied this area before you did. Be sure to use scientific citations when necessary. See Page 19 in the "Style Manual for Research Papers," but change the "page #" to the "year of publication."

4. *Method (Process, experiment, research).*
   In this section you *describe what you did* to find the answer to your question. Be very specific. Anyone who reads your report should be able to *duplicate your research* using this description of your research. How did you go about finding the answer to your question? Tell what information you were looking for, why you needed it, and how you went about trying to find it. This section may vary greatly depending on the type of project you do. It might describe how you constructed a model and tested it, or it might tell how you collected your own samples or data and how you analyzed what you found. Or, it might be how you collected data electronically, or from library resources.

5. *Results (Data and data analysis).*
   The "Method" section describes "HOW" you collected the data, and this section "SHOWS" the data you collected, and "WHAT YOU DID WITH IT." This would include any tables, graphs, charts, maps, images, etc., that you found or made. It also includes any calculations, drawings, graphs, charts, images, etc., that you made in your attempt to find out just what the data mean.

6. *Conclusions (Results).*
   What conclusions can you draw from the data you collected and analyzed? What did you find out about your original Research Proposal question? If you started your project with a specific point to prove or disprove, does the data you collected and analyzed "support" your original proposal/question? Or, did your analysis appear to be contradictory to what you thought it would be? If you were just trying to find out how something worked, or how things were related, what did you find out? *Specifically state how your data support/prove/disprove your original question/proposal.*

7. *Literature cited.*
   This is where you document all sources. *Anything you use that was created by someone else must be listed here.* To create a Literature Cited, follow the format in the [Lakeside] Style Manual for Science Ci-

tations (or, maybe even talk to an English teacher[!], librarian, or science teacher). *Be sure to include all the information you got electronically.* The format we will use will be:

Author (last name first). Copyright date. *Title of Web Page.* Application used. URL address

Example: Schimmrich, Steven H. 1995. The Structural Geology Home Page. Netscape. http://hercules.geology.uiuc.edu/~shimmri/geology/structure.html#data

Be sure to include your mentor if you have one, and personal conversations where you got information that you use in the research. *Basically, if there is something in your paper that you got from someplace other than being made up in your own brain, there should be a reference to it here*!

How Your Paper Is Graded.

TITLE PAGE	(5 Pts)
ABSTRACT	(10 Pts)
INTRODUCTION	(20 Pts)
METHOD	(20 Pts)
DATA & ANALYSIS	(10 Pts & 10 Pts)
CONCLUSION	(20 Pts)
LIT. CITED	(10 Pts)
STRUCTURE	(10 Pts)
(spelling, sent. struct., internal cit.)	
TOTAL POINTS =	(115 Pts)

NOTE

1. This deadline was moved back to accommodate the addition of a week and a half for students to complete a paper revision, which was due on Wednesday, January 24th, during finals. From January 29th through February 2nd, students prepared their presentations. From February 5th through February 9th, students gave their presentations.

References

Aikin, W. M. (1942). *The story of the eight-year study.* New York: Harper.

Alberty, H. B. (1927). *A study of the project method in education.* Columbus, OH: Ohio State University.

Alexander, R. M. (1989). *Dynamics of dinosaurs and other extinct giants.* New York: Columbia University.

Allen, C. (1993). Reciprocal evolution as a strategy for integrating basic research, design, and studies of work practice. In D. Schuler & A. Namoka (Eds.), *Participatory design: Principles and practices* (pp. 239–253). Hillsdale, NJ: Erlbaum.

Archer, R. L. (Ed.). (1964). *Jean Jacques Rousseau: His educational theories selected from* Émile, Julie, *and other writings* (pp. 19–54). New York: Barrons.

Au, K. H., & Mason, J. M. (1981). Social organizational factors in learning to read: The balance of rights hypothesis. *Reading Research Quarterly, 17,* 115–152.

Ayers, W. (1989). *The good preschool teacher: Six teachers reflect on their lives.* New York: Teachers College Press.

Ayers, W. (1993). *To teach: The journey of a teacher.* New York: Teachers College Press.

Ball, D. L. (1990). Reflections and deflections of policy: The case of Carol Turner. *Educational Evaluation and Policy Analysis, 12*(3), 247–259.

Ball, S., Hull, R., Skelton, M., & Tudor, R. (1984). The tyranny of the "devil's mill": Time and task at school. In S. Delamont (Ed.), *Readings on interaction in the classroom* (pp. 41–57). London: Methuen.

Bantock, G. H. (1984). *Studies in the history of educational theory.* London: George Allen & Unwin.

Blumenfeld, P. C., Soloway, E., Marx, R. W., Krajcik, J. S., Guzdial, M., & Palincsar, A. (1991). Motivating project-based learning: Sustaining the doing, supporting the learning. *Educational Psychologist, 26*(3), 369–398.

Bourdieu, P. (1990). *In other words: Essays toward a reflexive sociology* (M. Adamson, Trans.). Stanford, CA: Stanford University Press.

Brickhouse, N., & Bodner, G. M. (1992). The beginning science teacher: Classroom narratives of convictions and constraints. *Journal of Research in Science Teaching, 29*(5), 471–485.

Brown, A. L. (1992). Design experiments: Theoretical and methodological challenges in creating complex interventions in classroom settings. *Journal of the Learning Sciences, 2*(2), 141–178.

Brown, J. S., Collins, A., & Duguid, P. (1989). Situated cognition and the culture of learning. *Educational Researcher*, January–February, 32–42.

Brown, J. S., & Duguid, P. (1990). *Enacting design for the workplace.* Paper presented at Technology and the Future Conference, Stanford, CA, March 28–30, 1990.

Bruce, B. C., Peyton, J. K., & Batson, T. (Eds.). (1993). *Network-based classrooms: Promises and realities.* New York: Cambridge University Press.

Bruce, B. C., & Rubin, A. (1993). *Electronic quills: A situated evaluation of using computers for writing in classrooms.* Hillsdale, NJ: Erlbaum.

Bruner, J. (1963). *The process of education.* New York: Vintage.

Bruner, J. S. (1990). *Acts of meaning.* Cambridge, MA: Harvard University.

Cohen, D. K. (1988a). Educational technology and school organization. In R. S. Nickerson & P. Zodhiates (Eds.), *Technology in education: Looking toward 2020* (pp. 231–264). Hillsdale, NJ: Erlbaum.

Cohen, D. K. (1988b). Teaching practice: Plus que ça change. . . . In P. Jackson (Ed.), *Contributing to educational change: Perspectives on research and practice* (pp. 27–84). Berkeley, CA: McCutchan.

Cohen, D. K. (1990). A revolution in one classroom: The case of Mrs. Oublier. *Educational Evaluation and Policy Analysis, 12*(3), 311–329.

Cohen, E. G. (1994). Restructuring the classroom: Conditions for productive small groups. *Review of Educational Research, 64*(1), 1–35.

Cole, M., & Griffin, P. (1980). Cultural amplifiers reconsidered. In D. R. Olson (Ed.), *The social foundations of language and thought* (pp. 343–364). New York: Norton.

Cole, M., & Griffin, P. (1987). *Contextual factors in education: Improving science and mathematics education for minorities and women.* Madison, WI: Wisconsin Center for Education Research.

Collins, A. (1991). The role of computer technology in restructuring schools. *Phi Delta Kappan*, September, 28–36.

Collins, A. (1992). Toward a design science of education. In E. Scanlon & T. O'Shea (Eds.), *New directions in educational technology.* Berlin: Springer-Verlag.

Collins, A., Brown, J. S., & Newman, S. E. (1989). Cognitive apprenticeship: Teaching the craft of reading, writing, and mathematics. In L. B. Resnick (Ed.), *Knowing, learning, and instruction: Essays in honor of Robert Glaser* (pp. 453–494). Hillsdale, NJ: Erlbaum.

Condon, E. U., & Gillmor, D. S. (1968). *Final report of the scientific study of unidentified flying objects.* New York: Bantam.

Cremin, L. (1961). *The transformation of the school.* New York: Knopf.

Cuban, L. (1984). *How teachers taught.* New York: Longman.

Cuban, L. (1986). *Teachers and machines: The classroom use of technology since 1920.* New York: Teachers College Press.

Cuban, L. (1990). Reforming again, again, and again. *Educational Researcher, 19*(1), 3–13.

Cuban, L. (1993). Computers meet classroom: Classroom wins. *Teachers College Record, 95*(2), 185–210.

D'Amico, L. (1999). *The role of assessment infrastructures in crafting project-based science classrooms.* Doctoral dissertation, Northwestern University, Evanston, IL.

Dede, C. J. (1990). Imaging technology's role in restructuring for learning. In K. Sheingold & M. S. Tucker (Eds.), *Restructuring for learning with technology* (pp. 49–52). New York: Center for Technology in Education, Bank Street College of Education.

Dewey, J. (1895). Interest in relation to the training of the will. In J. J. McDermott (Ed.), *The philosophy of John Dewey, Vol. II: The lived experience* (pp. 421–442). New York: Putnam.

Dewey, J. (1897). My pedagogic creed. In J. J. McDermott (Ed.), *The philosophy of John Dewey, Vol. II: The lived experience* (pp. 442–454). New York: Putnam.

Dewey, J. (1901). The situation as regards the course of study. *Journal of the Proceedings and Addresses of the Fortieth Annual Meeting of the National Education Association*, 332–348.

Dewey, J. (1902). The child and the curriculum. In J. J. McDermott (Ed.), *The philosophy of John Dewey, Vol. II: The lived experience* (pp. 467–483). New York: Putnam.

Dewey, J. (1938/1950). *Experience and education*. New York: Macmillan.

Dow, P. (1991). *Schoolhouse politics: Lessons from the Sputnik era*. Cambridge, MA: Harvard University.

Doyle, W. (1979). Classroom tasks and students' abilities. In P. L. Peterson & H. L. Walberg (Eds.), *Research on teaching: Concepts, findings, and implications* (pp. 183–209). Berkeley, CA: McCutchan.

Dwyer, D. C., Ringstaff, C., & Sandholtz, J. H. (1991). Changes in teachers' beliefs and practices in technology-rich classrooms. *Educational Leadership*, May, 45–52.

Eccles, J. S. (1989). Bringing young women to math and science. In M. Crawford & M. Gentry (Eds.), *Gender and thought: Psychological perspectives* (pp. 36–58). New York: Springer-Verlag.

Eckert, P. (1990). Adolescent social categories—Information and science learning. In M. Gardner, J. G. Greeno, F. Reif, A. H. Schoenfeld, A. diSessa, & E. Stage (Eds.), *Toward a scientific practice of science education* (pp. 203–217). Hillsdale, NJ: Erlbaum.

Edelson, D. C., & O'Neill, D. K. (1994). The CoVis Collaboratory Notebook: Supporting collaborative science inquiry. In A. Best (Ed.), *Proceedings of the 1994 National Educational Computing Conference* (pp. 146–152). Eugene, OR: International Society for Technology in Education with the National Education Computing Association.

Erickson, F. (1986). Qualitative methods in research on teaching. In M. C. Wittrock (Ed.), *Handbook of research on teaching* (pp. 119–160). New York: Macmillan.

Farnham-Diggory, S. (1990). *Schooling*. Cambridge, MA: Harvard University Press.

Firestone, W. A. (1993). Alternative arguments for generalizing from data as applied to qualitative research. *Educational Researcher, 22*(4), 16–23.

Fishman, B. (1996). *High-end high school communication: Tool use practices of students in a networked environment*. Unpublished doctoral dissertation, Northwestern University, Evanston, IL.

Fishman, B., & D'Amico, L. (1994). Which way will the wind blow? Networked computer tools for studying the weather. In T. Ottman & I. Tomek (Eds.), *Educational Multimedia and Hypermedia, 1994: Proceedings of Ed-Media '94* (pp. 209–216). Charlottesville, VA: Association for the Advancement of Computing in Education.

Fishman, B., & Pea, R. D. (1994). Proactive policy for the internetworked school: A proposal emerging from the CoVis Project. *Technos: Quarterly of Education and Technology, 3*(1), 22–26.

Fullan, M. G., & Miles, M. B. (1992). Getting reform right: What works and what doesn't. *Phi Delta Kappan*, June, 745–752.

Geertz, C. (1973). *The interpretation of cultures.* New York: Basic Books.

Geertz, C. (1988). *Works and lives: The anthropologist as author.* Stanford, CA: Stanford University Press.

Gibson, J. J. (1986). *The ecological approach to visual perception.* Hillsdale, NJ: Erlbaum.

Glesne, C., & Peshkin, A. (1992). *Becoming qualitative researchers: An introduction.* White Plains, NY: Longman.

Gordin, D., Polman, J. L., & Pea, R. D. (1994). The Climate Visualizer: Sensemaking through scientific visualization. *Journal of Science Education and Technology, 3*(4), 203–226.

Guzdial, M. (1995, April). *Artifacts of learning: A perspective on students' learning processes and strategies through their learning products.* Paper presented at the Annual Meeting of the American Educational Research Association, San Francisco, CA.

Hall, E. T. (1976). *Beyond culture.* New York: Doubleday.

Harel, I., & Papert, S. (1993). Software design as a learning environment. *Interactive Learning Environments, 1*, 1–32.

Heath, S. B. (1983). *Ways with words: Language, life, and work in communities and classrooms.* Cambridge, UK: Cambridge University Press.

Hofstadter, R. (1963). *Anti-intellectualism in American life.* New York: Vintage.

Horn, E. (1920). What is a project? *Elementary School Journal, 21*, 112–116.

Houghton, J. R. (1996, July). Why do we need national skill standards? *NSSB Workwise*, pp. 1–2.

Hurricane/Tropical Data. (1995). [Online]. Previously available at: http://thunder.atms.purdue.edu/hurricane.html

Jackson, P. (1968). *Life in classrooms.* New York: Holt, Rinehart, and Winston.

Jackson, S. L., Stratford, S. J., Krajcik, J. S., & Soloway, E. (in press). Making system dynamics modeling accessible to pre-college science students. *Interactive Learning Environments.*

Kidder, T. (1989). *Among schoolchildren.* Boston: Houghton Mifflin.

Kidder, T. (1995). Invited lecture, Northwestern University.

Kilpatrick, W. H. (1925). *Foundations of method.* New York: Macmillan.

Kohl, H. (1967). *36 children.* New York: Plume.

Kotlowitz, A. (1991). *There are no children here.* New York: Anchor.

Krajcik, J., Czerniak, C. M., & Berger, C. F. (1998). *Teaching children science: A project-based approach.* Boston: McGraw-Hill.

Krieg, R., & Wheelan, C. (1995, February 12). Separate—but equal? *Chicago Tribune Magazine*, pp. 14–25.

Kushner, H. S. (1981). *When bad things happen to good people.* New York: Avon.

Kyle, W. C., Jr. (1984). What became of the curriculum development projects of the 1960s? How effective were they? What did we learn from them that will help teachers in today's classrooms? In D. Holdzkum & P. B. Lutz (Eds.), *Research within reach: Science education.* Charleston, WV: Appalachia Educational Laboratory.

Latour, B. (1988). Drawing things together. In M. Lynch & S. Woolgar (Eds.), *Representation in scientific practice* (pp. 19–68). Cambridge, MA: MIT Press.

Lave, J. (1990). Views of the classroom: Implications for math and science learning research. In M. Gardner, J. G. Greeno, F. Reif, A. H. Schoenfeld, A. diSessa, & E. Stage (Eds.), *Toward a scientific practice of science education* (pp. 251–263). Hillsdale, NJ: Erlbaum.

Lave, J., & Wenger, E. (1991). *Situated learning: Legitimate peripheral participation.* Cambridge: Cambridge University Press.

Lee, H. (1960). *To kill a mockingbird.* New York: Warner Books.

Lemann, N. (1995). The structure of success in America. *The Atlantic Monthly,* August, 41–60.

Lemke, J. L. (1990). *Talking science: Language, learning, and values.* Norwood, NJ: Ablex.

Leont'ev, A. N. (1981). *Problems of the development of mind.* Moscow: Progress.

Lepper, M. R., Woolverton, M., Mumme, D. L., & Gurtner, J-L. (1993). Motivational techniques of expert human tutors: Lessons for the design of computer-based tutors. In S. P. Lajoie & S. J. Derry (Eds.), *Computers as cognitive tools* (pp. 75–105). Hillsdale, NJ: Erlbaum.

Lewin, K. (1946). Action-research into minority problems. *Journal of Social Issues,* 2, 34–36.

Lightfoot, S. L. (1983). *The good high school: Portraits of character and culture.* New York: Basic Books.

McGee, S. (1996). *Designing curricula based on science communities of practice.* Unpublished doctoral dissertation, Northwestern University, Evanston, IL.

McLaughlin, M. W. (1990). The Rand change agent study revisited: Macro perspectives and micro realities. *Educational Researcher, 19*(9), 11–16.

Means, B., Blando, J., Olson, K., Middleton, T., Morocco, C. C., Remz, A. R., & Zorfass, J. (1993). *Using technology to support education reform* (Report No. ISBN 0-16-042048-2). Washington, DC: U.S. Department of Education, Office of Educational Research and Improvement and Office of Research.

Mehan, H. (1978). Structuring school structure. *Harvard Educational Review,* 48(1), 32–64.

Mehan, H. (1980). The competent student. *Anthropology and Education Quarterly, 11*(3), 131–152.

Mehan, H. (1989). Microcomputers in classroom: Educational technology or social practice? *Anthropology and Education Quarterly, 20,* 4–22.

Nasaw, D. (1979). *Schooled to order: A social history of public schooling in the United States.* New York: Oxford University Press.

National Research Council. (1996). *National science education standards.* Washington, DC: National Academy.

Neill, A. S. (1960). *Summerhill: A radical approach to child-rearing.* New York: Hart.

Newman, D., Griffin, P., & Cole, M. (1984). Social constraints in laboratory and classroom tasks. In B. Rogoff & J. Lave (Eds.), *Everyday cognition: Its development in social context.* Cambridge, MA: Harvard University Press.

Newman, D., Griffin, P., & Cole, M. (1989). *The construction zone: Working for cognitive change in school.* New York: Cambridge University Press.

Norman, D. (1988). *The psychology of everyday things.* New York: Basic Books.

Office of Technology Assessment. (1995). *Teachers and technology: Making the connection* (S/N No. 052-003-01409-2). Washington, DC: Office of Technology Assessment.

O'Neill, D. K. (1998). *Engaging science practice through science practitioners: Design experiments in K–12 telementoring.* Doctoral dissertation, Northwestern University, Evanston, IL.

O'Neill, D. K., & Gomez, L. (1994). The Collaboratory Notebook: A distributed knowledge-building environment for project-enhanced learning. In T. Ottman & I. Tomek (Eds.), *Educational Multimedia and Hypermedia, 1994: Proceedings of Ed-Media '94* (pp. 416–423). Charlottesville, VA: Association for the Advancement of Computing in Education.

O'Neill, D. K., Wagner, R., & Gomez, L. M. (1996, November). On-line mentors: Experimenting in science class. *Educational Leadership, 54*(3), 39–42.

Palincsar, A. S., & Brown, A. L. (1984). Reciprocal teaching of comprehension-fostering and comprehension monitoring activities. *Cognition and Instruction, 1,* 117–175.

Papert, S. (1980). *Mindstorms: Children, computers, and powerful ideas.* New York: Basic Books.

Patton, M. Q. (1990). *Qualitative evaluation and research methods* (2nd ed.). Newbury Park, CA: Sage.

Pea, R. D. (1985). Beyond amplification: Using the computer to reorganize mental functioning. *Educational Psychologist, 20*(4), 167–182.

Pea, R. D. (1992). Augmenting the discourse of learning with computer-based learning environments. In E. de Corte, M. Linn, H. Mandl, & L. Verschaffel (Eds.), *Computer-based learning environments and problem-solving* (pp. 313–344). New York: Springer-Verlag.

Pea, R. D. (1993a). The collaborative visualization project. *Communications of the Association for Computing Machinery, 36*(5), 60–63.

Pea, R. D. (1993b). Practices of distributed intelligence and designs for education. In G. Salomon (Ed.), *Distributed cognitions: Psychological and educational considerations* (pp. 47–87). New York: Cambridge University Press.

Pea, R. D. (1994). Seeing what we build together: Distributed multimedia learning environments for transformative communications. *The Journal of the Learning Sciences, 3*(3), 285–299.

Pea, R. D. (1997). Personal communication.

Pea, R. D., & Gomez, L. M. (1992). Distributed multimedia learning environments: Why and how? *Interactive Learning Environments, 2*(2), 73–109.

Pea, R. D., Gomez, L. M., Edelson, D. C., Fishman, B. J., Gordin, D. N., & O'Neill, D. K. (1997). Science education as a driver of cyberspace technology development. In K. C. Cohen (Ed.), *Internet links for science education: Student-scientist partnerships* (pp. 189–220). New York: Plenum.

Peshkin, A. (1988). Understanding complexity: A gift of qualitative inquiry. *Anthropology and Education Quarterly, 19*, 416–424.

Phillips, D. C. (1990). Subjectivity and objectivity: An objective inquiry. In E. Eisner & A. Peshkin (Eds.), *Qualitative inquiry in education: The continuing debate* (pp. 19–37). New York: Teachers College Press.

Powell, A. G., Farrar, E., & Cohen, D. K. (1985). *The shopping mall high school: Winners and losers in the educational marketplace.* Boston: Houghton Mifflin.

Progressive Education Association. (1943). *Thirty schools tell their story.* New York: Harper.

Ravitch, D. (1982). American education: Has the pendulum swung once too often? In D. Ravitch (Ed.), *The schools we deserve: Reflections on the educational crises of our times* (pp. 80–89). New York: Basic Books.

Resnick, L. B. (1987). Learning in school and out. *Educational Researcher,* December, 13–20.

Resnick, L. B. (1995, April). *Work, schooling and learning: A new future? What role for research?* Lecture presented as part of the SESP Dean's Distinguished Colloquium Series at Northwestern University.

Resnick, M., & Rusk, N. (1996). The Computer Clubhouse: Helping youth develop fluency with new media. In D. C. Edelson & E. A. Domeshek (Eds.), *Proceedings of the International Conference on the Learning Sciences* (pp. 285–291). Charlottesville, VA: Association for the Advancement of Computing in Education.

Rogoff, B. (1990). *Apprenticeship in thinking: Cognitive development in social context.* New York: Oxford University Press.

Rogoff, B. (1994). Developing understanding of the idea of communities of learners. *Mind, Culture, and Activity, 1*(4), 209–229.

Roschelle, J. (1992). Learning by collaborating: Convergent conceptual change. *The Journal of the Learning Sciences, 2*(3), 235–276.

Ruopp, R., Gal, S., Drayton, B., & Pfister, M. (Eds.). (1993). *LabNet: Toward a community of practice.* Hillsdale, NJ: Erlbaum.

Sadker, M., & Sadker, D. (1994). *Failing at fairness: How America's schools cheat girls.* New York: Charles Scribner's Sons.

Sarason, S. B. (1971). *The culture of the school and the problem of change.* Boston: Allyn and Bacon.

Scardamalia, M., & Bereiter, C. (1991). Higher levels of agency for children in knowledge building: A challenge for the design of new knowledge media. *The Journal of the Learning Sciences, 1*(1), 37–68.

Scardamalia, M., Bereiter, C., McLean, R. S., Swallow, J., & Woodruff, E. (1989). Computer-supported intentional learning environments. *Journal of Educational Computing Research, 5*(1), 51–68.

Schank, R. C. (1990). *Tell me a story: A new look at real and artificial memory.* New York: Scribner.

Schofield, J. W. (1990). Increasing the generalizability of qualitative research. In E. W. Eisner & A. Peshkin (Eds.), *Qualitative inquiry in education: The continuing debate* (pp. 201–232). New York: Teachers College Press.

Schön, D. A. (1982). *The reflective practitioner: How professionals think in action.* New York: Basic Books.

Schwab, R. G., Hart-Landsberg, S., Reder, S., & Abel, M. (1992). Collaboration and constraint: Middle school teaching teams. In J. Turner & R. Kraut (Eds.), *ACM 1992 Conference on Computer-Supported Cooperative Work* (pp. 241–248). Toronto, Canada: Association for Computing Machinery Press.

Scott, C. A. (1994). Project-based science: Reflections of a middle school teacher. *The Elementary School Journal, 95*(1), 75–94.

Secretary's Commission on Achieving Necessary Skills. (1991). *What work requires of schools: A SCANS report for America 2000* (Report No. PB92-146711). Springfield, VA: National Technical Information Service.

Sheingold, K., & Hadley, M. (1990). *Accomplished teachers: Integrating computers into classroom practice.* New York: Center for Technology in Education.

Shrader, G., & Gomez, L. (1997). [Aids to reforming toward project-based teaching]. Unpublished raw data.

Shweder, R. A. (1990). Cultural psychology: What is it? In J. Stigler, R. Shweder, & G. Herdt (Eds.), *Cultural psychology: Essays on comparative human development* (pp. 1–43). New York: Cambridge University Press.

Simon, H. (1981). *The sciences of the artificial* (2nd ed.). Cambridge, MA: MIT Press.

Simon, H. A. (1957). *Models of man.* New York: John Wiley.

Sproull, L., & Kiesler, S. (1991). *Connections: New ways of working in the networked organization.* Cambridge, MA: MIT Press.

Suchman, L. A. (1987). *Plans and situated actions: The problem of human-machine communication.* Cambridge, UK: Cambridge University Press.

Sunspace. (1997). The sunspace site [Online]. Available: http://www.sunspace.com

Tobin, K., & Garnett, P. (1987). Gender differences in science activities. *Science Education, 71*(1), 91–105.

Tyack, D., & Tobin, W. (1994). The "grammar" of schooling: Why has it been so hard to change? *American Educational Research Journal, 31*(3), 453–479.

von Glasersfeld, E. (1989). Cognition, construction of knowledge, and teaching. *Synthese, 80,* 121–140.

Vygotsky, L. S. (1978). *Mind in society.* Cambridge, MA: Harvard.

Wasley, P. A. (1994). *Stirring the chalkdust: Tales of teachers changing classroom practice.* New York: Teachers College Press.

Wertsch, J. V. (1991). *Voices of the mind: A sociocultural approach to mediated action.* Cambridge, MA: Harvard.

Wittgenstein, L. (1967). *Philosophical investigations.* Oxford, UK: Blackwell.

Wood, D., Bruner, J., & Ross, G. (1976). The role of tutoring in problem-solving. *Journal of Child Psychology and Psychiatry, 17,* 89–100.

Zilversmit, A. (1993). *Changing schools: Progressive education theory and practice, 1930–1960.* Chicago: University of Chicago.

Index

About the Author

Joseph L. Polman is an assistant professor in the School of Education at the University of Missouri-St. Louis. After working in the software industry, he became engaged in uses of computers and networking in education. His interests include the cognitive, social, and cultural aspects of project-based science and history learning in technology-rich environments. He completed his doctorate in the Learning Sciences at Northwestern University, and a postdoctoral fellowship in education at Washington University.